Wm. H. Owen
Yale '97

June 1941

HOLMES-POLLOCK LETTERS

LONDON: HUMPHREY MILFORD
OXFORD UNIVERSITY PRESS

F. Pollard

Holmes-Pollock Letters

*The Correspondence of Mr Justice Holmes
and Sir Frederick Pollock 1874-1932*

EDITED BY

MARK DeWOLFE HOWE
Professor of Law, University of Buffalo School of Law

WITH AN INTRODUCTION BY
JOHN GORHAM PALFREY

VOLUME 1

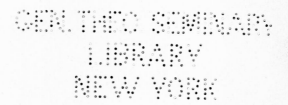
CAMBRIDGE · MASSACHUSETTS
HARVARD UNIVERSITY PRESS
1941

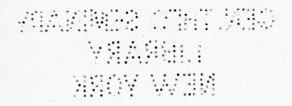
PRINTED AT THE HARVARD UNIVERSITY PRESS
CAMBRIDGE, MASSACHUSETTS, U.S.A.

PREFACE

THESE volumes might suitably carry the subtitle: "An Autobiography of a Friendship; the Biography of an Era." Intimate friendship between men of distinction is not uncommon, but it is seldom in the modern world that the instinct for intimacy finds its fullest expression in correspondence. Many apparent obstacles stood in the way of the friendship of Holmes and Pollock; geography and nationality might well have prevented its development; the extraordinarily heavy demands of the professional life of each would easily have excused the writing of that next letter on which the continuation of the friendship might depend. Readers of the correspondence will, I think, soon see why the excuse was not given and why the intimacy grew, despite the persistent obstacles. Holmes has described Pollock as a "true child of culture"; certainly the description was applicable to both men. As children of essentially the same culture Pollock and Holmes shared citizenship in the world of ideas — a world to which each gave his principal loyalty. That world, of course, is not one of nations and of boundaries, and if physical geography ruled out the possibility of the friends meeting, save infrequently, face to face, intellectual geography encouraged constant meetings of mind with mind.

The letters are the records of those meetings. Had Holmes and Pollock been neighbors in fact as well as in thought, no adequate picture of their intimacy would have survived. What we should lack would be not only the autobiography of a friendship but the biography of an era. For as truly as each man was the child of culture each was the father of thought, and the thought which they fathered became an important strand in the intellectual history of the last sixty-five years. Despite the public distinction of each man's life, the eminence of Holmes and that of Pollock shared a peculiar quality of insulated calm. From his special vantage point each was able to observe and to affect the course of history. Each was furthermore blessed with the talent of graceful, witty, and incisive expression. It is the combination of these elements which will, I believe, give lasting importance to these letters.

The readers of such a correspondence may find it helpful to know something of the general policy in the light of which specific editorial decisions have been made. The first endeavor has been to include all letters and all portions of each selected letter which were significantly expressive, in however small a degree, of the life, character, or thought of Holmes and Pollock and of their generation. Every omission, whether of a part or of the whole of a letter, is indicated.

Some readers, I believe, will regret the compromise decision which was reached on the debatable question of whether the letters should be printed *verbatim et literatim* or whether it was more appropriate to make corrections in spelling and punctuation. Holmes to a considerable extent and Pollock to a lesser degree tended in their letters to abbreviate words and phrases and to disregard orthodox rules of punctuation. I have attempted to translate the informal spontaneity of the originals to the printed page, but not to make the translation so relentlessly literal as to preserve obscurities of meaning or to spoil the appearance of the page. With those purposes in mind dashes, which in the originals served as hasty substitutes for commas and periods and which necessarily give a confused appearance to a printed page, have frequently been taken out and replaced by their more formal substitutes. Where easy understanding of a sentence required the addition of punctuation the addition has been made. Where abbreviation seemed likely to create obscurity for the general reader the full word or phrase has been substituted. Otherwise, the letters are printed as they were written, except that for reasons of space the full address of the writer, frequently given at the head of the letter, has generally been omitted. The difficulties of Holmes's handwriting, particularly in his later years, were so very considerable that no guarantee of absolute accuracy is possible. I believe, however, that all words not specifically noted as doubtful are accurate transcriptions.

In my annotation of the letters I have followed what seemed to me to be an appropriate rule of thumb — to give only such supplementary information as that fictitious character "the general reader" is likely to want. I have thought of him as partly Englishman, partly American, partly lawyer, and partly layman; I have made innumerable guesses, I hope not too inaccurately in too many cases, of the sort of information which this strange conglomerate is likely to want, and I have tried to give him just enough to satisfy his need. It is my hope that in the footnotes and in the index he will find the essentials.

Many persons have given me assistance in my editorial work. To all of them collectively I must express my warmest gratitude. To Mr. Richard W. Hale, Professor Samuel E. Thorne, and Miss T. E. Nadeau I am more indebted than anyone but they and I can know. Their careful preliminary work of assembling, copying, and indexing the letters made my task infinitely easier to perform than it would otherwise have been. Mr. John G. Palfrey, Holmes's executor, and Dean James M. Landis of the Harvard Law School, where the original letters are preserved, have at all times shown themselves generously willing to give me counsel and assistance. My wife, Mary Manning Howe, has on frequent occasions come to my rescue and prevented blunders which without her would have had to be corrected by someone else. But above all I am indebted to my father, M. A. DeWolfe Howe, for his constantly wise guidance. Needless to say, all errors of fact and of judgment are mine.

MARK DeWolfe Howe

Buffalo, New York
January 1, 1941

CONTENTS

VOLUME I

VOLUME II

ILLUSTRATIONS

VOLUME I

VOLUME II

INTRODUCTION

Among the papers which came to me as executor and legatee by the will of Oliver Wendell Holmes, second of the name,[1] was a remarkable series of letters to him from Sir Frederick Pollock, the third Baronet of that name, covering the greater part of a lifetime; and by great good fortune there is here joined the other side of the picture, the series of letters from Holmes to Pollock. Sir John Pollock, Bart., son of Sir Frederick, has warmly agreed to a consolidation of interests and joins with me in the presentation of these letters.

The mere preservation of the correspondence of two men through so long a period of time would be remarkable enough. Still more unique is the collection of the letters of two men of such distinction, with qualities so marked and with so many common interests. In spite of the inevitable differences between two men of pronounced personalities they had much in common. Both were endowed with inherited legal traditions. Both were deeply engrossed in the origin and development of the English Law. Both viewed its development in the imaginative manner, in its relations to the whole of life. Both looked at life through the glasses of philosophy, science, art and letters. Both possessed, each in his own way, the gift of phrase and the happy touch in lighter vein.

Holmes was four years Pollock's senior. He was born in Boston, Massachusetts, March 8, 1841, son of the distinguished father of the same name. His maternal grandfather was Charles Jackson, an Associate Justice of the Supreme Judicial Court of Massachusetts. He was in all respects a New Englander and all his grandparents traced descent from early Colonial settlers.

---

[1] "I leave to my executor the absolute use, disposition and control of all letters, papers and memoranda of mine including any unpublished letters or writings, and all my rights in letters written by me to others if there are any such in existence, subject always to the lawful rights of the recipients, and I give to my executor full authority to make such disposition or use thereof as he may approve, and I direct that he shall not be held accountable in any court for any destruction or disposition thereof, or for any use thereof, or for my rights relative thereto, whether by himself individually or by others."

Among his forebears was Thomas Holmes, a lawyer of Gray's Inn in London in the sixteenth century.

Holmes was educated at a small private school and at Harvard College, which he entered in the fall of 1857 with the class of 1861. Before his graduation the war between the states had begun, and he at once enlisted. He remained, however, in the vicinity of Boston and received his A.B. degree with his class.

During the war Holmes was thrice wounded, but recuperated and completed his term of service. In those years he lived an emotional lifetime, and the philosophy with which he was to face the rest of his life was profoundly affected.[2] He was mustered out July 17, 1864, and in September of that year he entered the Harvard Law School. He received his LL.B. degree in January 1866 and was admitted to the Bar in Boston in 1867.

Pollock was born December 10, 1845. He came of a famous English legal family which has included many distinguished jurists among its members. His grandfather, the first Baronet of the name, was Lord Chief Baron of the Court of Exchequer; his father, the second Baronet, was Queen's Remembrancer and Senior Master of the Supreme Court of Judicature. Pollock was educated at Eton and at Trinity College, Cambridge. He became a scholar of Trinity, and in 1865 he was awarded the University Pitt Scholarship; in 1867 he was second in the Classical Tripos, First Chancellor's Medallist, and sixth in the senior optimes of the Mathematical Tripos. He greatly valued his election in his second year to the Cambridge Conversazione Society, commonly called "The Apostles," a famous society of intellectuals with a secret ritual and a distinguished roll of members. Here friendships were formed which lasted a lifetime. In 1867 he received his B.A. degree and in 1868 was elected a Fellow of the College. He immediately prepared for the legal profession and was called to the Bar by Lincoln's Inn in 1871.

On graduating from the Law School, Holmes made his first visit to England. There his father had many friends and he made many acquaintances which became friendships. Many of the friendships thus formed he and Pollock were to hold in com-

---

[2] See *Speeches, by Oliver Wendell Holmes* (Boston: Little, Brown & Co.), esp. "Memorial Day," pages 1, 11, and "The Soldier's Faith," pages 56, 63, 64.

mon.[3] During the visit Holmes saw much of Leslie Stephen, whom he had already met in Boston when recovering from his third wound in 1863. He joined the Alpine Club (of which Pollock became an enthusiastic member) and went mountaineering in Switzerland with Stephen before returning to America.

Holmes made what is believed to have been his second visit to England in the summer of 1874, accompanied by his wife, and then the friendship between Pollock and Holmes began. As Pollock said, "There was no stage of acquaintance ripening into friendship; we understood one another and were friends without more ado." At this time the positions in the world of the two men were similar. Both had been recently married, Holmes in 1872 and Pollock in 1873.[4] They were in the early stages of the law practice, Holmes more actively than Pollock, and both were becoming legal scholars of the first magnitude.

Holmes was a partner in the Boston law firm of Shattuck, Holmes and Munroe. In 1870–71 he lectured on Constitutional Law at Harvard College and in the following year was University Lecturer on Jurisprudence. In 1870–73 he was editor of the *American Law Review* (vols. V, VI, and VII), and wrote articles for that review besides unsigned notes and reviews. At the same time he was editing and annotating the twelfth edition of Kent's *Commentaries*, published in 1873.

Pollock was deeply engrossed in the preparation of his first major legal work, *Principles of Contract*, the first edition of which was published in 1876.

Both men were in the early prime of life, strong in the qualities and appearance which they retained for so many years and for which they are still remembered. Holmes was strikingly handsome, of erect and distinguished bearing, vivid in thought

[3] There has been a tradition among Holmes's friends that he and Pollock met in the latter sixties, and his friends recall conversations with Holmes in which such a meeting with Pollock was understood to be referred to. (See Harold J. Laski, in *The Nation*, August 3, 1940.) No visits of Holmes to England in the sixties are authenticated except the visit of 1866, and the question suggests itself whether he and Pollock may not have met during that visit. Pollock, however, in his article on Holmes (48 *Harvard Law Review* 1277) states categorically that he first met Holmes in London a short time after he was called to the Bar in 1871; and in his letter of October 9, 1894, he refers to the first meeting as "just twenty years ago."

[4] Holmes married Miss Fanny Bowditch Dixwell, daughter of Epes S. Dixwell of Cambridge, Massachusetts, June 17, 1872. Pollock married Miss Georgina Harriet Deffell, daughter of John Deffell of Calcutta, August 13, 1873.

and speech. Pollock was vigorous and direct. If a certain brusqueness veiled a suggestion of shyness which made his casual conversation seem sometimes hesitating, there was nothing halting about his pungent and often caustic conclusions and expressions and his prepared addresses.

The details of their meeting during the summer of 1874 are left to the imagination; indeed the same is true of their later meetings. When in the same country they seldom wrote to each other, and then would come a gap in the series of letters. This series, however, so far as preserved, began in 1874 with a letter from Pollock while Holmes was in England.

The first letter as well as succeeding letters for some years may discourage the lay reader. They are almost wholly legal and significant mainly to the legal fraternity. The breadth of interests of both men soon crept into their correspondence, however, and the letters contain so much which has an appeal to all that they cannot fairly be characterized as merely legal.

The letters, like the lives of the two men, deal essentially with ideas; but the background of their lives and the more important activities, and their occasional contacts outside of letters, should be indicated with more emphasis than is possible by editorial footnote.

Holmes's life is the more capable of classification by reference to fundamental transitions and periods. There were three. The first was the period of preparation for and preparation and publication of his great work, *The Common Law*. This period had begun in a broad sense before 1874, and to his labors he gave his heart in the intervals permitted by his law practice, in which he was also making his mark. Much of the substance of *The Common Law* was delivered as a series of Lowell Lectures in Boston in 1880, and *The Common Law* was published in 1881.

During this period Pollock was equally indefatigable. As already stated he published *Principles of Contract* in 1876 and at once began the preparation of his second great work, *The Law of Torts*. At the same time he was preparing a series of essays which were published in 1882 under the title *Essays in Jurisprudence and Ethics*. In the meantime he brought out *A Digest of the Law of Partnership* in 1877, and he showed his versatility by editing with Leslie Stephen the *Lectures and*

Essays of W. K. Clifford (1879) and by writing *Spinoza, His Life and Philosophy*, which was published in 1880.

No further actual meetings are authenticated until 1882. The change in the familiarity with which the men addressed their letters to each other beginning in the fall of 1878 suggests that they may have met again, but this is only a conjecture.

A transition in Holmes's life as a background to these letters took place in December 1882, when he entered upon his judicial career. It is true that an intermediate period began in January of 1882, when he was appointed Weld Professor of Law in the Harvard Law School and contemplated a life as professor and teacher. He accepted the professorship, however, upon the express understanding that he should be free to accept a judgeship if one should be offered, and he was appointed an Associate Justice of the Supreme Judicial Court of Massachusetts on December 15, 1882.

From that time until his appointment to the Supreme Court of the United States in 1902 Holmes's work on the Massachusetts Court was the paramount business of his life. All other activities were subsidiary and there were few. He made occasional contributions to the *Harvard Law Review* and other legal periodicals, and a collection of his occasional speeches was published in 1891, to which in subsequent editions later speeches were added. He was appointed Chief Justice of Massachusetts in 1899. To him the appointment was in the nature of an accolade. It is true that his administrative duties were increased, and he undertook a larger proportion of the opinions of the Court, but his surroundings remained unchanged, and the current of his existence was not materially affected.

Pollock succeeded to the Baronetcy upon the death of his father, December 24, 1888. During the period from 1882 to 1902 he continued his great contributions as a legal writer and became prominent as a teacher. Unlike Holmes, he was not limited to one predominant occupation, and he threw himself magnificently into writing, teaching, and many incidental public activities. In 1884 he became Professor of Common Law at the Inns of Court, which professorship he held until 1889. He had already in 1883 become Corpus Professor of Jurisprudence at Oxford, which professorship he held until 1903.

In 1885 he was a founder of the *Law Quarterly Review*; he held the editorship until 1919 and continued as a contributor until the year of his death in 1937. He also contributed to other legal periodicals, including the *Harvard Law Review*. In 1887 his second major work, *The Law of Torts*, was published. In 1888 there was published *An Essay on Possession in the Common Law*, of which Pollock was the author in collaboration with R. S. Wright, later Mr. Justice Wright. It is said that the portion dealing with possession for purposes of civil as distinct from criminal law was written by Pollock himself. In 1890 he published his *Oxford Lectures and Other Discourses*. He drafted the Partnership Act of 1890 and published an annotated edition which embodied his earlier *Digest of the Law of Partnership*. In the same year *An Introduction to the History of the Science of Politics* was published. In 1894 Pollock traveled to India and there delivered the Tagore Lectures. In 1895 he became the first editor-in-chief of the Law Reports, a position which he held until his resignation in December 1935. The great *History of English Law before the Time of Edward I*, by Pollock and Maitland, was published in 1895. Although the larger part of the writing was done by Maitland, it is said that about one fifth was written by Pollock, and the work was planned in common and revised by both. During this period six editions of *Torts* and six editions of *Contracts* were prepared and published.

English commentators have indulged in some speculation as to Pollock's achieving the position at the Bar commensurate with his talents. The fact seems to have been that he soon became immersed in writing, teaching, and public activities, and by 1891 he had virtually ceased to hold himself out as a practising member of the Bar. Lord Wright sagely points out that no working lawyer could possibly have combined with his practice the study needed to acquire the equipment for Pollock's manifold activities.

During this period from 1882 to 1902 there were occasional actual meetings. Holmes went to England in 1882, and Pollock visited the United States in 1884. Holmes was in England in 1889 and Pollock visited the United States in 1895. Holmes was again in England in 1896, 1898, and 1901. In these visits sometimes they were accompanied by their wives, sometimes not. There are letters preserved between Holmes and Lady

Pollock, and several letters of Holmes to Lady Pollock are included in the letters here presented. Holmes had an affectionate interest in Pollock's son and daughter; he had no children of his own.

The second major transition in Holmes's life within the purview of these letters came with his appointment as Associate Justice of the Supreme Court of the United States in 1902. During that summer Mr. Justice Horace Gray had sent his resignation to the President and died on September 15, 1902. President Theodore Roosevelt appointed Holmes to fill the vacancy, and Holmes took his seat on the Bench December 8, 1902.

The complete change in environment served to emphasize the change in his work. He and his wife of course moved to Washington, and in 1903 he bought the house on I Street where he lived until his death. He continued to spend summer vacations at Beverly Farms, Massachusetts, but summers were moments of relaxation. His work was in Washington, and his work was predominant in his life. The breadth and variety of the cases which came before him and the occasional magnitude of the questions presented appealed to his imagination. He used to say, however, that he hated so-called great cases, and once in a dissenting opinion pointed out that they are called great "not by reason of their real importance in shaping the law of the future, but because of some accident of immediate overwhelming interest which appeals to the feelings and distorts the judgment." His own interest lay in the fundamental development of the law.

Holmes kept himself aloof from public affairs as a detached and remote observer. He delighted in keeping abreast of current thought and in seeing and talking to young men, whose ideas he found stimulating whether he agreed with them or not. For them his library became a center. His secretaries were a remarkable group of young men chosen successively and usually annually from the elect of the graduating class at the Harvard Law School, and their devotion to him continued after their terms ended. Among them was Mark DeWolfe Howe, the able editor of these letters, who is now Professor of Law and Acting Dean of the Law School of the University of Buffalo.

In 1920 Holmes published *Collected Legal Papers*, consisting of articles and addresses collected through the good offices of

Harold J. Laski. In 1922, in his eighty-second year, Holmes underwent a major operation, and while his recovery was satisfactory he then realized that he was an old man, and his limited outside activities were rigorously curtailed. In 1929 he suffered the most grievous loss in the death of his wife. He wrote to Pollock, "For sixty years she made life poetry for me."

There were published in 1929 and 1931 respectively two collections of Holmes's opinions, *The Dissenting Opinions of Mr. Justice Holmes*, arranged, with introductory notes, by Alfred Lief, with a foreword by Dr. Kirchwey, former Dean of the Columbia Law School, and *Representative Opinions of Mr. Justice Holmes*, arranged, with introductory notes, by Mr. Lief, and with an introduction by Harold J. Laski.

Throughout these later years Holmes took a whimsical pleasure in the increasing public recognition of his achievements, and his friends made an occasion of his ninetieth birthday. He was made Honorary Bencher of Lincoln's Inn. The *Harvard Law Review* devoted the March issue to paying him honor, and among the articles was one by Pollock. Holmes was touched by the many tributes.

A sense of failing powers led to his retirement on January 12, 1932. He continued to live in Washington and Beverly Farms, but this series of letters closes with Holmes's letter of May 15, 1932. His letters, like Pollock's, were always written in longhand, and his hand failed. His necessary correspondence he turned over to his secretary. Pollock continued to write occasionally and was kept informed, but the reciprocal quality of the series of letters was ended.

During the years following Holmes's appointment to the Supreme Court of the United States, Pollock's activities continued with vigor. *The Expansion of the Common Law*, a book of lectures, was published in 1904. In 1906 he published an annotated edition of the Indian Contract Act in collaboration with an Indian lawyer and judge. In 1912 he published *The Genius of the Common Law*, a book of lectures delivered at Columbia University; and in 1922, *Essays in the Law*, which included papers read in Oxford, London, Glasgow, and the United States. These were followed in 1927 by an entertaining book in lighter vein entitled *Outside the Law*. He devoted much time to the preparation of new editions of his principal works. *Torts* went through thirteen editions in his lifetime, the last prepared by him in 1929. *Contracts* went through nine editions during his lifetime, the last prepared by him in 1921.

Pollock became a Bencher of Lincoln's Inn in 1906, King's Counsel in 1921, and Treasurer of Lincoln's Inn in 1931. He was appointed the Judge of the Admiralty Court of the Cinque Ports in 1914, and was disappointed that no proceedings were instituted in that court before him.

During this last period the two friends still occasionally saw each other. In the summer of 1903 Holmes was again in England and Pollock came to the United States in the fall of that year. In the summer of 1907 Holmes visited England, and in August of the same year Pollock came to the United States for the meeting of the American Bar Association in Portland, Maine. In the summer of 1909 Holmes visited England and received the degree of D.C.L. at Oxford. In August of that year Pollock attended the meeting of the American Bar Association in Detroit, Michigan. In the fall of 1911 Pollock visited the United States and delivered the Carpentier Lectures at Columbia University. In 1913 Holmes visited England for the last time. The last meeting of the two friends face to face was in 1930, when Pollock visited the United States and he and Lady Pollock spent a week with Holmes at Beverly Farms.

It would be a serious omission if I should fail to recall the sincere interest which Pollock throughout his life showed for American law, American lawyers and writers, American law schools, and American law reviews following in the footsteps of his *Law Quarterly Review*. He was deeply interested in the development of the Common Law in the courts of the United States. In his own books he often cited American authorities and favored reciprocity on the part of the courts of one country in citing the decisions of the other. He lectured in the United States and contributed to the *Harvard Law Review* and other American law reviews. He maintained friendships here, and there are many who came to him as young men from the Harvard Law School or the *Harvard Law Review* who will never forget the cordiality and kindness with which they were received by him and by Lady Pollock.

It should also be added, as is indeed obvious from the letters, that both Holmes and Pollock were omnivorous readers. Their reading covered a wide range, from Bracton, Kant, Spinoza, and the classics to Wodehouse. I have in my possession a book in Holmes's hand in which he recorded the books that he read. This book is referred to by the editor as the "Journal," and is spoken of by some of the secretaries as the "Black Book." It began in 1876 with notations from works which Holmes consulted in his legal research. From 1882 on, he entered each year the books read during the year, with the infrequent addition of a note of an important event. The numbers of books recorded are almost incredible.[5]

Holmes died on March 6, 1935, two days before his ninety-fourth birthday. Pollock paid him tribute in articles in the *Harvard Law Review* and the *Law Quarterly Review*. Pollock lived long enough to take an active interest in the collection of this series of letters. He died on January 18, 1937.[6]

What has been written here, as already indicated, does not purport to be a complete biographical index of either of the two men or a complete bibliography of their writings.

The judicial opinions and writings of Holmes and the writings of Pollock are their monuments. Their legal significance, universally recognized as great, must be left to the legal historian; and events as well as the lights and shades of the ideas which constituted the greater part of their lives must be left to biographers except as reflected in the letters. The letters speak for themselves.

I wish to express the deepest gratitude to Mark DeWolfe Howe for undertaking the editorial work without which these letters could not have been presented, and to express the highest appreciation of his performance. Acknowledgment is due to Mr. and Mrs. Richard W. Hale of Boston for their invaluable contribution in first deciphering the letters. Acknowledgment is also due to the Law School of Harvard University and Dean James M. Landis for their generous sponsorship and assistance.

John Gorham Palfrey

Boston, Massachusetts
January 1, 1941

[5] A few copies of the "Journal" have been privately circulated, but the book has not been published.
[6] The greater part of the April number of the *Law Quarterly Review* is appropriately devoted to a series of articles on Pollock's life and works (53 *L.Q.R.* 151–206).

HOLMES – POLLOCK LETTERS

VOLUME I

I

1874-1894

BIDEFORD, July 3, 1874[1]

My dear Mr. Holmes:

Many thanks for your papers, which I have read in a slovenly way this morning, that being the only way at this distance from law books. There are many points you discuss or suggest which I should like to look more into—meanwhile I will give you some rough jottings as evidence that I have really read your articles. (You know the formula to thank an author for a work one means *not* to read — write off before you open the packet: "My dear xxx: Thanks, etc., etc. for your etc., etc. just received from the reading of which I hope to derive etc., etc.") On the notice anent Austin,[2] I thoroughly agree that the only definition of law for a lawyer's purposes is something which the Court will enforce. As to duty in cases of contract, I think the enforcement when practicable of specific performances clearly distinguishes the "sanction" from what you call a tax on a course of conduct.[3] As to the paper on Torts,[4] I am glad you so clearly expose the fallacy of treating legal negligence as a state of the negligent's consciousness. I wholly agree that both here, and in the nearly parallel cases you mention, where the question is whether a certain variation of a thing from the description it

---

[1] At the time when this letter was written Holmes was in England.

[2] 6 *American Law Review* 723 (1872). The notice was concerned with Pollock's article "Law and Command," 1 *Law Magazine and Review* (N.S.) 189 (1872), in which John Austin's definition of law had been criticized. Holmes's notice is reprinted in *Justice Oliver Wendell Holmes: His Book Notices and Uncollected Letters and Papers* (Shriver, ed. 1936), hereinafter cited as Shriver, p. 21, and in 44 *Harvard Law Review* 788 (1931).

[3] In this review Holmes had stated that "the notion of duty involves something more than a tax on a certain course of conduct." 6 *Am. L. Rev.* at 724; Shriver, at 26; 44 *Harv. L. Rev.* at 790.

[4] "The Theory of Torts," 7 *Am. L. Rev.* 652 (1873); reprinted, 44 *Harv. L. Rev.* 773 (1931).

was sold by amounts to difference in kind so as to annul the sale,
the true theory is that all attempts to get a scientific measure
are out of place and we can only seek a rough measure in "the
average opinion of the community" — or such of the community as are accustomed to dealings of the kind in question.
And by the way not only the juryman's verdict but the judge's
applications of "natural justice," "the reason of the law," *et hoc
genus omne*, really come to the same thing. As to the case which
professed to lay down a mathematical rule about rights to light
and air,[5] I think you will find that notion has been exploded by
several later decisions in the Appeal Court. (*N. B.* Our equity
cases in courts of first instance are for various reasons to be used
with great caution as authorities on questions of pure law.)

As to mercantile custom, see the important late case of
Crouch v. *Crédit Foncier*,[6] showing that the law merchant cannot now be extended by evidence of any modern custom: a
curious contrast to the time when the law was still so fluid that
the Court could take the evidence of merchants to satisfy itself
whether pirates were perils of the sea. On the other hand the
customs of particular trades as distinct from mercantile custom in general have of late years had more weight given to
them than ever before, *e.g. Fleet* v. *Murton.*[7] . . . Your classification of Wrongs [8] falls in partly with a notion I have had in
my head some time, thus: The text-writers say there is no intelligible distinction between the *delict* and *quasi-delict* of the
Roman lawyers. I think there is one. *Delict* proper being the
breach of a general duty, *i.e.* not arising from any special position of the party. (Whoever & whatever I am, I may not throw
things on my neighbour's head.) *Quasi-delict* the breach of a
particular duty (*i.e.* one which does arise from, etc.). (*As a
householder*, I may not let anybody throw things out of my
window on my neighbour's head.) I think that in English law
the somewhat anomalous action for a "tort arising out of a

[5] Beadel v. Perry, L.R. 3 Eq. 465 (1866).

[6] L. R. 8 Q. B. 374 (1873).

[7] L. R. 7 Q. B. 126 (1871).

[8] In his essay on "The Theory of Torts," Holmes suggested that the subject Torts
included Duties of All to All, Duties of Persons in Particular Situations to All, and
Duties of All to Persons in Particular situations. See his tabular analysis, 7 *Am. L. Rev.*
663; 44 *Harv. L. Rev.* 785.

contract," as against a carrier *e.g.*, must be explained in this way. Thus *Delict* would comprise your "Duties of All" and *Quasi-Delict* would coincide or nearly so with your "Duties of Persons in Particular Situations to All." Have you abolished special pleading of the ante-Common-Law-Procedure-Act kind in Massachusetts? If not, here is a gem from Viner's *Abridgment* somewhere in title Pleader, which may be useful to you. I think it is not generally known. I turned it out once by chance, looking for something else, and its oddity fixed it in my mind. A declaration in trover for bottles without naming how many bottles is ill: but a declaration for twelve pair of boots and spurs without naming how many spurs is well enough: for it shall be intended of the spurs that belong to the boots. I write at once in this disorderly fashion, as I don't know how long you are to stay in town or in England. I should like to have your Boston address before you go, for some day I propose to inflict on you a copy of a book I am now at work on which (if it ever comes out) will embody with improvements the most of what I wrote in the *Law Magazine*.[9]

My wife adds to my own her kindest regards for you and Mrs. Holmes.

Yours truly,
F. Pollock

London, May 2, 1876

My dear Mr Holmes:

I have been rather busy the last week or two, or I should have sooner thanked you for your very interesting paper on "Primitive Notions."[1] Your position seems well made out by evidence and analogy, and I think it a good piece of work in itself, and of just the kind now wanted to clear the way for an adequate handling of the general body of the Common Law. Whether it would be at all possible, until much more has been done in this way, to produce a really good institutional book, *quaere.* A Mr. Nasmith produced this last winter 2 vols. of so-

---

[9] Pollock, "Law and Command," *supra*, note 2.

[1] "Primitive Notions in Modern Law," Part 1, 10 *Am. L. Rev.* 422 (1876).

called *Institutes of English Private Law*. They had only the merit of good intentions. If you read our *Saturday Review*, you may have seen there what I thought of them.[2] It is wonderful how little we (on this side) have improved upon Blackstone. The tinkerings of his modern editors are mostly pitiful. Kent is a considerable advance, but leaves much to be desired.[3] For one thing, it is too large for a first book. I wonder from which side further advance will come. Prof. König of Bern, who has given my book a very handsome notice in the *Zeitschrift des Bernischen Juristen-Vereins*[4] (so you see I have a European reputation!) observes that American lawbooks are as a rule more scientific than English, & I suppose he is right, though I should not call Story's a happy instance. Anyhow, your *Law Review*[5] is far above anything of the kind here.

I don't think we shall mend matters by getting people who know nothing of the law of England to lecture on something they choose to call Jurisprudence: and the Inns of Court seem by the late changes in their arrangements in this behalf to have come to the same mind.[6]

You were good enough to ask about the chances of my coming to Boston. I should like it of all things (with or without further proceedings to the West: one may dream, while one is dreaming, of Yosemite valley & Sierra Nevadas), but don't see my way to it for at any rate the next year or two.

Yours truly,

F. POLLOCK

[2] 41 *Saturday Review* 54 (Jan. 8, 1876.)

[3] The twelfth edition of James Kent's *Commentaries*, edited by Holmes, had been published in 1873.

[4] *Principles of Contract* (1876), reviewed by K. G. König in 11 *Zeitschrift des Bernischen Juristen-Vereins* 289 (1876).

[5] The *American Law Review*, of which Holmes had been editor from 1870 to 1873.

[6] In 1873, following the recommendation of the Council of Education, the Inns of Court adopted a new system of legal education by which the six readerships on various subjects were done away with and in their place were established four professorships. The professors were to be assisted by tutors. In place of the Readership on Jurisprudence there was instituted a Professorship in Jurisprudence, including in that subject International Law, public and private, Roman Civil Law, Constitutional Law, and Legal History.

LONDON, July 26, 1877

My dear Mr. Holmes:

Many thanks for no. 2 of "Primitive Notions,"[1] which is very interesting & I think important for the scientific understanding of the law. The Select Committee of the House of Commons on Employers' Liability for Injuries to Servants (*i.e.* with regard to the doctrine of "common employment") has just published its report & evidence, which strongly bring out the difficulty of accounting for the general rule of vicarious liability for a servant's act unless as a survival. If you can get at English Blue Books this would I think interest you.

There seem to me to be two fictions mixed up in the doctrine. (1) The *personal* fiction that act of agent = act of principal — which properly belongs to the region of contract, but has got extended beyond it. (2) The *real* fiction (as pointed out by you) that the *thing* or instrument is liable. In the modern legal notion (1) prevails; historically I suppose (2) is almost or altogether the original efficient cause. . . .

Do you think Codification a humbug in the sense that codified arrangement of the law is undesirable *in itself*, or only that there is no advantage in doing it by legislative authority? In your article on "Theory of Torts"[2] you seem to desire "comprehensive arrangement" which I suppose means some more or less codified exposition.

I so far agree as to admit that the consideration of case-law as a pure science tends to make one look on codes as a kind of brutal interference with the natural process of legal reason. In 1874 I wrote a series of articles in the *Pall Mall Gazette* on "Case Law and Inductive Science"[3] which were I believe taken by several people as a covert argument against codification. They produced a long half-controversial letter from Sir James Stephen[4] & I had to explain that such was not my meaning.[5]

[1] "Primitive Notions in Modern Law," Part 2, 11 *Am. L. Rev.* 641 (1877).

[2] 7 *Am. L. Rev.* 652 (1873), reprinted 44 *Harv. L. Rev.* 773 (1931).

[3] Reprinted in Pollock's *Essays in Jurisprudence and Ethics* (1882), p. 237, *sub nom.*, "The Science of Case Law."

[4] Sir James Fitzjames Stephen, first baronet (1829–1894); Judge of the High Court of Justice, 1879–1891; author of *History of the Criminal Law* (1883); vigorous advocate of codification of the English law.

[5] Pollock's views at this time concerning the problem of codification were developed at some length in the introduction to his *Digest of the Law of Partnership* (1st ed., 1877)

(I pursued the analogy afterwards into the region of moral judgments, comparing the manner in which ethical standards are gradually refined & modified to the development of case-law by decisions [6] — this however has only a philosophical interest). Stephen met the supposed scientific objection with (as I think) the right answer: that laws exist not for the scientific satisfaction of the legal mind, but for the convenience of the lay people who sue & are sued. Now to say that law is for practical purposes more certain without a code than with one seems to me sheer paradox. Compare the Indian Penal Code with the amazing muddle English criminal law has drifted into through (among other causes) the combined meddling & timidity of the Legislature. However, I am not really in possession of your view: I hope you will put it into shape some day in the *American Law Review* or elsewhere. If so, I might be strongly tempted to reply — or could we (this as a mere conjectural suggestion) get up a sort of moot in print and have the two together? . . .

Yours truly

F. POLLOCK

LONDON, Nov. 26, 1878

Dear Holmes:

Sir H. Maine[1] tells me that he duly received your paper,[2] and was much interested by it but, being much exercised by the affairs of India and the two Universities, has not yet been able to acknowledge it as he would like. I don't know that I have any comment to make myself, as I agree with little or no exception. In the definition *ad fin.* how do you mean "exclude *others than* the owner" to be taken?[3] For a possessor, *e.g.* a

---

[6] See his essay "Ethics and Morals" in *Essays in Jurisprudence and Ethics* (1882), p. 287.

---

[1] Sir Henry Maine (1822–1888), author, *inter alia*, of *Ancient Law* (1861); *Village Communities* (1871); *Early History of Institutions* (1875); *Popular Government* (1885). In 1871 he had been appointed to a seat on the Indian Council, in 1869 he became Corpus Professor of Jurisprudence at Oxford, and in 1877 he was elected Master of Trinity Hall, Cambridge.

[2] "Possession," 12 *Am. L. Rev.* 688 (1878).

[3] The article had concluded with the following words: "But it is enough for the

termor, pledgee, or bailee having a lien, in many cases intends to exclude all the world *inclusive of* the owner. So that it should run, *semble*, "all persons or all persons other than the owner." I suppose you would hardly say that every possessor *is* owner *ad hoc*.

The first vol. of a new edition of Bracton, in the Rolls Series, is just out [4] & will I suppose find its way to you speedily. I fear it will be better used on your side of the ocean than on this. The editor is Travers Twiss. If he has used his mss. properly, they are all derived from an archetype which was itself carelessly written (some existing ones come by his account so near the date of the original that one can hardly talk of *corruption*). In Güterbock's *Henricus de Bracton*, p. 88, note 94, is a manifestly corrupt passage & the obvious correction, but the new print simply repeats the edition of 1569. In Bracton, fo. 16*b* (Güterb., p. 85) I strongly suspect that "*Tu eam quasi* TRADITAM *accipias*" is not a blunder of Bracton's but a clerical error for CREDITAM, which Bracton would naturally have written from the corresponding passage in the *Digest* cited by Güterbock. The new edition however gives TRADITAM with the vulgate. What is still odder, a few words before it gives "vel quid tal*i*" for "v. q. tal*e*" of edition 1569 — which is a change for the worse in sense. I shall make inquiries about Twiss's competence as a diplomatist; for it seems to me queer. It would be very annoying if it should turn out that so important a work is not being competently done. My opinion of Sir T. T.'s merits as a jurist, from what I have read of his, is pretty mean — but that proves nothing as to his care & accuracy in dealing with mss.

Did you ever hear the defunct Confederate States spoken of as the Lost Cause? They are so in a new (& otherwise rather silly) English book. Truly there is great virtue in capitals.

Yours truly,
F. POLLOCK

---

present if, with some incidental matters, it has been shown . . . that, except in the instance of servants as explained, one who manifests physical control over a thing with the intent and power (judged by the manifested facts) to exclude others than the owner from it, acquires possession, whether he has or has not the intent to deal with it as owner," *id.* at p. 720.

[4] *De Legibus* (6 vols., 1878–83).

BOSTON, December 9th, 1878

Dear Pollock:

... I of course agree with the doctrine suggested by your criticism of my final sentence, but I think you will find that the passage is not intended as a *definition* but simply a statement of the proposition I had sought to establish, *i.e.* of the more disputable part of a definition — leaving the rest to follow *a fortiori*.

I have been looking for Bracton for some time and had supposed that Twiss was a very good man for the semi-mechanical work of collation etc. If it should prove otherwise I should agree with you that we should be better off with the old prints and the *spes* of a critical edition by and by.

I am just now in a mild excitement. The judiciary of the U. S. (as distinguished from the State) is made up as follows.

1. The Supreme Court, sitting only to determine questions of law.

2. The Circuit Courts, the Circuits embracing several states & the Court having formerly been composed of a judge of the Supreme Court and the District judge, but most of the work being now done by local circuit judges (one for each circuit) not members of the Supreme Court who are of recent creation.

3. The District Court, held by a single judge appointed for the District. *This* District is coextensive with the State & known as the District of Massachusetts. Our local Circuit Judge having died last summer [1] there has been talk of promoting the District Judge Lowell,[2] and a good many of the bar have mentioned my name as Lowell's successor if he goes up.[3] The place is not desirable for the money, for the salary is only $4000. But it would enable me to work in the way I want to and so I should like it — although it would cost me a severe pang to leave my partners. But this morning from the papers it rather looks as if the Attorney General of the U. S.[4] was

---

[1] George Foster Shepley, circuit judge, died on July 20, 1878.

[2] John Lowell (1824–1897), United States District Judge for the District of Massachusetts from 1865 to 1878.

[3] Concerning the possible appointment of Holmes to the District Court, see George F. Hoar, *Autobiography of Seventy Years* (1903), II, 418–419.

[4] Charles Devens (1820–1891) was Attorney General of the United States, 1877–81,

Oliver Wendell Holmes, Jr.
1870

thinking of taking the Circuit Judgeship, which will of course settle the question, and there are other men in the field who have strong chances even if Lowell is promoted.⁵ But the way the bar here have spoken about me has given me much pleasure, and I can't help feeling nervous about the result until the thing is settled, although if I were appointed I should hardly know whether to be glad or sorry.

I heard rather a good story last night of an old judge who used to be fonder of quoting Latin than his knowledge of the tongue justified. He said "I will take up the question *de novo* — from the egg"!

Several of the State Courts have left equally amusing slips in the Reports. Old Redfield of Vermont has a simile in which he refers to the well known puzzle of Hercules and the lobster (meaning Achilles & the tortoise), and I have read in a California volume that the wife on marriage acquires an inchoate right of dower which by the death of the husband becomes choate.

But I must turn to more serious labors. This will reach you about the right time to present my wishes for a Merry Christmas.

Very truly yours,
O. W. HOLMES JR.

BOSTON, July 16, 1879 ¹

My dear Pollock:

I sent you the other day another article (Common Carriers) from this month's *Law Review*,² which as you will see is a sort of Appendix to that on Possession, and was easy to write after that. I intended it at first as merely a short note for the

---

and Associate Justice on the Supreme Judicial Court of Massachusetts, 1873–77, 1881–91].

⁵ Judge Lowell was appointed to the Circuit Court on December 18, 1878, and Thomas Leverett Nelson was named to take his place on the District Court, January 10, 1879.

¹ A letter of Holmes to Pollock, dated March 13, 1879, is omitted. Its contents consisted solely of a description of the Pennsylvania and Massachusetts statutes concerning the registration of partnerships.

² "Common Carriers and Common Law," 13 *Am. L. Rev.* 609 (1879).

Albany Law Journal, but I found as one always does that to say all I thought necessary took more space than I expected. I had the boldness to send copies to Sir A. Cockburn & Brett, L.J. as I had made their opinions my text [3] — although I know neither of those gentlemen & thinking I did not need an apology or introduction for such a purpose. It is my hope as you may have seen from the course of the pieces sent you, to take up the principal conceptions of our substantive law for the purpose of a new analysis so far as they seem to me to need it. When I have accumulated enough material I shall hope to rewrite them in the form of a book. But I can assure you it takes courage and perseverance to keep at a task which has to be performed at night and after making one's living by day. I have to thank you and other English friends for encouragement which has been very valuable to me. . . .

Very truly yours,
O. W. HOLMES JR.

LONDON, August 2, 1879

Dear Holmes:

Thanks for your letter and the article on Common Carriers which I duly received. I have not had time to consider it much, but it seems all right, & at all events to dispose of the Roman law theory.

About the same time I sent you a copy of the Partnership Bill I have been drafting.[1] In the new part (*Commandite*) I found the German Code more useful than anything else. All the statutes of American States (except those founded on old French law) seemed to me too timid and impracticably cautious.

Just now I have read Bigelow's[2] *Placita Anglo-Normannica* with much interest, and written a notice of it (not yet pub-

---

[3] Nugent v. Smith, 1 C. P. D. 19, Brett, J. (1875); reversed in 1 C. P. D. 423, Lord Chief Justice Cockburn (1876).

---

[1] For an account of Pollock's preparation of the Bill for the Consolidation and Amendment of the Law of Partnership, see his introduction to the second edition of his *Digest of the Law of Partnership* (1880), p. xxv, and the appendix to the fourth edition (1888), p. 161.

[2] Melville M. Bigelow (1846–1921); Professor of Law, Boston University, 1872–1921.

lished) for the *Saturday Review*,[3] in which journal I have also been testifying concerning the imposture committed by Travers Twiss in his new edition of Bracton,[4] which in every respect but cheapness is rather worse than the old one. I knew Twiss not to be a very accurate man, but did not expect such a piece of scamped work. The text is not edited at all, and the translation is full of schoolboy blunders. People interested in the subject ought to be warned as much as possible, since *prima facie* they might not unreasonably take the work on trust from the Record office. The worst is that it will now never be done properly, at least in our time.

Yours truly,
F. POLLOCK

LONDON, February 10, 1880

My dear Holmes:

Many thanks for the paper on Negligence.[1] I have not been able to give as much consideration to it as I should like. But I quite agree with your thesis that legal negligence is not a state of mind (as somebody says in Year Book quoted in Blackburn on *Contract of Sale*, the thought of man is not triable, for the devil himself knows not the thought of man), but falling short of an objective standard of conduct. Also I much like the exposition of modern doctrine and practice from this point of view. The topic has a certain philosophic interest as being on the borderland of law and ethics. The jury, aided & moderately controlled by the judge, play the part of Aristotle's φρόνιμος and I don't think the frankness and practical wisdom of his appeal to the judgment of reasonable men on concrete questions of duty — ὡς ἂν ὁ φρόνιμος ὁρίσειεν — has ever met with full justice from later philosophers.

To go back for a moment to Possession: have you ever noticed that in Gaius' account of the *actio furti* we find precisely the old Germanic rule of the bailee, not bailor, having the

---

[3] 48 *Saturday Review* 327 (Sept. 13, 1879).
[4] 47 *Saturday Review* 153 (Feb. 1, 1879), and *id.* 775 (June 21, 1879).

[1] Holmes, "Trespass and Negligence," 14 *Am. L. Rev.* 1 (1880).

remedy, and the same artificial reason given by a systematizing age? I wonder if there is any trace in Latin literature of the earlier stage: probably not. The passage is in Book 3, §§ 203–207. Observe that the reason for the rule is logically worked out, so that in the case of *depositum*, where the bailee is liable only for his own misfeasance, the *actio furti* is exceptionally given to the owner. My attention was called to this in looking through the excellent edition of Gaius and Ulpian brought out by Prof. Muirhead of Edinburgh. I have written a rather elaborate notice of it (at least for a non-technical journal) which will be in the *Saturday Review* sooner or later.[2]

Your Massachusetts statute for muzzling judges must be a curious piece of legislation.[3] Has it any special history, or is there anything like it in other States?

I hope Bigelow will give us some more historical work soon. Stubbs,[4] I hear, is not satisfied with his choice of authorities: but I don't know what in particular he objects to. Possibly B. might say that in many cases the specific authenticity does not matter so long as the record is near enough to its ostensible date to be typical.

Yours truly,
F. Pollock

Boston, June 17, 1880

My dear Pollock:

I should have written to you before this had I not been very hard driven with work, day and night. Practise of our mixed sort occupies my days, and my nights have been largely devoted to preparing a course of lectures for next winter in which

---

[2] James Muirhead, *The Institutes of Gaius and Rules of Ulpian* (1880), reviewed in 49 *Saturday Review* 286 (Feb. 28, 1880).

[3] In his article "Trespass and Negligence," at p. 35, Holmes had referred to the Massachusetts statute of 1860 (Gen. Sts., Ch. 115, Sec. 5) providing that "the courts shall not charge juries with respect to matters of fact, but may state the testimony and the law." For a description of the history of the statutory provision, as that history was known to Holmes, see "Remarks of Richard W. Hale," 11 *Mass. L. Q.* (No. 2) 57 (1926).

[4] William Stubbs (1825–1901); Bishop of Oxford; author of *The Constitutional History of England* (1874–1878); editor of *Select Charters of English Constitutional History* (2nd ed., 1874).

I hope to put together some of the ideas which I deem most important in a regular order looking forward at a later date to making a little book.[1] But as you will realize one gets ahead but slowly when his only chance is to sit down after dinner and after a day of more or less hard work. The frame of mind needful for successful speculation is so different from that into which business puts one.

I am much obliged to you for your reference to Gaius which had escaped me and which is very suggestive. It rather tends too to confirm a suspicion which I have often had that even the Roman law as the Roman lawyers understood it would give but partial support to the theories of German philosophers upon possession. I was content to assume for the purposes of my article that they were justified on their data but I have never felt quite convinced. If I remember it I will send you the outline of an argument which I recently made which involved a reference to the Roman doctrine. The case is important and has not been decided. I am afraid we shall lose it from the way the Court took my argument and yet I am not reconciled to doing so.[2] Bigelow is I suppose now in England finishing a book on Anglo-Norman procedure.[3] He is a man whom I greatly respect for his sincere love of learning which he has proved in spite of poverty etc., but there is nothing incisive or masterly about him — so that whatever he does will have to be done over again. He is, however, getting to be a really learned man.

I am just now writing that part of my course which deals with contracts and am struck anew with the value of your book.[4] I referred to your account of Consideration in one of my articles as the best which I had seen.

Yours truly,
O. W. HOLMES, JR.

[1] Holmes gave the Lowell Institute Lectures in Boston in the winter of 1880–81. The lectures were the basis of his volume *The Common Law* (1881).
[2] This case has not been identified.
[3] Melville M. Bigelow, *History of Procedure in England from the Norman Conquest* (1880).
[4] *Principles of Contract* (2nd ed., 1878).

BOSTON, March 5, 1881

My dear POLLOCK:

I have failed in all correspondence and have abandoned pleasure as well as a good deal of sleep for a year to accomplish a result which I now send you by mail in the form of a little book *The Common Law*. When a man is engaged all day at his office in practise it is a slow business to do work of this sort by night, but my heart has been deeply in it, and I am encouraged to hope by the way in which you have received articles which were precursors of parts of the volume that you will not think my time has been wasted. At any rate I have worked hard for results that seemed to me important. You are happy in being able to afford time to philosophy. I have to make my living by my profession and therefore have been compelled to approach philosophy indirectly through the door of a specialty, but all roads lead to Rome and I don't doubt that a man with the philosophic craving would find stuff to work upon if he was a hatter. I sometimes even think that there is a certain advantage in difficulties, and that one sails better with the wind on the quarter than when it is directly astern. I should like it very much if my book was noticed in England but I suppose there are few anywhere who interest themselves in such things. At least I find that Englishmen sometimes think that one has a better audience here for anything on the law which is not strictly practical, while I have been wont to look for companionship more to a few men on your side — although I should be unjust and ungrateful not to add some Americans in the same line.

Sincerely yours,
O. W. HOLMES, JR.

BOSTON, April 10, 1881

Dear Pollock:

Many thanks for your letter [1] and the advance sheets which I received a short time before it. We all appreciate your book

---

[1] The letter referred to is missing.

very highly here. I see that a hideous American reprint has made its appearance which is a practical evidence of its popularity. I congratulate you on reaching a third edition so soon.[2]

I gave a light touch to the question of bilateral contract by letter in my Eighth Lecture and also to one or two other things of which you speak. That particular question seems to me one which might probably be decided by tossing up without any particular harm. If there were a clear preponderance of convenience either way I should decide that way without hesitation and it seems to me that the telegraph furnishes a new argument for requiring actual receipt of the return letter. But so far as logic and the analogies of the law go I incline the other way. I should like you to see the Appendix to the 2d Ed. of Langdell's *Cases*, also published separately in a small book called (I think) *Elements of Contract*.[3] A more misspent piece of marvellous ingenuity I never read, yet it is most suggestive and instructive. I have referred to Langdell several times in dealing with contracts because to my mind he represents the powers of darkness. He is all for logic and hates any reference to anything outside of it, and his explanations and reconciliations of the cases would have astonished the judges who decided them. But he is a noble old swell whose knowledge ability and idealist devotion to his work I revere and love. I hope you will read my book. It cost me many hours of sleep and the only reward which I have promised myself is that a few men will say well done. I find it was sent to the *Saturday Review* & *Spectator*, but I fancy it is an accident whether it falls into the hands of people who will realize that the work is at least a serious one. If you come to America so as to be here September 1st or the last week in August, as I expect to take my usual three weeks vacation at that time I can put you and your wife if you have simple tastes up in our little place[4] in a way that I think you might enjoy

[2] The first American edition of Pollock's *Principles of Contract*, edited by G. H. Wald, was published in 1881, and was based on the second English edition of 1878. The third English edition was published in 1881.

[3] This supplement to the second edition of Christopher Columbus Langdell's *Selection of Cases on the Law of Contracts* (1872) was reprinted separately under the title *Summary of the Law of Contracts* (1880). Holmes had written reviews of the first edition; 5 *Am. L. Rev.* 539 (1871); 6 *id.* 353 (1872), reprinted Shriver, pp. 89, 92.

[4] At Mattapoisett, Massachusetts.

for a week. Let me know some time before if you come — as
I hope you will.

Yours truly,
O. W. HOLMES JR.

BOSTON, July 5, 1881

My dear Pollock:

I am exceedingly gratified and obliged by your good opinion
and your kindness in expressing it. The notice in the *Saturday
Review* [1] (which I had already attributed to you on internal
evidence before receiving the copy with your initials) was
worth a good deal of hard work, and the mention of my book
in your introduction to your new edition was even more intimately pleasing to me. [2] I do not think I should disagree with
any of your criticisms for I believe they all touch on points
upon which I sought to express myself with great caution. There
may be some things which I should like to discuss with you a
little but I doubt if there would be much. I think you will find
that I am right as to the *fact* that motion as such is pretty frequently mentioned in the older books, and if I can trust my
memory without my book before me, the latin phrase which I
quoted was not *movere ad mortem* but *omne quod movet cum eo
quod occidit hominem* — or words to that effect. [3] I cited that
particular phrase because it is evidently the original of a quotation which Blackstone gives as from Bracton and which people
have been puzzled to find there.

I feel almost ashamed to write of such matters when we are
feeling so much about the President. [4] It is at least a comfort to
believe that the attack had no political significance. If you and
Mrs. Pollock think of coming over here let me know in advance

---

[1] 51 *Saturday Review* 758 (June 11, 1881).

[2] In the introduction to the third edition of his *Principles of Contract* (1881), Pollock discussed at considerable length Holmes's chapters on Contract in his *Common
Law*.

[3] The phrase as quoted in *The Common Law*, p. 26, from Fitzherbert's *Abridgment*,
Corone, pl. 403, reads: "*omne quod movet cum eo quod occidit homines deodandum
domino Regi erit, vel feodo clerici.*"

[4] President Garfield was wounded by an assassin on July 2 and died on September 19,
1881.

when you are coming. We should be delighted to have you at
Mattapoisett if we are there. We expect to go there as usual
for about two weeks at the end of August and the first week in
September.[5] Be kind enough to remember me very kindly to
your father and mother.[6]

Sincerely yours,
O. W. HOLMES JR.

BOSTON, April 8, 1882

Dear Pollock:

If I can get a case argued at Washington in time as I hope
to do, — I shall sail with my wife for Liverpool on the *Parthia*
May 20 and be in London during at least the early part of June.

I don't yet give way too much to anticipation to avoid disappointment, but I think the chances are largely in favor of my
turning up. I therefore postpone writing for the present. I am
working like a beaver *ad interim* to get ready.

Yours ever,
O. W. HOLMES JR.

This is one of the advantages of the professorship.[1]

BOSTON, March 25, 1883

Dear Pollock:

I am not quite sure whether I have written you since hearing of your election to the Professorship of Jurisprudence or
not.[1] I have been in such a continuous whirl of affairs ever since
my appointment.[2] At all events I may say once or again as

---

[5] Pollock did not visit the United States in 1881.
[6] See *Personal Remembrances of Sir Frederick Pollock, Bart.* (1877), II, 264, for mention by Pollock's father of his meeting with Holmes in 1874.

[1] Holmes was appointed Professor of Law at the Harvard Law School on January 23,
1882. With his wife he made the contemplated trip to Europe in the summer of 1882.

[1] Pollock had recently been elected Corpus Professor of Jurisprudence at Oxford.
[2] On December 8, 1882, Governor John Davis Long had nominated Holmes an
Associate Justice of the Supreme Judicial Court of Massachusetts, and he had taken
office on December 15. On January 8, 1883, he resigned as Professor of Law at the
Harvard Law School.

you know without my saying that I am deeply delighted that you got the place. I of course wished you to have what you wanted if only because you wanted it, but I congratulate myself and all interested in the philosophy of law that you should be in a place which will give us a right to expect contributions from you which otherwise you could only make by stealing time from other work or from sleep. I know what that means, and know that no one can stand it long. I was sorely disturbed when in London,[3] to think that two friends whom I value as I do you and Dicey should find themselves in competition. And I am enchanted that you should be fellow workers at Oxford and that all is so well arranged.[4] Since my appointment I have been sitting in banc and writing opinions all the time. Next month I hold equity alone and the next (May) sit in divorce causes. I enjoy the work so far extremely. To mention one or two points in your letter:[5] Would you not call detinue an action of tort, or if not, would it not be necessary at least to understand the doctrines worked out through detinue to master the whole theory of tort? We use a simplified real action for the recovery of land in Massachusetts. It rather pleases me to remember that one of the most learned and best books on the subject was written by my grandfather, who once sat on our Supreme Bench.[6] (Jackson on *Real Actions*)

As to your draft I have only a word to say. I agree that the distinction between questions of the law of property and the law of torts is not without meaning. For besides conveyancing there is in the former the statement of the facts necessary to call this & that specific right into being, or to end it, etc. But in my old age I become less and less inclined to make much use of the distinction between primary rights duties and consequences or sanctioning rights or whatever you may call them. The primary duty is little more than a convenient index to, or

3 In 1882.

4 Albert Venn Dicey was elected in 1882 to the Vinerian professorship of English Law at Oxford.

5 The letter referred to is missing. It would seem likely, however, that Pollock had discussed matters which he was later to treat in the first chapter of his *Law of Torts* (1st ed., 1887), and, perhaps, that he had enclosed a draft of the chapter in his letter. The matters here referred to by Holmes were discussed at length in that first chapter.

6 Charles Jackson (1775–1855); Associate Justice of the Supreme Judicial Court, 1813–23.

mode of predicting the point of incidence of the public force. You may remember what you and Anson[7] thought an extreme application of this view when I dealt with contract in the purely legal aspect as only a conditional liability to pay damages, avoidable by performance. My inclination therefore, if I had time, would be, I think, to leave very little to be learned elsewhere about the primary rights supposed to be infringed by torts. I think (though this doesn't hit you) that some of your codifiers have an inclination to shove off what they don't want to talk about into some other part of the *corpus*. But then I don't attach much importance to the codifying furore — except for India.

I am reading Stephen's *Criminal Law*. My opinion of him as a law writer does not grow higher, as I read this or his former books. He knows nothing, it seems to me, of the scientific aspects of the history of law, and is to my mind rather a model of a fine old 18th century controversialist than a philosopher. He would knock the stuffing out of an antagonist upon a point of dogma I don't doubt, in the handsomest way. He is an adult male animal, but he hasn't the intuition of Maine or the higher class of writers.

I must stop. It is Sunday afternoon — I got up late — have written an opinion that there was evidence that a plaintiff was using due care and that the Judge did wrong in taking the case from the jury, and must now go and make a call or at least take a walk and get a little fresh air, a commodity of which I have precious little on week days. I have pretty well given up dining out, as I can't do it and feel as well and fit for work the next day and am amusing my evenings by reading a little *belle lettres*. "Ah, one of our Classics. We don't read them," as one of your countrymen once said to me when I quoted a line from *The Traveller*. I am meditating the perusal of your *Spinoza*.[8] Do you recommend it? Remember us most kindly to Mrs. Pollock and believe me

Sincerely yours,
O. W. HOLMES JR.

[7] Sir William Reynell Anson, (1843–1914); author, *inter alia*, of *Principles of the English Law of Contracts* (1st ed. 1879).
[8] Pollock, *Spinoza: His Life and Philosophy* (1880).

MATTAPOISETT, MASS.
August 27, 1883

Dear Pollock:

I have been so hard at work that I have neglected correspondence and everything but business until I got to this languid spot where I am apt to spend my vacations by the sound of the polyphloesbian, the mosquito and the crow. Here I have been for a month however and it is high time that I should remind you of myself. A week from today I shall again be in the whirl. Well, I like my work far more than I dreamed beforehand. The experience is most varied — very different from that one gets at the bar — and I am satisfied most valuable for an all round view of the law. I have written a lot of opinions of the full court, sat alone for some time in equity, disposed of a long divorce list and shall hold *nisi prius* soon after I leave here.

One sees too a good deal of human nature, and I find that I am interested all the time. We are very hard worked and some of the older Judges affirm that no one can do all the work without breaking down. I have not yet made up my mind — at all events it is more interesting than if we had less to do. The legislature has just given equity jurisdiction to the Superior Court which we hope will relieve us somewhat by throwing a good many things into that Court in the first instance subject to an appeal to us. I hope you will keep me informed of what is occupying your active mind. You do so many things that I never know whether next to expect a drama, a lawbook, a symphony or a system of philosophy. I hope and believe that you are happy in your new place. It must, I know by experience, be delightful and stimulating to expound to a lot of intelligent young men old enough to have serious opinions.

With kindest remembrances to Mrs. Pollock in which my wife joins, I am

Sincerely yours,
O. W. HOLMES JR.

BOSTON, November 5, 1883

My Dear Pollock:

I have so many things to say that I hardly know where to begin, but I will first mention that I have just received your admirable address.[1] I thank you most sincerely for your kind mention of me which gratifies me and warms my heart. I hope you will let me know something of your experiences and the methods which you adopt in your new place. I suppose that it is somewhat different from a law school intended to produce lawyers ready for the bar after a short time in an office, but I don't quite figure to myself what the differences are. . . . As to Lord Coleridge's visit[2] I think that he made a very pleasing personal impression by his very knowing and lightly touched speeches which mingled skillful flattery with occasional touches of more wholesome truth, but I don't believe that it was of any importance as an international influence if so intended. . . . I notice your observation as to Denman Ross. He is not a man of first rate ability, but he has I believe really studied the German sources at first hand for a long time, and after reading his book[3] I am not prepared to accept Sir H. Maine's wholesale condemnation of him (which I remember he expressed to me) without further knowledge. I cannot myself form an independent opinion, but I doubt if Maine himself has the necessary first hand knowledge for that, and I have been so much impressed by the way in which the German professors go down like a row of bricks before the last theory which some exceptional man has made fashionable that I don't bow prostrate before a consensus of them. The presumption is that Ross is wrong, but I must say that the more obvious parts of his arguments have always struck me as difficulties and as I have said I can't control what he offers as the data of the next books after Caesar and Tacitus.

[1] Undoubtedly his inaugural lecture delivered at Corpus Christi College, Oxford, October 20, 1883, entitled "English Opportunities in Historical and Comparative Jurisprudence." The lecture is printed in his *Oxford Lectures and Other Discourses* (1890). At pp. 45–46 he made reference to Holmes.

[2] Lord Chief Justice Coleridge (1820–1894) came to the United States in August 1883 as the guest of the New York Bar Association and, until his departure in October, traveled extensively and spoke frequently throughout the United States. The letter in which Pollock apparently had mentioned Lord Coleridge's visit and other matters referred to by Holmes is missing.

[3] Denman W. Ross, *Early History of Landholding among the Germans* (1883).

I read your *History of the Science of Politics* [4] with much profit and I have to thank you also for having put me upon Burke who certainly is marvelous great. . . . Our kindest remembrances to Mrs. Pollock as well as yourself.

> Yours ever,
> O. W. Holmes Jr.

Boston, March 9, 1884

Dear Pollock:

This Sunday morning our good old messenger has just brought me your letter [1] from the Court House and I accept it as a sort of birthday greeting — for yesterday I reached the venerable age of 43. I don't mind growing older for I think that I have found life as vivid as most people and have had my share so far of action and passion. If a man gets a year's life out of a year he can ask no more.

I need not repeat how delighted I am at this more definite assurance that you are coming here, and whenever it may be I shall do all in my power to see as much of you as possible. To answer your questions categorically I think that people generally get back to town from about the first to the middle of October. The College term begins in the beginning of the same month and the Cambridge people have to be on hand then.

We Judges have a different lot. We have no regular vacations and the fortune of any member of the Court in that regard depends on what he has to do and his assignments which are made by the C. J. and vary from year to year. We meet in Boston early in September and then five of the seven go off to hold Court in the country counties — generally we can get back to Boston for Sunday and perhaps one or two more days each week, but that depends. Whether I shall go this next September I don't yet know, but probably shall in time to write you. . . .

[4] Pollock's lectures on the *History of the Science of Politics*, delivered at the Royal Institution in 1882, were published serially in the *Fortnightly Review* from August 1882 to January 1883 and in book form in 1890.

[1] This letter is missing.

This letter was interrupted by two weeks a few lines back. I told Cabot Lodge the other day that you were coming and he expressed the hope that he should see you and said he'd agree to any theory of booked and unbooked laws. He has thrown over early law and gone into American history & politics, is chairman of the State Republican Committee and as such shares with Gov. Robinson the credit of having licked Butler. He is young rich and has a pleasant wife and house. He, like the greater part of Boston, lives within an hour or two of the city on the seashore in the summer time.

I am glad to hear of the prospects of the *Review*.[2] Of course for the present my investigations are at an end. I have however some memoranda touching the doctrines of early Equity (especially *uses*), a topic on which I always contemplate the possibility of writing more at length,[3] and I may perhaps be able to shape certain portions into an article. We will see. . . .

Give my love to Leslie Stephen & his wife. He is one of my oldest and dearest friends — yet I hardly ever write him nowadays or he me.

Goodbye
Sincerely yours
O. W. HOLMES JR.

LONDON, July 12, 1884

My dear Holmes:

In first week of September we are to cross into U. S. William James has asked us to spend a week in Keene Valley, Adirondacks, then we are for Cambridge and/or Boston. Should be happy to meet you on circuit, if so be.

Your copy of speech sent me must have miscarried (the N. H.

---

[2] Plans for the foundation of the *Law Quarterly Review*, under Pollock's editorship, were made during the year 1884, and the first issue was published in January 1885. For the story of its origins, see Pollock, 51 *L. Q. Rev.* at 6–7 (1935).

[3] Holmes contributed an article to the second issue of the *Law Quarterly Review*: "Early English Equity," 1 *L. Q. Rev.* 162 (1885), reprinted in *Collected Legal Papers* (1920), hereinafter cited as *C. L. P.*, p. 1, and in 2 *Select Essays in Anglo-American Legal History* (1908) 705.

one?).[1] I have seen Bryce's,[2] & we greatly admire it, & hope you will have another left for me.

Yours ever,

F. POLLOCK

BOSTON, November 2, '84

Dear Pollock:

. . . I have been very hard at work and have written opinions in some very interesting cases. I mentioned that of the foetus that wanted to recover (upon a statute) for making it a person prematurely by reason whereof it died.[1]

Another touched easements where the dominant estate was in Rhode Island and the *quasi* servient estate here & action brought here (for withdrawing water of stream). Held it would lie.[2]

Another is a most interesting case of homicide,[3] well settled by your law, and the other way by an old case of ours. If my opinion goes through it will do much to confirm some theories of my book. Next week (election week) we go to Salem. . . .

I have just received your draft on negligence[4] for which I thank you. It reached my hands but an hour ago so I can not

---

[1] Presumably Holmes's "Memorial Day," an address delivered May 30, 1884, at Keene, New Hampshire; printed in *Speeches of Oliver Wendell Holmes* (1934), hereinafter cited as *Speeches*, p. 1.

[2] James Bryce (1838–1922), Regius Professor of Roman Law, Oxford, 1870–93; British Ambassador at Washington, 1907–13.

---

[1] Dietrich v. Northampton, 138 Mass. 14 (1884). In an opinion by Holmes the Court held that a statutory action for the wrongful death of an infant, prematurely born alive, but dying almost instantly after birth, could not be brought by the child's administrator.

[2] Mannville Co. v. Worcester, 138 Mass. 89 (1884).

[3] Commonwealth v. Pierce, 138 Mass. 165 (1884). The unanimous opinion of the Court, written by Holmes, was delivered on November 24. Distinguishing the earlier case of Commonwealth v. Thompson, 6 Mass. 134 (1809), Holmes stated that the external standard of responsibility was applicable to criminal prosecutions as to civil actions, and that a doctor, though ignorant of the danger involved in his conduct, might be convicted of manslaughter when his reckless prescription of a dangerous remedy resulted in his patient's death.

[4] It is possible that Pollock had sent to Holmes a preliminary draft of Chapter XI of his *Law of Torts* (1887), that chapter being concerned with negligence.

criticize it yet. Give my kindest remembrances to Mrs. Pollock.

Sincerely yours,
O. W. HOLMES JR.

BOSTON, March 12, 1886 [1]

Dear Pollock:

I thank you for your letter.[2] I suppose a day or [two] later you received a newspaper containing the tail or end of a discourse on the choice of the law as a profession.[3] The difficulties and generally the things to be spoken of here are somewhat different from what they are with you. Your case suggests one on which I propose to deliver an opinion if it passes the criticism of my brethren.[4] Cattle are sold for cash at a market. The process of delivery takes some little time & is accomplished by weighing off, which also is necessary to ascertain the price, so that though the sale is a cash sale the cattle are delivered an hour before payments. In the interim the seller is induced to take a worthless check by false pretenses & the buyer is indicted for obtaining the cattle by false pretenses. I don't mean that the actual case is so simple as this, but in my view it comes to this. I think the man may be convicted and that it is not necessary to decide whether the buyer shall he held not to have gained possession while the sale is *in fieri* or whether it shall be held enough *under such circumstances* for one already in possession to obtain the title by false pretenses. But the case suggests curious speculations. I have had no time to read anything but some little poetry etc. for change of thought, as my work

[1] A brief note from Holmes to Pollock, dated February 6, 1885, is omitted. With the note he enclosed a copy of the speech "The Law" which he had delivered on the previous night at the Suffolk Bar Association. (See *Speeches*, p. 16.) Also there is omitted a letter from Holmes, dated April 5, 1885, in which he discussed briefly the circulation of the *Law Quarterly Review* in the United States, expressed admiration for Pollock's versatility in writing, and mentioned without comment his own opinions in Learoyd v. Godfrey, 138 Mass. 315 (1885), and Brown v. Eastern Slate Co., 134 Mass. 590 (1883).

[2] The letter referred to is missing.

[3] "The Profession of the Law — Conclusion of a Lecture Delivered to the Undergraduates of Harvard University on February 17, 1886." Reprinted in *Speeches*, p. 22.

[4] Commonwealth v. Devlin, 141 Mass. 423 (1886).

fills almost all my time. I notice in the review of Piggott on *Torts* in your *Review* [5] . . . you speak of conflicting theories as to rebutting malice in libel and slander and refer to 7 App. Cas.[6] I put the matter in my book p. 139. You speak of Stephen having written on it — where has he done so? I had supposed that I started the point for the first time. I have read your articles on Manors with much pleasure and interest.[7] I can't criticise them as I don't know enough. I am struck with what you say as to the continuity with the Saxon period (which indeed I believed before) because I think we get very little light on the general law from Saxon sources. I think our forms of action, our notions of contract, possession, tort, trust etc., come in the main through Normandy from the Franks, as I have endeavored to show.

Have you received John Gray's book on the *Rule against Perpetuities* for notice? I think so far as I have examined it that it is really a first rate piece of work of its kind, worthy of the great masters of real property law.

Will you please remember me to Sir Wm. Anson. I always recall what I saw of him with unmixed pleasure and could wish that he should not forget me. . . . Remember Mrs. Holmes & me to Mrs. Pollock and believe me always

Sincerely yours
O. W. HOLMES JR.

BOSTON, December 21, 1886

Dear Pollock:

. . . I have just finished the last opinion I have on hand to write — and have nothing to do till January 1, when I shall have a hard two months in Equity, followed by sittings in banc with other opinions to be written and then by the spring circuit.

Since the first of September until now I have been on the stretch all the time, and during the summer our life was sad and wearing for reasons which I have mentioned before. Father

---

[5] 2 *L. Q. Rev.* 95 (1896).
[6] Capital and Counties Bank v. Henty, 7 App. Cas. 741, 787 (1882).
[7] See Pollock, *Oxford Lectures and Other Discourses* (1890), p. 112.

is very well but somehow seems much more distinctly an old man than heretofore.

This and my mother's breakdown and the fact that I have started eye glasses all make me realize what otherwise I should often forget, that I have got well into middle life. But I am very happy and I always think that when a man has once had his chance — has reached the table land above his difficulties — it does not matter so much whether he has more or less time allowed him in that stage. The real anguish is never [?] to have your opportunity. I used to think of that a good deal during the war.

Please tell Mrs. Pollock that the Yale people made me an LL.D. the same day that Oxford gave father his Degree. I wrote her that I was expecting it.[1]

I must go out to make a few Christmas purchases.

I don't think the run of questions this autumn has been as interesting as usual. Still I've had some nice points. . . .

Give my love to Dicey and remember me most warmly also to Sir Wm Anson & so a merry Christmas & happy New Year to you all from

Yours sincerely,
O. W. HOLMES JR.

BOSTON, January 17, 1887

Dear Pollock:

I suppose you received my letter[1] saying with what pleasure I contemplated your proposed letter to me by way of opening gun to your *Torts*.[2] Since then I have received the article on History of Contract.[3] By a young man I imagine. I like to see them all try a cut at Hobbes' iron cap (there's arrogance for

---

[1] The degree of LL. D. was conferred on Holmes by Yale University on June 30, 1886. For his speech on receiving the degree see *C. L. P.*, p. 33; *Speeches*, p. 26.

---

[1] Both this letter and the one from Pollock to which it was responsive are missing.
[2] The first edition of Pollock's *Law of Torts* (1887) contained a prefatory letter addressed to Mr. Justice Holmes.
[3] Probably an article by John W. Salmond, "The History of Contract," 3 *L. Q. Rev.* 166 (1887).

you) but I think the old pot will serve for a few days longer, still.

My work is so hard that I don't dare attempt outside things. When a few days leisure come I want to fall to and probably should, but my wife comes down on me with a picture of death as imminent if I do. So I fill such moments with talk about life, and reading poetry aloud, and French novels to myself. I wax impatient sometimes to think how much time it takes to do a little fragment of what one would like to do and dreams of. Life is like an artichoke; each day, week, month, year, gives you one little bit which you nibble off — but precious little compared with what you throw away. I enjoy it as keenly as most people however, I rather think. And I do despise making the most of one's time. Half of the pleasure of life consists of the opportunities one has neglected. But already I have idled too long in making these few cosmical observations.

Yours ever,

O. W. H. Jr.

Boston, March 4, 1888 [1]

My dear Pollock:

I have been a little slow in thanking you for your kind letter [2] because having been somewhat upset and a little delayed in my work I had to make up for it and have been very busy. My mother's death [3] was not to be regretted on her account but such an event whenever it happens must be a shock and give one a tug that goes far down to the roots.

Father seems well and takes his loss as I would have him. My sister [4] will live with him and he will be happy.

---

[1] A note from Holmes, dated September 2, 1887, is omitted. The note stated that Holmes enclosed a letter which he had recently received from General Benjamin F. Butler, whom Holmes described as "a very remarkable man, whatever you may think of him." The letter from Butler mentioned Pollock's recent volume on torts and criticized the tendency of the Supreme Court of the United States to abandon precedents and to make new law. It is preserved with the Holmes and Pollock letters at the Harvard Law School.

[2] This letter is missing.

[3] Holmes's mother died on February 6, 1888.

[4] Mrs. Turner Sargent (Amelia Jackson Holmes, 1843–1889).

Maine certainly is a great loss.[5] I think he had the gift of imparting a ferment which is one of the marks of genius and that his first book[6] most brilliantly caught and popularized in the form of established propositions the ideal ends toward which more truly scientific students on the continent had long been striving. He seems to have been impatient of investigation himself and I do not think will leave much mark on the actual structure of jurisprudence, although he helped many others to do so.

I should write to Maitland if I knew him. I wish you would express to him my opinion that his work on legal history is of the truly scientific kind — accurate investigation of details in the interest of questions of philosophical importance.

His criticism of a phrase of mine in 4 *L. Q. R.* 35 is right I doubt not. I had noted some references in my copy to the same point before I saw his article.[7] I don't know anybody here who is doing anything to speak of in that way, perhaps because I am too busy to know.[8] There is what seems an excellent study of the development of actions for loss of service in 22 *Am. Law Rev.* 765–[9] [*sic*] in the midst of other matters less important. Ernest Young (one of the *Essays on Anglo-Saxon Law*)[10] a learned young man, just made full professor, "died suddenly" it says in the papers, killed himself I am told, the night before last. Laughlin,[11] another of them, is broken down with work I hear (probably the trouble with Young), and Royce, one of our most promising philosophers, has had to stop work for the present.

I think I haven't written to you since I read your *Torts*. It's an admirable piece of work not at all adequately praised by

---

[5] Sir Henry Maine died on February 3, 1888.

[6] *Ancient Law* (1st ed. 1861).

[7] "The Beatitude of Seisin," 4 *L. Q. Rev.* 24, 286 (1888).

[8] On the outside of the envelope enclosing this letter Holmes had written: "I should have excepted Ames in what I say within. He is giving some very careful and instructive lectures on the history of laws." James Barr Ames (1846–1910) was Bussey Professor of Law, Harvard Law School, 1879–1903; Dane Professor of Law, Harvard Law School, 1903–09; Dean of the Harvard Law School, 1895–1909.

[9] John H. Wigmore, "Interference with Social Relations," 21 *Am. L. Rev.* 764 (1887).

[10] Author of "Anglo-Saxon Family Law" in *Essays in Anglo-Saxon Law* (1876), pp. 121–182; Professor of History, Harvard University, 1874–88.

[11] J. Laurence Laughlin (1850–1933), author of "Anglo-Saxon Procedure," *id.* pp. 183–305.

saying that it is much the best there is so far as my knowledge goes.

I have written a good many decisions on which I have been much interested. I may mention *Fairbanks & Snow*, 145 Mass. 153 (not yet published), to be seen in the various periodical reporters, on duress of a 3d person, not disclosed to the contractee. I have to get away from Lord Coke in *Thoroughgood's Case*[12] & from some N. Y. decisions to establish what principle and analogy required.

Our reporter[13] has just been made a judge of the Superior Court and since the last sentence was written I have received two of the numerous candidates for the office. Such occasions make you realize in a painful way how many clever agreeable men are on the verge of failure in the battle of life.

Remember me most kindly to Mrs. Pollock.

Sincerely yours,
O. W. HOLMES JR.

BOSTON, February 23, 1890[1]

Dear Pollock:[2]

I was truly sorry at the piece of bad news your New Year letter gave me as to your term being held not continuable.[3] I did not quite know whether it was settled beyond revision. If it gave you more time to work with Maitland on the history of the law I should not regret it except for the money. I have been very hard at work — rather harder than usual because of the Chief Justice's illness.[4] But on Friday I wrote my last

---

[12] 2 Rep. 9 (1582).

[13] John Lathrop (1835–1910), appointed an Associate Justice of the Supreme Judicial Court on January 24, 1891.

---

[1] In the summer of 1889 Holmes had been in England.

[2] Pollock's father, Sir William Frederick Pollock, Bart. (1815–1888), died on December 24, 1888, and Pollock succeeded, as third Baronet, to the title.

[3] The letter from Pollock is missing. It seems probable that it referred to the termination of Pollock's professorship of Common Law at the Inns of Court. From 1884 through 1889 he had received appointments to that office from the Council of Education. The normal term of a professor's office was three years. See 6 *L. Q. Rev.* 228, 229 (1890).

[4] Marcus Morton (1819–1891); Justice of the Supreme Judicial Court, 1869–82; Chief Justice, 1882–Aug. 27, 1890.

decision and am ready to meet the boys in consultation on Tuesday. Then to sit again and load up with more cases to be decided.

I was glad of the little notice of Lambertenghi's translation of my book in the *L. Q. R.*[5]

The cases which I have had this year have not been remarkable for universal interest — although there is always the pleasure of unravelling a difficulty. Here is one. The Executors of a deceased quack (I should suppose) doctor gave the plaintiff his formulas and trademarks, "Dr. so & so's Queen of Pain" etc. by word of mouth alone. The defendant has learned the formulas honestly and has a right to make the medicines; he proposes to use the trade marks. I should add that the plaintiff does not continue any manufactory or anything of that sort of the late inventor & the trademarks no more indicate the plaintiff's than the defendant's manufacture.[6] I hope to persuade the brethren that if (like the *res nec mancipi*) modern forms of incorporeals unknown to the old law of which delivery is impossible can be given at common law without a deed or Ms. (as to which our law has been rather more conservative than yours) yet that the plaintiff has no right to protection, as otherwise the right to the exclusive use of a collocation of words for advertising purposes would be erected into a new species of property far superior to that of poets in their verses, lasting as long as a certain class of goods is manufactured & transferrible in gross, wholly irrespective of any fraud, etc, etc. I had occasion to read some of Lord Westbury's judgments on the matter, with renewal of my old impression that I didn't quite see what there was to admire in him. . . .

My winter has not been sprightly, what with not feeling very well, and the adjustment to a new situation — living in my father's house instead of in my own,[7] etc. But all goes well and things seem far more cheerful now than they did. Remember me always with affectionate regard to Lady Pollock and also

[5] *The Common Law* was translated into Italian by Francesco Lambertenghi and was published in Sondrio in 1888–89 under the title *Il Diritto Comune*. The volume was briefly reviewed in 6 *L. Q. Rev.* 106 (1890).

[6] Chadwick v. Covell, 151 Mass. 190 (1890). Holmes wrote the Court's opinion.

[7] Following the death of his sister Amelia, on April 3, 1889, Holmes and his wife moved from 9 Chestnut Street to his father's house at 296 Beacon Street, Boston.

do not fail to tell old Dicey that I still live and think of him. . . .

Yours ever,
O. W. HOLMES JR.

BOSTON, January 17, 1891

Dear Pollock:

I have only a moment to return in fullest measure your good wishes[1] to you and to Lady Pollock. Would that I could have both of you here or be with both of you there this snowy day. Poor old Devens of our bench has just died and I am pressed with some extras, having been pretty busy before. He had seen the elephant pretty thoroughly in his time. He commanded a division during the war and was Attorney General of the U. S. under President Hayes. . . . I watch with a deep interest every step you and Maitland take in history. I can't help thinking that it will be a mistake to spend much time on Anglo-Saxon Law. It has seemed to me from all that I have ever read that, however it may be with institutions, our *corpus juris* and procedure are Frankish (with a varnish of Roman), and think the most profitable sources before the Conquest are on the Continent. Of course there is a generic identity in the Ang. Sax. laws with other *leges barbarorum*. But back of the year books I think you learn most from the *Lex Galica* and its successors and German commentators. But dear me I am so absorbed in the actualities and immediacies that I can only envy your learned explorations. . . .

I wrote a decision which has just been sent down[2] that in an action for enticing away a man's wife (without slander by mere advice), the defendant had a right to testify that his advice was honest, since unless it was dishonest he was privileged — intimating that probably also he was not liable unless he actually intended to produce separation, the latter intimation being on the ground that when there intervenes between the defendant's act and the consequences complained of another wrongful

---

[1] The letter referred to is missing.
[2] Tasker v. Stanley, 153 Mass. 148 (1891).

act as a *sine qua non* then defendant is not chargeable unless he actually intended the result. I think this is the ground of a great number of cases, but I only gave a hint of my general view which is all I can do now. . . .

Yours ever,
O. W. HOLMES JR.

BOSTON, March 22, 1891

Dear Pollock:

I have been delayed in answering your letter[1] by the fact that I am under a high pressure of work with the full court. In the way of a single book which will give you a general out-line of prevailing views, a reference to the special treatises, together with citations of important texts on the history and content of Frankish, etc. law, I can recommend *Lehrbuch Der Deutschen Reichs- und Rechtsgeschichte* von Dr. Joh. Friedrich von Schulte. My edition is the 5th (probably there is a later one), Stuttgart — Wilhelm Nitzschke, 1881. I did not have it when I was writing but I bought it at Heidelberg in '83[2] and read it and thought it an admirable compendium and starting point for almost anything you want. . . . Since then I believe Heusler has published a good general book, and perhaps Brun-ner, and for all I know others. The Germans are model text-book makers.

I send you herewith *Tasker* v. *Stanley*. It was thought ad-visable to cut down the discussion in which I aired some of my views. So you will see that it only gathers a lot of references which in my mind converge to further conclusions. What I have in mind beside the immediate point of privilege for honest advice is this. The general criterion of liability in tort for which I have contended as you know is the tendency of an act under the circumstances known to the actor — according to common experience. If the probability of harm is very great and manifest the act is called malicious or intentional. (See *White & Duggan*, 140 Mass. 18, 20.)[3] If less but still sufficient

---

[1] This letter is missing.   [2] Probably a slip. Holmes was in Europe in 1882.
[3] In his opinion for the Supreme Judicial Court in this case Holmes said: ''A specialty deriving its validity from an estoppel *in pais* is perhaps somewhat like Nebu-

to impose liability it is called negligent. But forthwith the objection arises if *tendency* is the general test why is not a man who sells firearms liable *civiliter* & *criminaliter* when someone is shot by one of his customers, since it is pretty certain according to common experience that murderers and trespassers will buy his pistols for their purposes? It is commonly said that the law stops with the first responsible cause in the ascending line, which is true generally speaking. But why? Again it is commonly said because the last actor is in a legal sense the cause of the results. But an innocent actor intervening later, is as much a cause as a wrongful one — yet if the intervening actor is innocent the earlier wrongdoer may be held. *E.g.* a privileged repetition of a slander. See *Elmer* v. *Fessenden*, 151 Mass. 359, 362,[3] and generally *Clifford* v. *Atlantic Cotton Mills* 146 Mass. 47, 49.[4] The true ground, I think, is that a man is *presumed not to contemplate illegal conduct of others* and is not liable unless it

---

chadnezzar's image with a head of gold supported by feet of clay. But if the case is properly put on that ground, then, as was pointed out in Commonwealth v. Pierce, 138 Mass. 165, the difference between intent and negligence, in a legal sense, is ordinarily nothing but the difference in the probability, under the circumstances known to the actor and according to common experience, that a certain consequence, or class of consequences, will follow from a certain act; and it follows that the question when an estoppel will arise is simply one of degree."

[3] The case was an action for slander brought by an employer against a doctor who was alleged to have advised the plaintiff's employees that the materials upon which they worked in the plaintiff's factory were poisoned. It was charged that as a result of this information the employees abandoned their employment. The plaintiff argued that the defendant was answerable not only for his own statements concerning the materials but also for damage suffered from the repetition of the story by others. Discussing that contention, Holmes said: "The general rule that a man is not liable for a third person's actionable and unauthorized repetition of his slander, is settled. . . . If the repetition is privileged, the question becomes somewhat different. It is true that the fact that the sufferer has no action against one person is not a sufficient reason for giving him one against another, even if otherwise he is remediless. But the case is withdrawn from the principle applied in many instances, that the law will look no further back than the wrongdoer who is the proximate cause of the consequence complained of." It was then found to be unnecessary to resolve the suggested problem because the repetition of the slander was not privileged.

[4] It was held in this case, in an opinion written by Holmes, that the owner of a building who let it to a tenant was not liable to a passer-by who was injured by snow falling from the steep unguarded roof, even though the tenant had made no covenant to repair, and the owner had reserved the right to enter the premises to repair them or to determine whether they were being properly used. In the course of his opinion Holmes said (pp. 48–49): "There is no doubt that a man may sometimes be liable in tort, notwithstanding the fact that the damage was attributable in part to the concurrent or subsequently intervening misconduct of a third person. . . . But the general tendency has been to look no further back than the last wrongdoer, especially when he has complete and intelligent control of the consequences of the earlier wrongful act."

is shown that he actually did contemplate it, — this class of cases marking an exception to the general external test of tendency, although no doubt the Jury may find actual intent from the plainness of the tendency. I think this explains the cases as to repetition of slander, the dog spear cases, the law of landlord & tenant explained in *Clifford* v. *Atlantic Cotton Mills*, *supra*, what I suppose to be the criminal law as to accessories before the fact, etc., etc. I sent you the first half of a discourse on Agency[5] (including master & servant) written nine years ago and now published in the *Harvard Law Review* to please the young chaps who edit it. I told them I had no time to write but if Ames thought the old ms. worth printing they might have it. Now that I see it in print I think it pretty good, the first half at least. I've not yet seen the second.[6] But I should hope that you and Maitland might some day run across some texts which would throw new light. . . . I have had a turn or two of not being as well as I could wish, which warns me to be careful. This month I have passed the equator of fifty. Life grows more equable as one grows older; not less interesting, but I hope a little more impersonal. An old man ought to be sad. I don't know whether I shall be when the wind is west and the sky clear.

Sincerely yours,
O. W. HOLMES

BOSTON, June 7, 1891

Dear Pollock:

Many thanks for your letter [1] and my sincere commiserations for your illness. I have had some more trouble, since I wrote you I think, and at the same time have been very hard at work, as the Chief Justice [2] has had to take a rest and hand over his cases, and W. Allen the senior side judge after having been ailing and requiring partial relief from the rest of us died

---

[5] 4 *Harv. L. Rev.* 345 (1891), reprinted in *C. L. P.*, p. 49.
[6] 5 *Harv. L. Rev.* 1 (1891), reprinted, *id.*, p. 81.

---

[1] This letter is missing.
[2] Walbridge A. Field.

suddenly four days ago. *Tasker* v. *Stanley* in itself was plain enough as you say. Its interest to me was as a step toward a formula I was wishing to expound. First I had a case of *Clifford* v. *Atlantic Mills* . . . where I justified a previous Mass. case [3] (that a landlord is not liable for the fall of snow from a roof which the tenant might and ought to have prevented) on the general principle that the law stops with the last wrongdoer having intelligent control of the consequences complained of. Then in *Elmer* v. *Fessenden*. . . . I intimated that a man might be liable for a privileged repetition of his slander. Then came *Tasker* v. *Stanley*, and now I have fired off a later decision not yet in print (I forget the names — I'll try to find it —), in which I stated what I had in mind. Action *vs.* a town for a defect in a highway; [4] statutory liability, as construed for many years (probably originally on general notions of liability but now standing as a special principle) confined to cases where, as it has been put commonly, the town's neglect is the sole cause. The jury might have found that there was a defect in a highway — *viz.* a telegraph wire hanging close to the ground — that plaintiff was using due care, that the wire got entangled in the wheels of a wagon driving the opposite way from the plaintiff but that the driver of that wagon did not know it. The plaintiff was hurt in driving under the wire. I took occasion to indicate that the innocent third person is as much a concurring cause as a guilty one, but that the law considers the third person not *qua* cause but *qua* wrongdoer, and that the doctrine as to towns is only an extreme application of the general principle that within limits not yet exactly defined a man is presumed to expect lawful conduct from his neighbors even if he is acting wrongfully and therefore is not liable for results which would not have come to pass but for their later, or, in case of towns at least, concurrent, wrongdoing. Innocent acts of a third person of a kind which the town was bound to contemplate are no excuse. So at last I've got it in. There has been an awful lot of rot talked about causes by judges and presumably by gents like Wharton. [5]

[3] Leonard v. Storer, 115 Mass. 86 (1874).

[4] Enclosed in the letter were the advance sheets of Hayes v. Hyde Park, 153 Mass. 514 (1891).

[5] Francis Wharton (1820–1889); author of numerous treatises including *The Law of Homicide* (1st ed., 1855); *A Treatise on Criminal Law* (1st ed., 1846); and *The Law*

I want to get it all on the footing of the reasonably-to-be-contemplated, and to explain at the same time the exception which is perfectly settled here at least in cases like the wrongful repetition of a slander, etc., when it would not be enough, I apprehend, to show that the defendant as a reasonable man might have expected the repetitions — which is generally true — if he did not expect it in fact.

Give my kindest regards to Lady Pollock. I think of you both often, in the midst of much strenuous toil.

Yours ever,
O. W. HOLMES, JR.

BOSTON, July 8, 1891

Dear Pollock:

I enclose you, or rather send you by this mail, an opinion of mine reported in 146 Mass. 545,[1] (see *Goreley & Butler*, 147 Mass. 8.) which has lately been reversed by the Supreme Court of the U. S., together with Lamar's opinion.[2] It is the only case written by me & almost the only one I've sat in for these 9 years that has gone to the Supreme Court (it involved a federal ques-

---

of Negligence (1st ed., 1874), to which was added an appendix on Causation, published separately in 1874, under the title *A Suggestion as to Causation*.

[1] Heard v. Sturgis. The plaintiffs in this case, during the Civil War, had paid enhanced premiums for war risk insurance on their vessels and cargoes. In 1875 they assigned all their property to the defendants as assignees in bankruptcy. In 1874 Congress had made provision for the payment of claims directly resulting from damage caused by Confederate vessels which had sailed from British ports. Thereafter, in 1882, when all claims for such direct injury had been paid, Congress made provision for the distribution of unappropriated funds to persons who had paid war risk insurance on their vessels. Holmes, in an opinion for a majority of the Court, held that the plaintiffs, rather than the defendant assignees in bankruptcy, were entitled to the award, since at the time of the assignment the plaintiffs had no vested right of any kind, supported by a moral consideration, to receive compensation from Great Britain or the United States for the enhanced premiums. The award of the Commissioners, under the act of 1882, Holmes considered to be a pure gratuity, distinguishable from awards to those persons whose property had been destroyed by the Confederate vessels.

[2] Williams v. Heard, 140 U. S. 529 (1891), reversing Heard v. Sturgis, *supra*, note 1. Mr. Justice Lamar, for the Supreme Court, held that there was at all times "a moral obligation on the part of the government to do justice to those who had suffered in property" (140 U. S. at 540–541), and that though the plaintiffs' rights were not enforceable until 1882, they had existed from the first and were property which passed to the assignee in bankruptcy in 1875.

tion). I think it an interesting case and one which I could have written the other way, but I confess I think the ground adopted by the U. S. Court one which is quite irreconcilable with primary juridical notions. My view (you will see there was a dissent)[3] carried the Supreme Court of Maine which has been tending the other way and the Court of Errors and Appeals in New York. So that in everything but technical authority the weight is on my side. I should like to show it to Bowen[4] but as you told me he had been ill I thought I would not trouble him. I merely send it to you as an amusement for your leisure moments. My vacation is just beginning. I am in very fine health again and everything smiles. My very kindest remembrances to Lady Pollock.

Sincerely yours,
O. W. Holmes

Boston, Oct. 21, 1891

Dear Lady Pollock:

I hope this week to send you my pamphlet[1] and as I have a moment's leisure I write to you now to recall myself to you and yours. Work has begun in good earnest, and as the Chief Justice is off duty still, and another judge is under the weather and there are only seven of us in all there is a chance of high pressure. However, the immediate result is that I have two or three idle days so we cannot make a full court for this week. Idle days are apt to be the busiest as you know, no doubt, and I am between two errands when I sit down to this reminder. I have seen the first volume of your husband's *Revised Reports*[2] but have had no time or chance to examine it; another man told me that it was done as well as possible which gave me pleasure. As to people, I have scarcely set eyes on a soul outside the bar.

[3] In the Massachusetts Court Mr. Justice Field wrote a dissenting opinion in which Mr. Justice William Allen concurred. 146 Mass. at 552.

[4] Lord Bowen had recently considered an analagous problem in *Ex parte* Huggins, 21 Ch. Div. 85 (1882).

[1] The first edition of Holmes's *Speeches* was published in 1891.

[2] The first volume of *The Revised Reports*, edited by Pollock with the assistance of R. Campbell and O. A. Saunders, was published in 1891.

OLIVER WENDELL HOLMES
ABOUT 1890

I expect to be rather an anchorite this winter and neither drink wine or make love but to be happy and content if I am able to do my work and keep well.

I long to come to England and to see you all again but frame no plans. Meantime don't forget your affectionate friend

O. W. HOLMES JR.

Don't answer till you get the book.

LONDON, November 11, 1891

My dear Holmes:

We are very glad to have your discourses neatly collected. Several of them are old friends, notably the first,[1] which we admire as much as ever.

I have been boiling down the law of trade combinations for the use of the Labour Commission (which I send you); and I am lecturing on Anglo-Saxon law in Oxford to three men and an Indian lady (one of the men York Powell, who can give me a good many points in construing the texts); and I have been helping to found a Fencing Club in that same seat of learning.

Also at odd times I am writing on the Early History of Mountaineering (a fascinating subject, but requiring many books and minute care) for a forthcoming volume in the 'Badminton' Series. The library of the Alpine Club will thereby justify its existence, I hope. And today I hear of my (incepting) election to 'The Institute' — a club of forty real property lawyers whose existence is hardly known even to the majority of the Equity Bar.

That young New Zealander Salmond has brought out a little volume of essays:[2] the right sort of stuff, and the faults those of youth. He sticks, against both you and Ames, to what I now think the least probable of all the historical theories of Consideration. . . .

I need not tell you that America in the divine person of Miss

---

[1] "Memorial Day" (1884).

[2] John W. Salmond, *Essays in Jurisprudence and Legal History* (1891).

Rehan has again captured the British stage, and *The American*[3] seems like to survive its critics. . . .

St. Martin hath sent us a storm of wind and rain instead of his summer.

Yours ever,

F. POLLOCK

BOSTON, April 15, 1892

Dear Pollock:

I am constantly in your debt for good and charming things. I have received your book of verse now.[1] How sincerely I admire them I told you long ago. The Greek awakes sad recollections in me. I was a tolerable Grecian once myself but since I graduated mighty little have I looked at save a play or two by Aeschylus with a pony and the *Iliad* ditto. I always think of the Frenchman's answer when he was asked if a gentleman must know Greek & Latin: "No, but he must have forgotten them." I must not write long, for this morning I must prepare to give my opinion to the legislature whether they can authorize municipal wood & coal yards — a step towards Communism. I am likely to be in the minority and to think that they can, but I may come out the other way or the rest of the 7 may agree with me.[2] I will send you a case on embezzlement which I wrote some time ago.[3] There was no difficulty with the decision but I tried to explain a bit of history about it. No very great or burning questions have been before me although a good many fairly interesting ones. I am growing or rather am stouter than I ever have been since I last was wounded and am very well

---

[3] Henry James's *The American* had opened in London on September 26, 1891.

[1] *Leading Cases Done into English* (1892). A number of the verses in the volume were in Greek. An earlier edition had been published in 1876.

[2] See Opinions of the Justices, 155 Mass. 598 (1892). Chief Justice Walbridge A. Field and Justices Allen, Knowlton, Morton, and Lathrop advised the legislature of Massachusetts that it had no such power. Mr. Justice Barker concurred with them in part. Holmes, in a brief opinion, stated that he was "of opinion that when money is taken to enable a public body to offer to the public without discrimination an article of general necessity, the purpose is no less public when that article is wood or coal than when it is water, or gas, or electricity, or education. . . ." 155 Mass. 607.

[3] Presumably Commonwealth v. Ryan, 155 Mass. 523 (1892).

although I have to be pretty careful. I had a touch of the enemy of the year before, last February — a kind of inflammation in my insides — but time and care will put him down. I saw Sara Bernhardt in the *Dame aux Camélias* last night and am a wreck today. Give my sincerest regards to Lady Pollock.

Yours always,
O. W. HOLMES JR.

BOSTON, April 26, 1892

Dear Pollock:

   ... The article on malice by Ormsby [1] ... seems to have waked up rather late.

I believe I sent you a case *Hayes* v. *Hyde Park* [2] in which I developed the exceptional importance of actual intent when there is an intervening wrongdoer between the damage & the act complained of, and the importance of the intervening party being a wrongdoer, showing the futility of the usual modes of discussion in terms of *cause*. I once remarked that ignorance was the best of law reformers. I think the observation applies to *Claridge* v. *South Staffordshire Tramways Co.* [3] ... which somebody pointed out to me. The Judges didn't know much history and used their wits with no bad effect. I decided substantially the same point the other way in *Brewster* v. *Warner* 136 Mass. 57.

The portrait of you is excellent. [4] ...

Yours ever,
O. W. HOLMES JR.

My affectionate homages to Lady Pollock.

---

[1] W. E. Ormsby, "Malice in the Law of Torts," 8 *L. Q. Rev.* 140 (1892).
[2] 153 Mass. 514 (1891).
[3] [1892] 1 Q. B. 422. The case raised the problem of whether a bailee in possession could recover damages for a negligent injury to the bailed chattel, and if so what damages were recoverable.
[4] A photograph of Pollock was published as a frontispiece to volume 8 of the *Law Quarterly Review* (1892).

BOSTON, January 20, 1893

Dear Pollock:

I am for the moment in the position of a bloated capitalist; two cases have come on in which I can't sit because of interest and while they are finishing the last one I send you a line. I have only my usual story to tell — of living like a recluse and working hard, just hard enough, that is. Solitude, socialism and solitaire. I made the acquaintance of one of our labor leaders some time ago, made a pilgrimage to his very humble shrine and bid him sit and deliver his sentiments. "Sir," I said, "I am Judge H. of the Supreme Judicial Court. I have no ulterior motives and no particular questions to ask or observations to make, but I thought in the recently published interviews you talked more like a man of sense than the rest, and as a Judge and as a good citizen I like to understand all phases of economic opinion. What would you like if you could have it?" So we have discoursed several times with some little profit. Organization, the 8 hour law, and the Swiss referendum seem to be his particular objects.

For the last 3 months apart from law, Hobbes's *Leviathan*, and a few stories, I have read mighty little, having been mainly occupied in playing solitaire — a form of decadence I should not have believed possible before-hand — but it is a relief to one's eyes, etc. I have begun Karl Marx's book, but although he strikes me as a great man I can't imagine a combination less to my taste than Hegel and political economy. I just received the proofs in our very slow reports of an old case which it struck me might interest you . . . , *Graves* v. *Johnson*.[1] Sale "in view of" a violation of laws of another state. It gave me a chance to have a touch at the theory which I have written to you about in tort, as it affects contract.[2] . . . I hope you are all well. Give my affectionate remembrances to Lady Pollock and believe me

Yours ever,
O. W. HOLMES JR.

---

[1] 156 Mass. 211 (1892).
[2] "As in the case of torts, a man has a right to expect lawful conduct from others In order to charge him with the consequences of the act of an intervening wrongdoer you must show that he actually contemplated the act." *Id.* at 212–213.

HIND HEAD COPSE,
SHOTTERMILL, SURREY
August 9, 1893

My dear Holmes:

. . . My paper on Maine is out in the *Edinburgh*.[1] I think I sent you a separate copy of it addressed to Boston but am not quite sure. That he did not make any specific discoveries of importance I should on the whole agree, but I think he did what was more important than any particular discovery. However I 'crave leave to refer' to what I have said in print.

My voyage to the Indies is practically fixed. A certain rich Bengali by name Tagore had a son who became a Christian. Wherefore he cut him off (raising in the High Court of Calcutta, to the great comfort of the profession, the whole question of a Hindu's testamentary powers)[2] and left his money to charities, one of which is the foundation of an annual law lectureship in the University of Calcutta. One of the subjects proposed for this winter's course was the law of Fraud etc. in British India, which suits me exactly,[3] as I have gone over the ground in Contracts to please myself, and in Torts in drafting a code for the Government of India.[4] The Law Faculty of the said University (so called — it is modelled on the sham University of London) has recommended me to the Senate, which always elects as it is recommended. . . . Good introductions are promised me, and it is bound to be an interesting experience anyway. . . .

You would like our company here, though I say it. Mrs. Clifford[5] has taken a ruined priory a few miles off. A brilliant Irish family are near neighbours . . . . Pity we can't have you and the William James's too. Wright, J.[6] is five miles off in

[1] 178 *Edinburgh Review* 100 (July 1893); an unsigned review of a number of books on Sir Henry Maine.

[2] Ganendra Mohan Tagore v. Upendra Mohan Tagore, 4 Bengal L. Rep. 103 (1869); 9 Bengal L. Rep. 377 (1872); 1 Indian Appeals 387 (1874).

[3] The lectures were published in a volume entitled *Fraud, Misrepresentation and Mistake in British India* (1894).

[4] Pollock's draft of a Code of Civil Wrongs for India was first included as an appendix to the second edition of his *Law of Torts* (1890), p. 517.

[5] Mrs. W. K. Clifford, English novelist and playwright and friend of Holmes and Pollock. In 1879 Leslie Stephen and Pollock had edited and published the *Lectures and Essays of W. K. Clifford*, in two volumes, with an introduction by Pollock.

[6] Sir Robert Samuel Wright (1839–1904); Justice of the Queen's Bench Division of the High Court of Justice, 1890–1904; author, with Pollock, of *An Essay on Possession in the Common Law* (1888).

Hampshire, and will preside at his village flower show next week.

Yours ever,
F. POLLOCK

August 31, 1893 [1]

My dear Holmes:
I agree with your dissenting opinion.[2] The proper question, I think, was whether a reasonable man, reading the article with the ordinary knowledge of a citizen of Boston, would naturally and reasonably read it as applying to the plaintiff. It would be a question of law whether there was *any* evidence of this, and, if yes, then a question for the jury whether the article did, in that sense, defame the plaintiff.

But Nemesis is upon us. The reasonable man and the "external standard" have filtered down to the common examination candidate, who is beginning to write horrible nonsense about them.

Yours ever,
F. POLLOCK

I sail September 15.

CALCUTTA, December 11, 1893

My dear Holmes:
When did I write to you last? I can't remember anything I did in Europe except that I generally wound things up to go of themselves till my return. I have amplified my knowledge

[1] The original of this letter was found in Holmes's copy of Volume 159 of the Massachusetts Reports (1894). If Holmes had written to Pollock concerning the case discussed, the letter is missing.

[2] Holmes's opinion in Hanson v. Globe Newspaper Co., 159 Mass. 293, 299 (1893). The defendant newspaper company had published an article describing a criminal trial of "H. P. Hanson, a real estate and insurance broker of South Boston." The person so tried was in fact A. P. H. Hanson. The plaintiff, H. P. Hanson, who was also a real estate and insurance broker in South Boston, brought an action of libel. The trial court denied him recovery, and the majority of the Supreme Judicial Court, in an opinion by Knowlton, J., sustained the ruling. Holmes wrote a dissenting opinion in which Morton and Barker, JJ., concurred.

of jurisdictions; just now I am where the Common Law prevails (as regards European British Subjects) by statute: and I have been where it is received as 'justice equity and good conscience,' *viz.* anywhere in British India outside the Presidency towns, also where law is mostly in the breast of the native Prince and the Resident between them, *viz.* the minor States of Rajputana, also where there is no law, or at least no *lex terrae* at all, *viz.* the Khaibar Pass beyond British territory and before you came to the Amir's.

De facto there are posts of the Khaibar Rifles, an irregular military police, and two picturesque and much armed Sawárs of that force ride with one's trap: and the tribes keep the peace of the pass faithfully enough, being well paid by us. But it was quaint to see how, when the sapper in charge of our posts was going over Ali Masjid Fort (which is an elevated fort, mudbuilt like everything there, commanding a goodish view), and I sat down on a ruined tower for the view, a Khaibar Rifleman with grass sandals and a very ancient rifle anxiously hovered within ten feet of me. That N. W. corner of the Empire is not exactly beautiful, but one gets the feeling of Central Asia and sees types one would not see elsewhere.

They live, so far as we let them, in a Dark-Ages condition of infinite bloodfeud and no settled scales of wergild; which leads to complications with modern penal justice.

Rajputana is a dream of medieval splendour — cities with not a stone modernized (the British Residency is always detached), and the most gorgeous harmonies of colour living and moving in a brilliant sun. A fine people too.

The Maharaja of Jodhpur is as princely a gentleman as you shall see.

Likewise I have seen "Agra and Lahore of Great Mogul" as Milton saith. Fatehpur Sikri, the deserted but noways ruined palace of Akbar, is a marvellous thing: decoration in stone (red sandstone it is) carried to the farthest point without niggling — exquisite adaptation of Hindu detail by Mahometan designers and a certain 'Lofty Gate' to the great mosque which is a real flight of architecture. . . .

The great Sikh temple at Amritsar is a sight to remember, not so much for the temple as for the pilgrims coming and going: Hinduism is elastic and all manner of Hindus treat it as a holy place. One element which does not contribute colour to a Hindu religious crowd is the fakirs, as they wear nothing but caste marks and ashes. But there are not many of them.

As to the Taj Mahal at Agra — the one piece of Indian architecture that many good folk have heard of — its supremacy is quite deserved, though no reproduction does it justice.

Ask me not of Calcutta: it is a sham European city with a squalid native city grown round it. The river, the shipping, and the maidan, which is a fine open space between the river and the quarter of European houses (much like a magnified St. John's Wood), are the only features of any interest. The 'cold weather' climate is of bright days with treacherous evening chills: I am down with one, and the Babus have to do without two lectures: but indeed, as Maitland observed, they should not need to be taught much of Fraud and Misrepresentation. . . .

I am trying to start on Persian, which is worth learning. Urdu (Hindustani as it is commonly but improperly called) has no literature and is therefore not worth pursuing for a visitor not likely to return to the country. Persian seems to be about as simple in grammar and rich in idiom as English. In N. India too the grammatical breakdown of Sanskrit in the vernacular is greater than that of Latin in the Romance Languages. The Urdu verb is a mere rudiment eked out with auxiliary constructions.

Dec. 12. The doctor has given me a clean bill. He thinks he is on the track of a new infection present in these cases, not malarial but some other specific little devil of a microbe. There is a new drug called phenacetene with a wonderful power of reducing temperature.

Anglo-Indian hospitality is the one thing in the world that equals American, unless peradventure they do the like in Australia, which may be. I have spent just one day (not counting days in the train) as an ordinary traveller at my own charges. Here I am staying with old friends.

I am not satisfied that anybody knows very much law here; certainly they are not great at equity to judge by reported cases. They seem to have a way of aiming at the obviously right result by elaborate judgments of ten pages professing great hesitation: still, so far as I have observed, they oftener come right than not.

My enemy *Derry* v. *Peek*[1] has not been so much as cited in court here — certainly nothing like a judicial discussion.

I expect to be home again before the end of January, so London will be my next address.

Yours ever,
F. POLLOCK

Do echoes of the cow-killing troubles reach you? There is no doubt somebody is trying to brew mischief deeper down in the Hindu population than it has ever been tried before. Happily our eyes are wider open than they ever used to be. I have just been reading the Mutiny documents edited and summarized by my friend G. W. Forrest.[2] The greased cartridge business is one of the incredible truths of history: I believe the evidence is now fully published for the first time.

13th. I hear today from my wife that Bowen is looking ill and old, for which I am sorry.

F. P.

. . . At Benares I saw a real gymnosophist — a Brahman ascetic who lives in a garden all by himself & wears no clothes — he was beautifully clean and his manners most distinguished. Benares has been I think a little overrated and over-described. But it is worth while to see what a queer tangle of things of all sorts modern Hinduism is. It all runs to grotesque.

I heard Lord Lansdowne make a memorable speech at Agra: he praised the townsmen for having had no row, but did not mention (what I heard afterwards) that the field battery quartered there (European, of course — the only native artillery since the Mutiny are a few mountain batteries) had been ostentatiously marched through the town. . . .

---

[1] 14 App. Cas. 337 (1889). Pollock had criticized the decision at some length in 5 *L. Q. Rev.* 410 (1889) and in the second edition of his *Law of Torts* (1890), p. 254 *et seq.*

[2] Sir George William Forrest, *Selections from the Letters, Despatches and Other State Papers Preserved in the Foreign Department of the Government of India, 1772–85* (1890).

BOSTON, April 2, 1894

Dear Pollock:

I have waited too long to answer a very nice letter you wrote me from India. When I received it I had inside of me for the first time a dose of the drug you mentioned in it, for I was ill and aching with the *grippe*, or influenza as you call it — odd coincidence. . . .

I have known and done almost nothing but law. The next *Harv. Law Rev.* will have an article of mine, "Privilege Malice & Intent," [1] a supplement to the doctrine of the external standard. Little more than platitudes, yet things not generally known. The last two or three years I have found myself separated from my brethren on some important constitutional questions; the last a few days ago on the power of the legislature to pass an act subject to approval of the people by vote (the *referendum* of Switzerland about which the workingmen here are beginning to make a row). My brethren deny it & I affirm it,[2] and among the respectable there are some who regard me as a dangerous radical! If I had seen fit to clothe my views in different language I dare say I could have been a pet of the proletariat — whereas they care nothing for me and some of the others distrust me. The issues might become very grave, but in actual fact I don't expect anything particular will happen to any of us on that score.

Why is not the true doctrine that title passes by judgment (for substantial damages) in trover not by satisfaction? [3] I am aware of the remarks of your Willes, Blackburn *et al.*,[4] but why is not the true theory (undealt with by them) that as against the converter one may have the value of the chattel in damages or the chattel at his election but not both, and that judgment *determines the election.* Trespass and trover on the one side and replevin on the other stand on opposite ground. As the old books put it the former *disaffirm* the latter *affirms* property in

---

[1] 8 *Harv. L. Rev.* 1 (1894); reprinted in *C. L. P.*, p. 117.
[2] Opinions of the Justices, 160 Mass. 586, 593 (1894).
[3] See Holmes's dissenting opinion in Miller v. Hyde, 161 Mass. 472, 478 (1894).
[4] In Brinsmead v. Harrison, L. R. 6 C. P. 584; L. R. 7 C. P. 547 (1872). Sir James Shaw Willes (1814–1872) was a Justice of the Court of Common Pleas, 1855–72. In the summer of 1870 Pollock was his Marshal on his Western Circuit. See Pollock *For My Grandson* (1933), p. 164.

the plaintiff. The former, that is, say the property is in the defendant *now* by his wrongful act & I demand damages for the act which divested my property. The latter says I have the *right* of property and demand restitution. Newton in Y. B. 19 H. VI, 65, pl. 5; Vavisor in 6 H. VII, 8, *et seq.*; 18 Vin. Abr. 69 E (cited in Sergeant Manning's note, 6 Man. & Gr. 640); Maitland & Ames on Disseisin of Chattels [5] which explains the meaning of the books referred to. The question arises here. We have no binding authority, and I am pressing the above argument, but I fear some compromise expression. The other notion is an arbitrary dealing with trover in an attempt to effectuate an executory sale to be executed by payment — relying on some language in Jenkins, 4th Cent. Case 88 if my memory is right. Observe the trace of what I think the new rule, in the notion that upon payment, the defendant gets title by relation from *date of conversion.*

I have read some philosophy (especially Windelband's *History of Philosophy*, an extremely good book, translated, & published by MacMillan), novels, and confusing arguments on bimetallism [6] etc., and have been a recluse. I come in with the juries tomorrow, and have some promise of having Bob Ingersoll [7] before me in a will case. We always begin our sittings with a prayer. Do you have anything like that or is it a relic of Puritanism?

Remember me most affectionately to Lady Pollock.

Yours ever,
O. W. HOLMES

LONDON, May 11, 1894

My dear Holmes:

Thanks for your advices. Just now I am involved in a course of lectures on "Jurisprudence," in which I am deliber-

---

[5] Maitland, "The Seisin of Chattels," 1 *L. Q. Rev.* 324 (1885); Ames, "The Disseisin of Chattels," 3 *Harv. L. Rev.* 23, 313, 317 (1889–90).

[6] In Holmes's Journal he includes among the books read in 1894 F. W. Taussig, *The Silver Situation in the United States* (1892), and Edward Suess, *The Future of Silver* (Robert Stein, tr.; Senate Mis. Doc. 95; 1893).

[7] Robert G. Ingersoll (1833–1899); famous atheist.

ately burning the gods of the so-called English school. It means putting into shape a lot of notes I have been making, and using in lectures on special branches of the subject, in the last ten years — and doing it against time to some extent. Ultimately I hope it will become *A First Book of Jurisprudence for Students of the Common Law*. Part 1: The General Notions of Law. Part 2: Legal Authorities and their use.[1] . . .

Meanwhile Maitland and I have a whole volume of history in type, and we ought to have two vols. ready some time next year.[2]

The Tagore lectures have become one of the (corporeally) thinnest law books ever seen,[3] but I think I have put some things in fresh lights that may be useful to Anglo-Indian students and perhaps amuse the learned. You shall have one of my copies when I get them. . . .

Thanks for the extra copy of *Harvard Law Review*, with your article. I have not been able to read it properly yet.

Yours ever,
F. POLLOCK

Postal Card; Pollock to Holmes

June 16, 1894

Bryce and I were talking of tenures the other day, and wondering whether you had quite abolished them. Do you consider that in your Commonwealth land is allodial, or held of the Commonwealth of Mass. in free and common socage (presumably by fealty only)?

Have you such a thing as a corporation sole still about you? I never heard that your Governor was one, though the sole real *Excellency* in the U. S. as Lowell [1] once told me.

What think you of the nature of a thing in action? Is an

---

[1] The first edition was published in 1896. The introductory chapter was published in 10 *L. Q. Rev.* 228 (July 1894).

[2] Pollock and Maitland's two-volume *History of English Law before the Time of Edward I* was published in 1895.

[3] Pollock, *The Law of Fraud in British India* (1894).

---

[1] Presumably A. Lawrence Lowell.

exclusive franchise (several fishery, ferry, copyright, patent) a thing in action? *A ma entente semble que nemque.* I suspect our "thing in action" is really very near the Roman "obligation." Hence you will perceive that I am on the warpath of "General Jurisprudence."

F. P.

June 26, 1894

Dear Pollock:

I am away from law books until next Tuesday. I am not sure whether it is not still our theory that we have a tenure (we certainly have the Statute *Quia Emptores*) but I know of no consequences peculiar to it. Practically I should think our ownership was allodial. I will try to remember to inquire.

I don't know of any corporation sole.

I read Williams's article on Choses in Action [1] with pleasure. My only criticism would be that I didn't quite understand the purpose of the inquiry. Most emphatically I do not think an easement or a patent a chose in action any more than a five acre lot. A patent is property carried to the highest degree of abstraction — a right *in rem* to exclude, without a physical object or content. It is matter reduced to Boskievitch [2] (qu. sp.?) points.

I have often thought of writing about a page on copyright. The notion that such a right could exist at Common law or be worked out by it seems to me imbecility. It would be intolerable if not limited in time and I think it would be hard to state a basis for the notion which would not lead one far afield. *Non obstant* the long-winded judgments in the old cases.

I have dissented and asserted the proposition that a judgment in trover passes title, politely hinting that the trouble with Willes, Jessel, and our U. S. Supreme Court was that they didn't know quite enough. I will try to send you the case when it is printed. [3]

[1] T. Cyprian Williams, "Is a Right of Action in Tort a Chose in Action?," 10 *L. Q. Rev.* 143 (1894).
[2] Roger Joseph Boscovich, 1711 (?)–1787.
[3] Miller v. Hyde, 161 Mass. 472, 478 (1894).

I hope you will read my article [4] as it adds a supplement to the notion of the external standard which I have gradually worked out in a series of decisions. Also I insinuated that one of your late English decisions [5] — since Bowen's steamship case about a combination of merchants [6] — really only expressed class sympathy.[7] So you see generally I have been stamping about. . . .

Yours ever,
O. W. H.

I sincerely regret the loss of Bowen.[8]

TRINITY COLLEGE, CAMBRIDGE
October 9, 1894 [1]

My dear Holmes:

This morning we learn that your father — a man more loved by more fellow-men who never saw him than perhaps any other writer of our language in our time — has passed away, in fulness of years, peacefully, among his own people, as was fitting and as he must have desired it.[2]

I cannot bring myself to apply the common terms of lamentation to the close of one of the longest, most complete, most

---

[4] "Privilege, Malice and Intent," 8 *Harv. L. Rev.* 1 (1895); *C. L. P.* 117.

[5] Temperton v. Russell [1893] 1 Q. B. 715. Holmes summarized the holding by saying that "it seems to be unlawful for the officer of a trade union to order the members not to work for a man if he supplies goods to the plaintiff, for the purpose of forcing the plaintiff to abstain from doing what he has a right to do," 8 *Harv. L. Rev.* at p. 7; *C. L. P.* at p. 127.

[6] Mogul Steamship Company v. McGregor, Gow and Co., 23 Q. B. D. 598 (1889). The dissenting opinion of Bowen, L.J., is at p. 611. Holmes summarized the holding of the case in the following words: "In England, it is lawful for merchants to combine to offer unprofitably low rates and a rebate to shippers for the purpose of preventing the plaintiff from becoming a competitor, as he has a right to do, and also to impose a forfeiture of the rebate, and to threaten agents with dismissal in case of dealing with him." *Id.*

[7] "The ground of decision really comes down to a proposition of policy of rather a delicate nature concerning the merit of the particular benefit to themselves intended by the defendants, and suggests a doubt whether judges with different economic sympathies might not decide such a case differently when brought face to face with the issue." 8 *Harv. L. Rev.* at p. 8; *C. L. P.* at p. 128.

[8] Lord Bowen died April 10, 1894.

---

[1] Pollock visited the United States in the summer of 1894.

Dr. Holmes died on October 7, 1894.

beneficent and I think I cannot be wrong in saying happiest lives of this century; nor, if I have read you at all right since we made, just twenty years ago, the acquaintance which ripened into friendship on your next visit to England, would you thank me if I tried. Let words be as they will — you will have plenty, of all varieties of good meaning, before you get these lines — and think of us as with you in spirit. . . .

Yours ever,
F. POLLOCK

BOSTON, October 21, 1894

Dear Pollock:

You write with a tender and charming touch and I thank you sincerely. I face rather solemnity than sadness. My father had had all that he could have from life and he quietly ceased breathing as Mrs. Holmes and I stood by his side, after a serene and happy summer, just as I was apprehending that the future had only suffering in store for him. The marks which I have seen of universal affection for him here and a widespread similar feeling with you give me much pleasure.

I have been delayed in acknowledging and in examining your new edition of *Contracts*, but you know my high opinion of the book. Give my love to Lady Pollock. With love and affection.

Yours ever,
O. W. HOLMES

II

1895-1899

BOSTON, January 31, 1895

Dear Pollock:

I am delighted to hear your news — both parts of it.[1] I had heard that you were coming here [2] and was on the point of writing to you. Of course I shall expect to see much of you. . . .

I trust that the Law Reports will pay you well? [3] I envy you your talk with Brunner, still more if you did them in German; your diabolical allroundness makes it possible to suspect you of it, but I hope not, enviously. Have you seen Nordau, *Dégénérescence*, original, German, but I read it in French. It gratifies all the most malevolent impulses of one's heart and abounds in shrewd things, if you don't take him too seriously. A German the other day quoted apropos of him their saying that in the vulgar herd there is one more than each of us suspects and said that Nordau also was a *dégénéré*.

Feb. 1. This morning we hear that our old associate Judge Hoar has died. A tale of him a few days ago strikes me as pretty large. He was lying comatose, and some one having occasion touched him to wake him. "Are you the Messenger?" said he (meaning of Death of course). "I am ready." Then he realized where he was and added "I was glad to see you wore a fur hat." . . .

My love to Lady Pollock, and *au revoir* to you.

O. W. H.

---

[1] If Holmes had recently heard from Pollock, the letter is missing.

[2] Pollock had been invited to address the Harvard Law School Association at the exercises celebrating the twenty-fifth anniversary of C. C. Langdell as Dean of the School on June 25, 1895. At the Commencement exercises Harvard University conferred on Pollock the degree of LL.D.

[3] Pollock had recently been appointed editor of the Law Reports, the official publication of the reports of the English courts.

Holmes to Lady Pollock

BEVERLY FARMS, July 2, 1895

Well My Dear Lady:

Your Frederick has come and gone, has covered himself with glory and departed.[1] He gave everyone great pleasure and I heard nothing but good of him on all sides. I grieved not to see more of him but it seemed inevitable that he should be occupied somewhat officially, and should be in Cambridge most of the time. He and John Gray and I received our LL.D's together which was pleasant, although, apart from the association, the degree comes to me too late for me to care much for it except negatively. I take it as a mark that the President[2] has buried the hatchet and no longer bears me malice for giving up my professorship for a judgeship — which I expressly and in writing reserved the right to do (in accordance with advice of one who knew him better than I) but which he was inclined to let people understand was not fair. He is a valuable man and I am on most friendly terms with him and can be so long as he has no power of any kind over one. I have settled down to a vacation routine already, taking a little drive and a little read, and a little nap and a little walk every day, but I dilate with vast potentialities in the way of schemes. I meditate on learning the bicycle (notice the *on*, I have not got further than thinking *about* it). I consider whether it would be worth while to collect some of my legal essays into a book. I think of joining a Country Club. I purpose to read Frederick and Maitland's noble work.[3] And so on. If you read this last to F. he would wonder that I had not begun it already in view of what I said to him, but I must finish H. Spencer's *Sociology* first, as I began it last winter — and possibly one other short unfinished book. H. Spencer you English never quite do justice to, or at least

---

[1] At the Harvard Law School exercises on June 25, Pollock delivered an address, "The Vocation of the Common Law," printed in his volume *The Expansion of the Common Law* (1904), p. 1, and in 4 *Harvard Graduates Magazine* 1 (1895). At the luncheon of the Law School Association, following Pollock's address, Holmes, among others, made brief remarks which may be found in 4 *Harvard Graduates Magazine* 47–48 (1895); *Speeches* (1934), p. 67; *C. L. P.*, p. 138.

[2] Charles William Eliot (1834–1926).

[3] Pollock and Maitland, *History of English Law before the Time of Edward I* (1895).

those whom I have talked with do not. He is dull. He writes an ugly uncharming style, his ideals are those of a lower middle class British Philistine. And yet after all abatements I doubt if any writer of English except Darwin has done so much to affect our whole way of thinking about the universe. Of course he often is no more than a *vulgarisateur* but that was still more true of Sir H. Maine, and Sir H. M. covered so much less space. I presume you received a second Memorial Day Speech from me,[4] made 10 or more years after the first [5] which is in my little book of speeches. . . . I notice that my relations have done their share to give Punch material, without the latter's knowledge of his debt. My cousin years ago said "Many happy returns" to a man on his second marriage — or told me he did — wishing to say something pleasant. *Vide* late Punch. And my uncle John Holmes, an old bachelor, accounted for his *bad quarters* by the want of a *better half* which Punch got hold of a year or two ago. I have kept this in my drawer for several days, have missed my mail and generally have left undone all the things that I ought to have done, but let my faithful remembrance of you and yours cover all.

Sincerely yours,
O. W. HOLMES

I fold this queerly to have nothing private legible through the envelope.

BEVERLY FARMS, August 11, 1895

Dear Lady Pollock:

I did not write to you at once on receiving your letter thinking that possibly I might get another after you had received mine and that it was better to get running in good order. I wish I heard oftener from you. I am a recluse. Yours is one of the very few voices that reach me from outside my cavern and it is always dear and charming. You have the advantage

---

[4] "The Soldier's Faith," an address delivered on May 30, 1895, at Harvard University; *Speeches*, p. 56.

[5] See *supra*, pp. 25–26, 41.

of me as correspondent. There is an infinity of facts, gossip if you like, that you can tell me about, whereas I have no information on any theme short of the Cosmos. Oh yes — there is one — but I am getting tired of it: that Frederick of yours keeps doing some new thing which is entitled to praise. The other day, Eliot Cabot,[1] a learned Hegelian hereabouts, commended to me F.'s notice of Balfour's book,[2] which had given him much pleasure. It is delightfully touched, possibly treating B. a little more seriously than he deserves, and yet perhaps sufficiently indicating even that. Also the short leisure left me from the routine of every day is devoted to the *History of the Common Law*. I have read into the second half of Vol. 2 with continued unqualified satisfaction. It is a truly first rate piece of work, and I have no doubt will be accepted at once as such. Somewhat too much, methinks, of the virtues of Aristides. His success over here was enough for a time.

What else have I done? I have taken one lesson on the bicycle and I am stiff from it this morning and I feel as if I never should learn. Violent exercise upsets an old sportsman who has done nothing more vigorous than a quick toddle for years.

12th

While I was taking my lesson some friends of mine walked by and with them a girl with a roving eye who seemed to take more notice than the usual tame bird. So the next day, to wit, after beginning this letter, I strolled up to my friend's house and soon was at it hammer and tongs with m'mselle. Of course she had been brought up in London, though of an American mother. You may say what you like about American women — and I won't be unpatriotic — but English women are brought up, it seems to me, to realize that it is an object to be charming, that man is a dangerous animal — or ought to be — and that a sexless *bonhomie* is not the ideal relation. I always say you can get your tragedy of any desired length in England, from thirty seconds to a life-time. I had one adorable one of twenty-nine minutes by the watch. At the end of that time I started for my train. Woman I'd had a glimpse of in London — walk.

[1] James Elliot Cabot (1821–1903); author of *Memoir of Emerson* (1887).
[2] Pollock reviewed Arthur J. Balfour's *Foundations of Belief* in 20 *Mind* 376 (1895).

She sat on a style, I below her, gazing into her eyes — then, "remember this lane," "while memory holds its seat, etc.." "Adieu." And I still do and ever shall remember her, and I rather think she does me a little bit. What imbecilities for an old fellow to be talking. But if one knows his place and makes way for younger men when he isn't sure, it is better perhaps not quite to abandon interest in the sports of life. . . .

Your affectionate friend,
O. W. Holmes

August 23, 1895

My dear Holmes:

Actual malevolence is there, no doubt, as part of certain causes of action, and good reasons can be given for this; notwithstanding, it makes an inconvenient sort of issuable matter, and tempts judges with semi-political theories to strain the law.[1] Wright has considered your article in *Harv. Law Rev.*; he thinks it profitable, but criticizes you for not providing for such a case as this. A takes a long shot at B, knowing (as the fact is) that a hit is very unlikely, but wishing to shoot B; the shot is lucky and he does hit B. Clearly A may not say that the consequence was not probable. I suppose you would answer that the questions to which the "external standard" applies don't arise when we are dealing with intention proved *aliunde*, and that you gave the reader credit for knowing this. I am pleased to hear of my comments on Balfour being approved by a philosopher; that was a rather ticklish bit of work.

I find I cannot be content with one scrap. I want to tell you how little of the *History of English Law* is my writing: *viz.* the Introduction (not quite all), the chapter on Anglo-Saxon law, and the bulk, not the whole, of the chapter on Early History

---

[1] In his article on "Privilege, Malice and Intent," 8 *Harv. L. Rev.* 1, 2 (1895), reprinted in *C. L. P.* (1920) p. 117, 118, Holmes had stated that, "in some cases, a man is not liable for a very manifest danger unless he actually intends to do the harm complained of. In some cases, he even may intend to do the harm and yet not have to answer for it: and, as I think, in some cases of this latter sort, at least, actual malice may make him liable when without it he would not have been."

of Contract, which is expounded and rearranged from an article in *Harv. Law Rev.*[2]

The *Mirror of Justices* is the queerest of books.[3] I can't believe Andrew Horn or any rational Englishman wrote it — and I suggest a silly and conceited Continental (? Gascon) clerk living in England, and hugely gulled as to Anglo-Saxon antiquities by some learned friend who could not resist the joke.

Yours ever,
F. P.

I am reading the *Agamemnon* with Jack [4] — if the audience could construe the choruses even in their state of uncorrupt innocence at a first hearing, an Attic audience must have been terribly clever.

BOSTON, September 13, 1895

Dear Lady Pollock:

I am at work again, sitting in equity alone here in Boston while five of my brethren are circuiting about the State to hear questions of law in the different Counties. I always miss it if I do not go up to Pittsfield in Berkshire County, the western end of the State. I have a lot of friends there. My great great grandfather [1] owned pretty much the whole town and we used to own a remnant of 300 acres where I had much fun as a boy. I enlisted soldiers there, and went there when wounded and made love to all the available girls and generally I love the place. But it is easier to keep well here. On Friday, *viz.* today in 3/4 of an hour, I go back to Beverly Farms until Tuesday A.M. and then, (did I tell you?) I have shared the common lot and begun to learn the bicycle. I haven't had such a gleam of boyish joy for years as I get from my little runs of 5 miles or so, all that I have ventured as yet. Even tumbling off was a pleasure — to find that I could do it and not break! A Catholic lawyer told

---

[2] 6 *Harv. L. Rev.* 389 (1893).

[3] The Selden Society had just published a new edition of *The Mirror of Justices*, edited by W. J. Whittaker, with an introduction by Maitland. Pollock reviewed the volume in 11 *L. Q. Rev.* 393 (1895).

[4] John Pollock, Sir Frederick's son.

---

[1] Jacob Wendell.

me that the Pope had been consulted as to the propriety of a clergyman doing it, and hinted a question as to a judge of the Supreme Court. I told him it depended on the shape of the judge. If he measured a yard across it would be improper, but that I looked enough like the run of riders not to be ridiculous. I am not quite resolved whether to do it in town. My house is so near the park that I could get there with much comfort and have pleasant sport. After I had read the *History* I hinted to Little & Brown that if it was wished that I should notice it for *The Nation* I might do it — they having spoken to me earlier when I dared not promise — but they answered that *The Nation* now had made its arrangements. I hope it will get a more competent hand than did my book in the same sheet many years ago.[2] . . . Did you ever read a life of St. Francis of Assisi by Paul Sabatier? It has been translated (in this country I think). It gives one a very striking picture of a holiness which one loves none the less for disbelieving what it was founded on in the way of beliefs. . . . I have kept well this year again — August and the first half September being the time of dread — which makes three during which I have been all right. But I still have to be careful. I don't dare speculate much as yet about next summer. Sometimes I have thought that I might get over, and again have doubted. I need not say that I long to see you all. Forgive me if this time I put a word of law, etc. on the next page, to your husband, as my time is short if, as I hope, I am to catch today's mail. My trouble when I am at home is to get time for the leisurely feeling without which one can't write.

> Affectionately yours,
> O. W. HOLMES

Dear F.

I dealt pretty nearly with the case put by Wright, J. in *Common Law*, 161.[1] The reason one resorts to the external

---

[2] 32 *Nation* 464 (June 30, 1881).

[1] "Take a case like the glancing of Sir Walter Tyrrel's arrow. If an expert marksman contemplated that the arrow would hit a certain person, *cadit quaestio*. If he contemplated that it would glance in the direction of another person, but contemplated

standard is to determine the minimum consequences which a man *must* contemplate under given circumstances. If he actually contemplates more the ground for his escape is wanting, *viz.* that as life is action a man cannot be charged for the consequences of his living beyond what in a general way might be contemplated as the result of choosing this course rather than that. I read the *Agamemnon* with a pony a year or two ago with much pleasure. Aeschylus is the only one of them I have any articulate ideas about worth mentioning, and those hardly so. As to Homer I confess I prefer the *Peau de Chagrin*, and I think it is true that the Classics are dead, (saving all just exceptions & allowances). An enormous amount of knowledge is necessary not to "dilate with the wrong emotion," or at least to get the *nuance* of feeling which the writer had & meant to convey. I could discourse much on this theme as applied to the Old Testament & to Mr. Browning as he will strike posterity, etc. etc. . . .

Yours ever,
O. W. H.

London, November 13, 1895

My dear Holmes:

We have judicial authority for cycling here too. Sir Francis [1] and Lady Jeune may be seen wheeling, and it seems he is enthusiastic about it. My children and I, with Lord Macnaghten's younger son Malcolm, now a rising member of the Common Law Bar, spent part of the early hours of Sunday morning — after coming home from the play — in wheeling round the empty streets. We went straight east as far as the Royal Exchange, and came back by the Embankment, Pall Mall and Park Lane. . . .

---

no more than that, in order to judge of his liability we must go to the end of his foresight, and, assuming the foreseen event to happen, consider what the manifest danger was then. But if no such event was foreseen, the marksman must be judged by the circumstances known to him at the time of shooting."

[1] Francis Henry Jeune, Baron St. Helier (1843–1905); Judge of Probate, Divorce, and Admiralty Division of the High Court of Justice, 1891–92; President, 1892–1905.

Lord Russell of Killowen has made a vigorous attempt to stir up the Inns of Court in the matter of legal education. The mass of the profession seems to be as indifferent as ever, and I see no sign of any effective public opinion outside. On the whole I almost despair of living to see any serious improvement.

Yours ever,

F. POLLOCK

BOSTON, October 21, 1895

Dear Pollock:

Thirty-four years ago today was my first battle. I was shot through the breast at Ball's Bluff & it always seems something of an anniversary to me. I thought I was a gone coon, remembered *The Children of the New Forest* (Marryat), read in my then not distant youth, and expected to die to slow music like a character in that tale. I happened to have a bottle of laudanum in my pocket and resolved if the anguish became unbearable to do the needful. A doctor (I suppose) removed the bottle and in the morning I resolved to live.

I am glad you like Sabatier's book.[1] I forget whether I mentioned it but I read it somewhat more than a year ago and was much uplifted by it. A very different work I have just received. Our Brooks Adams's *Law of Civilization & Decay*, published by your Swan (qu. sp?) & Sonnenschein. I wonder if no American would print his Godless pages. I only received it two days ago but read it in a flash. It is about the most (immediately) interesting history I ever read. Remotely others like Windelband's dull *History of Philosophy* have more inward nourishment for me. It hardly strikes me as science but rather as a somewhat grotesque world poem, or symphony in blue & gray, but the story of the modern world is told so strikingly that while you read you believe it. The English if they notice the book will make fun of it. The matter of course way in which he treats the English Church as an accessory to a great land grabbing scheme and the Christian Church in general as be-

---

[1] Any letter from Pollock expressing this liking is missing.

longing to the time when men believed in magic, and sorcery had a money value, is enough to make an owl laugh, but hardly will please the established powers. I won't spoil the reading by mentioning his notions but I think it will pay you to run through it.

As to *Flood* v. *Jasper*² [*sic*] which I have looked at, I am afraid you would think me arrogant if I should say how little importance I attach to the discussions of the run of judges, whether English or American, on matters involving general theory — beyond the *fact* that in a given jurisdiction they do so and so. I made my remarks on the *Temperton case* ³ in the article I sent you some time ago.⁴ The question is not one to be solved by the general theories of law (to my mind), but as I said there, a question of policy dependent on particular circumstances; the question *viz*: how far a given act known to have detrimental consequences shall be privileged. I have no doubt that in some cases the motive, actual malevolence on the one hand, self seeking through harm to a neighbor on the other, properly may be allowed to mark the limit of the privilege.

I have run against your Lord Chief Justice lately in a queer way. *The Youth's Companion* (a sheet having a circulation of half a million) got an article about the law as a profession out of him,⁵ and then persuaded me to write an American counterpart ⁶ (neither yet published). His was rather of the conventional sort, and incidentally lauded the study of the Roman Law and insisted on the need of a University education. I said, (of course most politely) that I didn't think a University education necessary for a fighting success and that I didn't believe in increasing the difficulties of one historical study by adding

---

² Flood v. Jackson [1895] 2 Q. B. 21. The plaintiffs were shipwrights, employed from day to day, in a shipyard. The defendants were officers of a union of iron workers. The action was brought to recover damages resulting from the malicious inducement of the plaintiffs' employers by the defendants to discharge the plaintiffs, under threats that the members of the union would cease work if the plaintiffs were not discharged. In the Court of Appeal the judgment of Kennedy, J., for the plaintiffs, was sustained.

³ Temperton v. Russell, [1893] 1 Q. B. 715.

⁴ "Privilege, Malice and Intent," 8 *Harv. L. Rev.* 1, 7–8 (1894); *C. L. P.*, pp. 117, 127–28.

⁵ Lord Chief Justice Coleridge, "The Bar as a Profession," 70 *Youth's Companion* 79 (Feb. 13, 1896).

⁶ Holmes, "The Bar as a Profession," *id.*, 92 (Feb. 20, 1896); reprinted, *C. L. P.*, p. 153. In 1889 Holmes had published an article in 62 *Youth's Companion* 73 (Feb. 7, 1889) entitled, "Just the Boy Wanted in the Law."

another (the Roman Law). In short rather did a little Philistin-
ism. The editor showed my piece to him which moved him to a
reply [7] with a slight touch of subterranean warmth. I told the
editor I did not care to rejoin except to explain in two lines of
postscript what I meant by saying that the origin of our law
in the main was Frankish.[8] No more at present from

Yours ever,
O. W. H.

Remember me to Lady Pollock who owes me say ½ a letter
in reply to a poor one of mine.

Boston, December 27, 1895

Dear Pollock:

I received the *Pelias* [1] with oft renewed admiration of your
versatility. The classics may be dead, but not all that is written in Latin. Well — alas — I can't go on with gaiety but I
too must speak of Venezuela; [2] with regard to the manners of
the President's message I agree with you most heartily.[3] As
towards your country the tone was premature to say the least
and as to ourselves I confess it makes me indignant to have an
attitude assumed on a public question that I never heard of
and to be told that patriotism requires me to back it up, before
I have had a chance to consider the matter at all.

For purely world-reasons, I think we ought to be readier to
fight with any other nation; no doubt our two countries aggravate each other from time to time but on the whole each
comes nearer the other's notion of what is good and right than
any other blood can.

[7] 70 *Youth's Companion* 92 (Feb. 20, 1896); *C. L. P.*, p. 160.
[8] *Ibid.*; *C. L. P.*, p. 163.

[1] This reading of the title is doubtful. The piece referred to has not been identified.
[2] The letter in which, apparently, Pollock discussed Venezuela is missing.
[3] President Cleveland on December 17, 1895, delivered a special message to Congress discussing the boundary dispute between British Guiana and Venezuela and expressed his opinion that it would "be the duty of the United States to resist by every
means in its power . . . the appropriation by Great Britain of any lands or the exercise of governmental jurisdiction over any territory which after investigation we have
determined of right belongs to Venezuela."

With regard to the substance I don't know. Of course I know nothing about the boundary. To an outsider it looks as if your people were feeling round the Isthmus a good deal in one way and another. After all the nation is not bound by the President's message to Congress, and I think there is some force in what one of the leading men in the House said, that it avoided bitter and hasty talk to pass the bill for the Commission at once and in silence. I don't know what to think of the future; there is an unknown element. I fear that in the West there is a pretty widespread willingness for a fight with England — a very little thing might stir up a general feeling. Hereabouts I think all the sensible men I know feel as I do but regard the situation as more or less serious. Fancy my speech of last Memorial Day being treated as a jingo document! Greatly to my disgust it was put over in the *Harvard Magazine* and only came out a few days ago.[4] I quarrelled with the editor [5] about it in the summer, but now it seems to some of the godly as if I were preaching a doctrine of blood! My classmate Wendell P. Garrison, Editor of *The Nation* (I suppose it was he), a most watery person but one who is, was, and ever will be a flat, walked into me with a blunt knife in *The Post* and *The Nation*,[6] and I surmise that Godkin [7] backed him in a No. 2[8] which was too clever for poor Wendell. I met the great Edward Atkinson [9] this very morning and he shook his head & said, "I don't like it. It's bad morals and bad politics." To which I civilly replied that I didn't care, but on reflection called his attention to my speech being on Memorial Day, not now. There have been many things which I have meant to speak of but they have fled. This is but a sigh — and an affectionate

[4] Holmes's speech, "The Soldier's Faith," was printed in 4 *Harvard Graduates Magazine* 179 (December 1895).

[5] William Roscoe Thayer.

[6] See an anonymous editorial in the New York *Evening Post*, Dec. 16, 1895, p. 6, entitled "Sentimental Jingoism," and 61 *Nation* 440 (Dec. 19, 1895). The editorial was the same in the *Post* and *The Nation*.

[7] Edwin Lawrence Godkin (1831–1902); editor of the New York *Evening Post*, 1883–1900.

[8] See an anonymous editorial entitled "Force as a Moral Influence," New York *Evening Post*, Dec. 17, 1895, p. 6.

[9] 1827–1905; industrialist and economist; author of numerous pamphlets and magazine articles on political and economic matters.

remembrance to you and yours — to all of whom I wish a happy New Year.

Yours ever,
O. W. H.

CORPUS CHRISTI COLLEGE, OXFORD
February 1, 1896

My dear Holmes:

Last week I found that book by Brooks Adams lying at the Athenaeum and looked through it — clever, as the book of a smart young man full of one idea is clever — but his one idea is inadequate and I think often wrong. I wonder if he is a socialist, or a silver man, or both. As I don't profess to know the whole history of the world I can't test all his facts. But *e.g.* no educated man ought nowadays to accept Macaulay's libel on Warren Hastings as a base for general inferences about the conquest of India. Also Brooks Adams seems to think the Church was always a homogeneous body with one solid interest *contra mundum*, which is very funny to any one who knows any medieval history or literature.

Also I have read *The Red Badge of Courage* — the psychology seems to me artificial and forced. If a recruit did go through all those complex emotions he would never remember them. For the general picture you can bear witness — but I guess the discipline must have been better in your regiment. . . .

For the last 3 weeks I have been hard at work drafting a statement of our case in the Venezuelan affair to introduce a print of the most material evidence.[1] It would make a pretty assize of novel disseisin — or rather writ of right considering the lapse of time, descents cast, etc. The Venezuelans count on the seisin of the King of Spain and say our ancestors the Dutch were seised if at all *injuste & per vim*. We say that the said King was never seised in fact (with as much actual possession as the nature of the *locus in quo* admitted) before the Treaty of Münster, and that by force of the said Treaty which amounts

[1] See Documents and Correspondence relating to the Question of the Boundary between British Guiana and Venezuela (Blue Books, No. 1-5, 1896).

to a release & quitclaim by Spain of whatever they then possessed, they were then in as of right. We also say that a series
of Spanish acts and official documents show acquiescence in
the Dutch possession and title. Most of the evidence has
never been published. I shall be curious to see how it strikes
lawyers and publicists on your side. It is to be laid before
Parliament as soon as possible; if I have any copies at my dis-
posal I will send it you. It has been an interesting bit of
work and I am not sorry to find that this old brain-machine
(50 last December) can still do a fast spin without creaking.
The thing had to be done against time — I should have liked
to have 2 or 3 months instead of 3 weeks.

Yours ever,
F. Pollock

Hind Head Copse
Shottermill, Surrey
May 29, 1896 [1]

My dear Holmes:

Your letter [2] and judgment find us rusticating for the
Whitsun week. . . .

In your case [3] I think we should hold here (the few judges
of the QBD. who know the law) that (1) the boy's well meant
delivery to the defendants as bailees for his master appropriated
the possession to the master, if he had not done so already;
(2) the fact of the defendant's fraudulent intention being
found, there was no real delivery and they could be convicted
of "larceny by a trick" at common law. Not that I think the
doctrine would have been allowed by Brian [4] and his com-

---

[1] A letter from Pollock, dated May 20, 1896, is omitted. It dealt with various small
matters concerning Holmes's impending visit to England.

[2] The letter referred to is missing.

[3] This case is evidently Commonwealth v. Rubin, 165 Mass. 453 (1896). "A horse
was bought for *A*, and his servant engaged a boy to take it to him in another town.
On his way the boy fell in with *B*, who said he would deliver the horse for him, to
which the boy assented. *B* then paid the boy what he was to receive from *A*, and the
boy, who was innocent, left the horse with *B*, who misappropriated the horse, which
afterwards was found on his premises." (Headnote.) The Court, in an opinion by
Holmes, held that *B's* conviction under an indictment for larceny should be sustained.

[4] Thomas Brian, Chief Justice of the Common Pleas, 1471.

panions. It dates from *temp.* Geo. III. In the alternative I suppose it might also be the statutory "larceny by a bailee."

I am not quite clear about trespass *ab initio* being founded on any presumption of intent.[5] The older view (cases on finding, *Isaack v. Clark*[6] etc.) seems to be that possession of (or intermeddling with) another man's goods (or land) is fully justifiable only under his own authority, and that good intentions ("charity to save the thing for the true owner"), and even authority of law, make the possession excusable but excusable only; if the intruder deprives himself of excuse by abusing the authority, the latent trespassory character of his possession comes out in full force, and, if combined with original asportation and supervening *animus furandi*, may make the taking felonious. (*Riley's case*,[7] per Parke, I think.)

This way of thinking is in substance, I believe, as old as the latter part of the 15th century. But I must look up the case you cite from Hen. IV[8] and see what is the earlier stage of the doctrine disclosed by it.

Harriman has sent me a book on Contracts[9] in which he tries to make out that consent is quite immaterial and that the common law view is that the promisor is bound by a one sided *willenserklärung*. Applying this to informal contracts leads him, of course, into fictions quite as violent as any that he avoids: and he seems to forget that in early Germanic law you can have no jurisdiction at all without consent. But it is mighty clever. Also he forgets the extreme antiquity of *fides* and its Germanic equivalents.

Let us know your ship and date of sailing a mail or two in advance if you can.

We are all awheel here.

Yours ever,

F. POLLOCK

---

5 In his opinion in the Rubin case Holmes said, "The rule that, if a man abuse an authority given him by the law, he becomes a trespasser *ab initio*, although now it looks like a rule of substantive law and is limited to a certain class of cases, in its origin was only a rule of evidence by which, when such rules were few and rude, the original intent was presumed conclusively from the subsequent conduct." 165 Mass. at 455.   6 2 Buls. 306 (1614).

7 Regina v. Riley, Dears. 149 (1853), *per* Pollock, C. B., and Parke, B.

8 Y. B. 11 Henry IV, 75, Pl. 16.

9 Edward Avery Harriman, *Elements of the Law of Contracts* (1896).

October 2, 1896 [1]

My dear Holmes:

I have been exploring primeval forests and deserted grass-grown tracks beyond Selborne, and as I pushed my machine among ruts and loose flints (having fondly steered by map and finger-post) I tried to console myself with memories of the title in the Abridgments — *Chimin, quand serra dit foundrous*; but the common law right of using the adjoining land is not of much use to the wheelman. Talk of holidays — I have read Dicey's gigantic book and written a review thereof (not yet out) for the *Spectator* [2] My own little book [3] seems to be well received.

Yours ever,
F. POLLOCK

I wish Dicey had more sense of history: he is not clear of the damnable heresies of Austin. But it will be a most useful book.

HIND HEAD COPSE
SHOTTERMILL, SURREY
December 29, 1896

My dear Holmes:

We have not much news save of the wettest fall known these many years. As for our litigious cranks, we have enabled somebody — I forget at this moment what high judicial authority — to prevent them from bringing actions without special leave.[1] Curious to think how intolerable this would be except under an effective democratic constitution, and how we take it as a matter of course.

I have been trying my hand at an arrangement of the law

[1] Holmes had visited England and Ireland in the summer of 1896.
[2] The anonymous review of A. V. Dicey's *A Digest of the Law of England, with Reference to the Conflict of Laws* (1st ed. 1896) appeared in 77 *Spectator* 433 (Oct. 3, 1896).
[3] Pollock's *First Book of Jurisprudence* was published in July 1896.

[1] By an amendment to Order XXX of the Supreme Court of Judicature, which went into effect in 1897, it was provided that a plaintiff who wished to deliver a pleading should not be allowed to do so without an order from a Master. It seems likely that it was to this amendment which Pollock referred. See Odgers on *Pleading and Practice* (10th ed. 1930), p. 80.

intended to be fairly rational without breaking up the well-known practical categories. It is to serve as an introduction to a "New Abridgment" of the Common Law,[2] which is no doubt being duly advertised on your side. As I mention in a note, I owe a good deal to your old papers in the *Amer. Law Rev.*, I don't know just how much, for I thought it best now to write the thing out as it has settled itself in my own mind for better or worse during several years' ripening.

Have you read *Weir of Hermiston*? I took it up only this Christmastide and finished it yesterday. (I mean all there is of it). It was going to be Stevenson's best work and a really great novel.

The H. L. will not decide *Flood* v. *Jackson* much before Easter.[3] I am not sure that the Court of Appeal decided wrongly on the facts, but I feel pretty sure that their reasons would make the conduct of life impossible. Esher wants to restore the old doctrine of conspiracy: he tried it on in the Mogul S. S. Co.'s case but was happily overruled.[4] . . .

Here our young friends are committing a dramatic perform-ance in the name of local charity. My son is most martial to behold as an 18th century corporal arresting supposed Jaco-bites. He is just going to the dress rehearsal.

Yours ever,
F. Pollock

Boston, April 11, 1897[1]

Dear Lady Pollock:

I am off on Tuesday for a couple of weeks Circuit work at Worcester and before I go I will touch off a line in reply to

---

[2] See 1 *Encyclopedia of the Laws of England* (A. W. Renton, ed., 1897), p. 1.

[3] In the House of Lords the decision of the Court of Appeal, [1895] 2 Q. B. 21 was reversed, *sub nom.* Allen v. Flood, [1898] A. C. 1. See *supra*, p. 65.

[4] Lord Esher, M. R., had written one of the three opinions in Flood v. Jackson in the Court of Appeal; in the Mogul Steamship case, he wrote a dissenting opinion in the Court of Appeal, 23 Q. B. D. 598, 601, but the decision of the majority was sus-tained in the House of Lords, [1892] A. C. 25.

---

[1] A post card from Pollock to Holmes, dated February 24, 1897, is omitted. It dealt exclusively and briefly with Holmes's recent address, "The Path of the Law," delivered at Boston University, January 8, 1897, reprinted in 10 *Harv. L. Rev.* 457 (1897), and in *C. L. P.*, p. 167.

yours which I recd. yesterday and which gave me joy as all your letters do. I am glad you liked the Vierge book. I sent it because I think him the greatest living illustrator and do not suppose this book to be published except here. I am glad too that Macnaghten was pleased at my sending him an address of mine. I sent one also, or meant to — I am very sure I did — to the Pollock[2] who was with us on our charming river trip, but I wasn't quite sure about his address. They are two such nice chaps, and I was so delighted when in a semi shy way they came up and asked us to dine with them, before it was settled that we should dine with you on our arrival at town. I look back to that whole expedition and the grand finale in town with a sort of enchantment. Remember me sometime to the fair Miss Robins[3] if she hasn't forgotten the old Judge. I had Lehmann[4] to dine the other day with some bigwigs for the sake of his sister Lady Nina Campbell at whose feet I somewhat vainly laid the devotion of an ever faithful heart. We had some charming moments together, but my back once turned she lapsed into silence — arctic silence, I might say as that figure comes easily into my mind after reading Nansen's *Farthest North*. . . . I have been carried away both by the narrative itself and the reflections to which it gives rise. What a divine thing is adequate vitality — to be gay in the face of death and, almost worse, *ennui* — to be capable, though a complex and civilized man, to lark like a boy and to rejoice over a bellyful of blubber. I will not repeat reflections which I have made before and which one feels guilty in making as if for the first time. But this I have not said — *viz.* my respect for food has been revivified and refreshed. It is surprising with what interest and sympathy one follows grave speculations on the chances of a walrus. They seem more real than all our philosophy and teach us to be modest. I do not mean however to adopt Brooks Adams's simple summary of man as a destructive animal governed by greed and fear.

[2] Probably Dighton Nicholas Pollock (1864–1927).
[3] Presumably Elizabeth Robins, actress; author of numerous novels, and editor of *Theatre and Friendship: Some Henry James Letters* (1932).
[4] Rudolph Chambers Lehmann (1856–1929). Holmes spoke at the Tavern Club dinner in honor of Lehmann on November 24, 1896. His speech is printed in M. A. DeWolfe Howe, *Semi-Centennial History of the Tavern Club* (1934), pp. 74–76.

April 15, Worcester. I was interrupted at this point and am finishing my letter at the Worcester Club of a morning before going down to court and charging the jury in a will case. I shall expound to them what the meaning of undue influence is (so far as I know myself) and if they don't sustain the will I probably shall set the verdict aside. The man who wants a jury has a bad case — as an old Australian Judge said to me last year. I think there is a growing disbelief in the jury as an instrument for the discovery of truth. The use of it is to let a little popular prejudice into the administration of law — (in violation of their oath). I am putting up at a very comfortable little club where I am monarch of a morning and in the evening they give me dinners. I feel in these days that I would pay a dollar and a half and go across the street to see a good stiff prejudice of any kind. They have them in this place which is uncommonly strong in local feeling, and I find it a pleasant thing for a change. I like to hear of the various great men of the neighborhood who are believed in without too much pallid cosmopolitanism, and they have some strong chaps here. Forgive my details and remember me as always your affectionate friend,

O. W. H.

Now I must think for a few minutes on what I am going to say to my jury.

Love to Fred and the children.

BEVERLY FARMS, July 20, 1897

Dear Lady Pollock:

It is long — much too long — since I last wrote to you. . . . I just have been looking over Jowett's life [1] and am struck by the curious skeptical non-committal sort of consolations which he wrote. He always has struck me as no more than a retail dealer in notions, not the originator of large ideas, but I feel as I read that I have been somewhat prejudiced notwithstanding the remembrance of a very pleasant breakfast with him

[1] Evelyn Abbott and Lewis Campbell, *The Life and Letters of Benjamin Jowett* (2 vols., 1897).

in '66 when I was staying at Balliol with that Eminent Church-
man Edwin Palmer [2] (whom I do not remember in that capacity — but only as a kind host). Latterly I have spent a
fortnight driving up into the hills of New Hampshire and back
to be present at my nephew's wedding to a granddaughter
of Mr. Evarts.[3] Then there was speechifying and heat and
hullabaloo amid the charming scenery of the Connecticut
Valley and to the sound of many bobolinks singing in the
meadow below the house, as well as a nearer band of music.
The drive was perhaps the most delightful experience of my
life. The conditions were all as good as possible and my wife
who hasn't by any means got back to where she was before
her rheumatic fever, was wonderful in her resources of imaginative humor and forethought and seemed to awaken to a life
and joy which she has not known for a good while, — so I
was more than happy. I am settling down now to my usual
summer routine but so set free and enlarged by the bike. At
last I have one of my own and almost daily increase my dis-
tances though I don't emulate Frederick that mighty wheelman
before the Lord. The great thing is that it frees the imagination
and takes away the confined feeling which formerly used to
bore me here, but no longer does. I am laboriously picking
out a German lawbook (Heusler's *Institutionen*, which I suppose F. read long ago). And what with that and solitaire, and
little drives with my wife, and reading aloud, and talk with a
neighboring philosopher, and the bicycle, and guests, etc.
I am kept pretty busy. My wheel is an American Humber,
which we think about the best, with a gearing of 70 which I
agree with F. in thinking rather high. Tell me of any books or
gossip. You generally have something which you talk about
in London which doesn't get into the shops. . . . I went to
Brown University the other day to make a little speech at their
Commencement Dinner [4] supposing when I accepted the invitation that it meant a degree, which it didn't — so I missed both
earthly and heavenly reward, but I was well treated. I forget
whether I sent you a newspaper slip of what I said as to my

---

[2] Edwin Palmer (1824–1895); Archdeacon of Oxford.
[3] On July 8, 1897, Edward Jackson Holmes was married to Mary Stacy Beaman,
granddaughter of William Maxwell Evarts.
[4] *C. L. P.*, p. 164.

late partner Shattuck,[5] a big fellow, to whom I was much indebted and attached. Please give my love to the children and to Frederick. It was a satisfaction to find that I could stand the driving tour. That and my experiences in England last year make me feel that I am well — but never freed from the necessity of caution. How and where is Mrs. Clifford? Goodbye dear friend. You have given me a great deal of happiness for a long time and I am always

Yours affectionately,
O. W. Holmes

August 9, 1897

My beloved Frederick:

I have this moment received and had a charming letter from you,[1] and no farther ago than yesterday morning I all but was writing to you & was thinking about you. But inward disturbance disabled me and I didn't — mind not body. On Friday I lost my father's watch and the advertisement in the paper was wrong on Saturday and worse on Sunday after I had corrected by wire. But now all is serene. At noon a little humpback whom my man saw pick it up and drive off with it (of course, not knowing it was mine or what it was at the time) drove up to the door asked if I was *A*. W. Holmes and on my identifying by mentioning an adorable gold monkey on it (japanese — given me by one of my best girls) handed it over took his $25 and left me — both of us happy.

I like the damned arrogance of your mock modesty about the wheel. I feel pretty well pleased with myself for going 20 miles, over pretty bad roads to be sure. Brooks Adams is my companion, and a mighty entertaining one. He accepts the position of a crank. But he is full of pessimistic suggestions and can tell you history with inimitable vividness not unmixed with enhancing profanity. Thanks to him I have had more fun out of the crusades than any of the actors in them ever

---

5 *Speeches*, p. 70.

1 This letter is missing.

did, and he is really fine when he gets going on the Church of England. Also his presentation of the Catholic priesthood as medicine men is tickling to the malevolent fancy. I remember Davey telling me about *Allen* v. *Flood*.[2] I suppose it is the same case. He was free spoken in a semi confidential way. . . . I have finished Heusler — be he accursed. 200 pp. on the question which of the Little Pedlingtons on the Rhine had the regime of community and which only a right of reversion in the heirs — leaving me at the end wondering which and what was Eastphalia & which West — was somewhat more of a good thing than I wanted. I decided to hang up Brunner's *History*[3] to wait for better days. I don't know the case in the U. S. Supreme Court you mention, on the theory of contract. It is caviar to the general — and on any question involving the differential calculus of law I shouldn't expect much from them. . . . I am familiar with the notion you mention of *debt* — as if the coins of payment already belonged to the creditor — but I always have doubted and still doubt whether it is the real view of the old law. I meditate some day uttering a few generalities more on the origin of contract. Heusler is the first man whom I have seen who recognizes in his discourse that the generalization contract was not already given and present in the beginning and that special cases of what we now call contract presented themselves in their particularity ungeneralized, as bailments, warranty, suretyship (to us a modern word with somewhat different meaning), etc., etc. — a thought I dwelt on in my book and in my article on Early English Equity.[4] Apropos of debt, one of the things I don't know and suggesting a parallel to the views you mention is whether the early Roman law in dealing with a failure to pay the price of goods as = theft, looked at it as *quasi* a theft of the *goods* or of the *price*. I think that a significant question. You mention Mahan.[5] I tried to get him at a dinner I gave Lehmann when I had some of the local illustrious, but he was engaged. He

---

[2] Lord Davey concurred in the reversal of the decision of the Court of Appeals, [1898] A. C. 1, at 169. See *supra*, pp. 65, 72.

[3] Heinrich Brunner, *Deutsche Rechtsgeschichte* (1887–92).

[4] 1 *L. Q. Rev.* 162 (1885); *C. L. P.*, p. 1.

[5] Presumably, Alfred Thayer Mahan (1840–1914); author of *The Influence of Sea Power upon History* (1889).

wrote a pleasant letter to me also. . . . There is a (relatively) new book by Tarde — an *improvisatore* (qu. sp.?) on the Universe — whom I much like, *L'Opposition Universelle*. I mean to read it but have not yet done so.

Aug. 11. I have read 100 pp. of it. He is uncommon strong in suggestions of the *maybe's* of existence. But if one agrees with my friend Eliot Cabot in what I think the excellent statement that possibility means something of the existence of which we have some evidence, such suggestions are rather amusements for a rainy day, like today. But Tarde is so fertile that I feel much indebted to him. W. James's book *The Will To Believe* has interested me but more for its admirable writing and revelation of the essential Irishness of the writer than for the philosophic worth of its contents. He has a vivid feeling for the incident — the manifold in life — and also I think looks to Spiritualism as the one possible way of breaking away from a to him terrible necessitarian unification of the world. There are other influences also which I won't stop to enumerate. The result to my mind is chaotic, but useful as a check on the unifying tendency. I don't think he is as strong in dialectics as he is in vivid presentation and enumeration. So his books seem to me to belong on the side of art and *belles lettres* rather than to the opposite pole, philosophy. Boissier, *Cicéron et ses Amis*, is giving me a mild pleasure. The character of Atticus is not a very burning question, but classical gossip is entertaining. . . .

Well — goodbye. Remember me to Lady Pollock and the children.

Yours ever,
O. W. HOLMES

HIND HEAD COPSE
HASLEMERE, SURREY
September 17, 1897

My dear Holmes:

Thanks for your letter of divers dates.

As to the realistic conception of debt, I should have thought the identity in form of the writ of debt with the writ of right was sufficient proof of antiquity, though perhaps you might not have to go many centuries back to find the time when debts could not be recovered at all by any secular process.

The oldest theory of contract is I think negative. People in the 12th — 13th century could of course think and talk about promises, and even about agreement (*pactum*) as creating *some* kind of duty. But they held that promises, as such, were not enforceable in the King's temporal jurisdiction (inferior courts *did* enforce them, even by specific performance, see the King's Ripton and Littleport Rolls published by the Selden Society).[1] *Privatas convenciones non solet curia domini regis tueri.*

As to early Roman law, its analogies are risky unless one is careful to remember that the earliest Roman law for which we have more than conjectural restorations (huge volumes of Voigt on the XII. tables)[2] is in many ways less archaic than our medieval law. I don't believe any Roman lawyer would have thought of regarding the fraudulent purchaser of goods as stealing the price: it is his possession of the goods that is fraudulent and therefore, as the Scots say, "theftuous" — the Roman Law of *furtum* not being perplexed by anything like our extremely inconvenient doctrine of trespass and asportation. But I am speaking without book.

The modern Germans regard specific performance as the normal remedy and payment of damages only as a substitute where specific performance is impracticable. (This is now in their Civil Code.) They certainly did not get this from classical Roman law, but I am not prepared to suggest that they had any ancient Germanic tradition to work upon.

There is a good deal of speculative interest about the writ of covenant. Its failure to become a general remedy on contracts, perhaps with specific performance (see the schedule to the *Statutum Walliae*, where the modern narrowing has not yet been finally determined), is strong evidence of the incapacity of law in relatively early stages for anything like big generalization.

The inventors of assumpsit clearly thought that breach of

[1] *Select Pleas in Manorial and Other Seignorial Courts* (Maitland, ed., 2 Selden Society Publications, 1889), p. 99; *The Court Baron, Together with Select Pleas from the Bishop of Ely's Court of Littleport* (Maitland and Baildon, eds., 4 *id.*, 1891), p. 119.
[2] Moritz Voigt, *Die XII Tateln* (2 vols. 1883).

contract was *wrong* — not merely an election to pay damages rather than perform.

Again: if the obligation is, as you maintain, only alternative,[3] how can it be wrong to procure a man to break his contract, which would then be only procuring him to fix his lawful election in one way rather than another? (Fixing one's election in a particular way, *e.g.* voting for a particular candidate where there is no test of merit and no duty to choose the fittest, is a good consideration). Thus *Lumley* v. *Gye*,[4] and your cases as well as ours which have confirmed it, would be all wrong. But this is surely not now arguable except in the Langdellian ether of a super-terrestrial Common Law where authority does not count at all. You can't put it on the Statute of Labourers [5] — the later decisions leave no room for that view. . . .

Raymond [6] wheeled with me to the inn at Chiddingfold which has 14th-cent. timbers in the roof, and Munroe Smith [7] to the classic village of Selborne, where a humane parson leaves the church open for one to read the epitaphs of Gilbert White and his ancestors, and there is a passing great yew tree by the side of which we seem pretty ephemeral creatures.

We made them all teach us piquet, my wife and I having determined that we must lay in a game for two against our old age when the children have flown. (They are at this moment on a visit in Yorkshire).

We are pleased with R. H. Davis's *Soldiers of Fortune* — a rattling good story which I read through at a sitting.

Yours ever,
F. POLLOCK

[3] In his address, "The Path of the Law," delivered at Boston University January 8, 1897, Holmes had stated that "the duty to keep a contract at common law means that you must pay damages if you do not keep it — and nothing else." 10 *Harv. L. Rev.* 457, 462 (1897); *C. L. P.*, at p. 175. *Cf.* his statement in *The Common Law* (1881), p. 301: "The only universal consequence of a legally binding promise is, that the law makes the promisor pay damages if the promised event does not come to pass."

[4] 2 El. & Bl. 216 (1853).

[5] 25 Edw. III (1350–1).

[6] Robert L. Raymond; editor of the *Harvard Law Review*, 1897.

[7] Professor of Roman Law and Comparative Jurisprudence, Columbia University, 1891–1922.

My dear Holmes:

You are to have a belated New Year's (or rather early Lenten) gift from the Law Reports in the shape of (I guess it will come to) 80 or 90 pages of judges' opinions, mostly wrong.[1] In the House of Lords Herschell, Watson and Davey are very well, but Macnaghten's is the judgment which posterity, if it be wise, will study side by side with yours in *Vegelahn* v. *Gunter*.[2] I trust we shall get out the report with the February issue: the reporter is learned but rather old, and it will be a longish job. Only the organs of extreme capitalism (not having the wit to see that the contrary decision would have cut both ways) have expressed any dissatisfaction.

Karl Pearson[3] is to me a pretty disappointing person — a case of great power spoilt by fads or partisan twists — and I can take little interest in what he writes nowadays.

My third five-year term at Oxford is coming to an end: if I am re-elected I shall try a course of elementary history of English law, which is now possible. But please don't mention this to anyone at present. It may come to a short book in time. . . .

Yours ever,

F. P.

Dear Pollock:

As we don't shut up bores, one has to listen to discourses dragging slowly along after one has seen the point and made up one's mind. That is what is happening now and I take the

---

[1] Allen v. Flood, [1898] A. C. 1; reversing Flood v. Jackson. See *supra*, pp. 65, 72, 77.

[2] Vegelahn v. Guntner, 167 Mass. 92, 104 (1896). In this case a majority of the Court held that Holmes, sitting at *nisi prius*, had erred in refusing to enjoin the peaceful picketing of the plaintiff's place of business by members of a labor union who wished to increase the wages paid by the plaintiff. Mr. Justice Allen stated that "a combination to do injurious acts expressly directed to another, by way of intimidation or constraint, either of himself or of persons employed or seeking to be employed by him, is outside of allowable competition, and is unlawful." 167 Mass. at 99. Holmes in a dissenting opinion contended that the peaceful conduct of the defendants for a legitimate end was not unlawful and should therefore not be enjoined.

[3] In Holmes's Journal there appears among the books read during 1897 Karl Pearson's *The Chances of Death, and Other Studies in Evolution* (1897).

chance to write as I sit with my brethren. I hope I shall be supposed to be taking notes. I have just received your note on *Allen* v. *Flood* [1] which gives me much pleasure. I have read the whole case and while I find many shrewd remarks and able observations I feel a lack of articulate theory and fundamental analysis — if I may venture to say so.

I should have been glad to see the directions of Kennedy, J, which I have not been able to find anywhere except so far as they are set out in some of the judgments. I do not feel clear whether under his directions the jury's finding of malice did necessarily import that the final motive was malevolence or only, as in *Temperton* v. *Russell* [2] if I remember right, an intentional infliction of the harm complained of, leaving open the possible justification of trade war on which Lord Shand relied I believe. If the latter is the meaning of the finding the scope of the decision is different from what it would be if the finding means malevolence pure and simple, I should think. I feel some difficulty in making up my mind what the decision establishes although it affords ground for pretty confident prophesying on a number of points.

The first question in logical order, whether the plaintiff suffered a temporal damage which the law can recognize as such, is one which with the ensuing questions I think possibly might have been decided differently if there had been a sequence of cases before the house in the following order. (1) Slander of a man in his business. (2) A Catholic priest without any false statements malevolently warns his parish not to employ a doctor, intimating that he would not administer the sacraments while the doctor is under the roof, *per quod* the doctor loses all his business at one blow. (See *Morasse* v. *Brochu* 151 Mass. 567, where I never could find any slander or false statement [3]). (3) A malevolent act in the present case, as the first step in depriving plaintiff of all business, there being no trade fight in the matter. I can't believe that the House of Lords would deny an action in (2); and although a distinction might be taken between injury to credit or his chance of being dealt

---

[1] Possibly Pollock's brief article in 14 *L. Q. Rev.* 129 (April 1898).
[2] [1893] 1 Q. B. 715.
[3] A majority of the Court held, in an opinion by C. Allen, J., that the priest's words were actionable. No dissenting opinion was written.

with by the public *generally* and that of being employed by
one, I doubt whether if it had given judgment for plaintiff in
(2) it might not have done so in (3). I am glad of the decision,
but I don't attach much weight to the argument that the
remoter person could not be liable because the employer was
free to do as he liked. It seems to me that the true view is
that an intervening *right-doer* stands like the forces of nature,
and that the former may be used wrongfully as well as the
latter. In the case of a slander repeated where the repetition is
privileged I take it the slanderer may be liable for the repetition if it was a probable consequence of the original act. This
seems to test the principle. On the further questions, whatever
the results reached, I can't help thinking that it might have
been argued more keenly; but I won't bore you — you know
my notions about it. . . .

Paul Viollet sent me a volume of his history of French
executives & offices. I don't give the title rightly.[4] He is a
master. Also I am reading or rather just have begun Brandes,
Shakespeare, 2 vols., 8 vo., Macmillan, which promises to be
charming — also Froude's *Erasmus* which I never had read.
Mrs. Holmes & I read them aloud together. The bikers begin
to be seen in the streets but I have not yet ventured forth. I
saw Miss Robins last Sunday. It was a great pleasure to
see her charming face again. She shone in the odd little
gathering where I called on her like a small sun. Most of those
present looked out of drawing and failed to realize their types.
Which set her off — also she had on a pretty hat. I turned 57
the other day, but still feel the spring. Well goodbye. Other
bores are talking now from those with whom I began, but it is
another case which one makes up his mind on in 10 minutes
& then is jawed to for an hour and a half. Remember me affectionately to Lady Pollock & the infants.

Yours ever,
O. W. H.

I remember you put the point about possession in a note
when I was in England [5] which I never answered, and it has

---

[4] *Histoire des institutions politiques et administratives de la France* (3 vols., 1890–
1903).
[5] The note referred to is missing.

worried me ever since — just lost the note. I have thought at times that you didn't allow quite weight enough to identification by the senses as against all supposed elements of description.[6]

LONDON, March 30, 1898

My dear Holmes:

Your letter comes at a singularly appropriate moment. I am *inter apries juris*, writing an article on Torts for the *New Encyclopedia of English Law*,[1] *i.e.* practically trying to warn people of how many things the dicta in *Allen* v. *Flood* have unsettled. I fully agree with you that the arguments (in the old-fashioned sense, including the judicial reasoning) are not satisfactory. If a stronger man than Kennedy had got the first handling of the case it might have gone differently. However he was bound, in any case, by the wrong decisions (and worse reasons) of Esher & Co.

The Lords talked too much and about too many things — except Macnaghten. Why throw doubt which they can't at present satisfy on *Lumley* v. *Gye*, which was not before them? I don't know that overruling it would work much practical injustice: there have been very few actions of the kind here: but it would be inelegant, at least, for the law as a science: though I believe old Willes, a very great lawyer, thought *Lumley* v. *Gye* wrong.

Your views are I think a little too fine-drawn to be put in the hands of average judges, not to say jurymen: otherwise I should be much disposed to accept them. What I take *Allen* v. *Flood* as really deciding is that competition with all its incidents is a matter of common right and not of privilege and therefore not examinable as to motives: though the House of Lords might perhaps have reversed the bad law and worse facts of the Court of Appeal in the case at bar without deciding even so much: and that decision I think is the only safe one for a world of people who mostly get muddled over subtle

---

[6] See *infra* p. 85, footnote 2 (March 30, 1898).

[1] 12 *Encyclopaedia of the Laws of England* (1898), p. 189.

distinctions and think them unjust whenever they can't understand. . . .

I did not agree with your Court about "identification of sight and hearing" where the person "identified" is somebody else [2] — is that the point you mean? . . .

Yours ever,
F. POLLOCK

BOSTON, May 13, 1898

Dear F.:

Just a thank you for all your sendings.[1] I am occupying a 48 hours of leisure in looking into the early cases as to calling in the jury in negligence cases and the like.[2] The suggestion in *Weaver & Ward* [3] that the defendant might set forth his case with the circumstances for the court to judge was the line adopted as to *reasonable cause* which has been kept by the court to this day, and so as to *necessaries, reasonable* penalty, *reasonable* time, etc.

I don't like to be told that I am usurping the functions of the jury if I venture to settle the standard of conduct myself in a plain case. Of course, I admit that any really difficult

---

[2] In Edmunds v. Merchants' Despatch Transportation Company, 135 Mass. 283 (1883) the court was called upon to determine whether a swindler who, appearing in person pretended to be a reputable merchant by giving a false name, acquired title to goods sold to him by the defrauded seller. Morton, C.J., held for the court that title was acquired by the swindler. "The minds of the parties met and agreed upon all the terms of the sale, the thing sold, the price and time of payment, the person selling and the person buying. The fact that the seller was induced to sell by fraud of the buyer made the sale voidable but not void. He could not have supposed that he was selling to any other person; his intention was to sell to the person present, and identified by sight and hearing; it does not defeat the sale because the buyer assumed a false name, or practiced any other deceit to induce the vendor to sell." 135 Mass. at 283–284. For Holmes's and Pollock's views on this problem see Holmes, *The Common Law*, pp. 312–313; Pollock, *Principles of Contract* (10th ed., 1936), p. 472.

[1] Any letters from Pollock between March 30, 1898, and the date of this letter from Holmes are missing.

[2] Perhaps in preparation for the address which he delivered before the New York State Bar Association on January 17, 1899. The matter discussed in this letter was developed further in that speech. See, "Law in Science and Science in Law," 12 *Harv. L. Rev.* 443, 457–460 (1899); *C. L. P.*, pp. 210, 233–238.

[3] Hobart, 134 (1607).

question of law is for the jury, but I also don't like to hear it called a question of fact. . . .

Goodbye. Your letters give me great pleasure.

Yours,
O. W. H.

BOSTON, May 13, 1898

Dear Ly. Pollock:

I have just recd. a charming letter from you and I am Fred's debtor almost hopelessly. England has behaved nobly to us it seems to me and I hope we may draw closer together.[1] . . . Now we are waiting to hear news of another big fight which seems likely, and one lives over a sort of subterranean anxiety. I hear the sound of music as I write these words; probably some fellows going off, or it may be only down to some of our seacoast defences — but such sounds are frequent and recall old days. It gives one a certain ache. It always seems to me that if one's body moved parallel to one's soul, one would mind campaigning less as an elderly man than as a young one. If you are killed as a young one you feel that you haven't had your chance (the *bull* is merely external). At least that was the way I felt; but when one has had a try at life, has shown what he can do, and has come to some understanding with himself, to die a little sooner is only to lose pleasure, not to miss the point of being. But alas one's insides don't learn such good lessons from experience. I suppose a night on the ground would send me off with appendicitis. My old fellow lieutenant in Co. A., 20th Mass. Vol. Inftry., Charles Whittier, has gone on General Lee's staff, and if he does not have to rough it too much I should think might do some good work still. But, if a war should last any time on land, I think you would see all the old fellows replaced in a little while by younger ones, unless in some extraordinary instances. A general of 45 and a private of 30 are old. Everything in daily life goes on very quietly here. The only thing

[1] Since the outbreak of the Spanish-American war the British government and people had vigorously favored the American cause.

Sir Frederick Pollock

1897

that would suggest anything unusual is the multitude of flags from the windows of the houses, etc. I am going to the juggler's tonight. I still enjoy seeing wonderful feats. It is said that some of the tricks used by jugglers are of immemorial antiquity which reminds me that the account of Elijah's encounter with the priests of Baal as really turning on the use of kerosene, wh. I always had thought to be a little joke of Mark Twain's, is made serious by a similar story in the Apocrypha which says that the place is called Naphtha (if my memory is right) to this day. . . . I observe that I have used abbreviations freely in this letter. Do you think them low? I do rather. A lady I know, telling her host that she drank coffee for breakfast he said "Hopelessly middle." I feel somewhat that way as to abbreviations but friendship suffereth much and is patient so I rely on you not to chuck me. It does not look like England for me this year unless something happens pretty soon. With all affectionate remembrances to you and yours

Yours always,
O. W. H.

BOSTON, June 9, 1898

Dear Lady Pollock:

I am still hanging in the wind as to coming abroad, if England be abroad. Mrs. Holmes has begun to favor it just as I have been making up my mind that I ought not to do it — so I don't know. If I do I shall sail from New York by (Umbria?) on June 25 which I suppose would bring us to London by the following Saturday July 2. . . .

Brooks Adams has just been talking to me. He thinks this war is the first gun in a battle for the ownership of the world, through Control of the East Coast of Asia in which you and we and Japan will proceed to bottle up and kill the rest of mankind.

I confess to pleasure in hearing some rattling jingo talk after the self-righteous and preaching discourse, which has prevailed to some extent at Harvard College & elsewhere although

I do not yield myself except for the pleasure of the moment to B. A.'s theories.

A day has passed since I began this. I must send it off today and still I don't know what to say but still feel that probably I shall give it up — the theme is too absorbing. I long so to see you all again that I can't write about more indifferent themes. If I do not come, don't forget me and sooner or later I shall see your dear face again. I don't know whether I have said it before, but I do not know any man who does so many kind things as your Frederick and hardly anyone, not more than one, who has done so much according to his opportunities to promote good feeling between these two countries.

Affly Yours,
O. W. HOLMES

LONDON, November 30, 1898

My dear Holmes: [1]

For weeks I have meant to write to you, but we go on with many small occupations and no definite history, thinking there will perhaps be some resting point next week — well, let now be next week, or it may be never.

You will be glad to know that we have excellent accounts of Maitland from the Grand Canary (don't you feel tempted to annex it and him too?) where he has been sent to avoid the risks of an English winter. There is nothing organically wrong, and I do hope a good rest may put him in better case than he has been for some years. University routine, committees etc. on the top of his proper and really important work had quite run him down.

The Chancery Bar Lodge counts four Master Masons more, of whom I am one. The ritual of masonry is a perfect illustration of Selden's wise remark about the use of ceremonies in his *Table Talk*: they are like a penny glass to a cordial, of no value in itself, but the liquor is lost if you break the glass. For the

[1] Holmes had been in England and Ireland in the summer of 1898. Two brief post cards from Pollock, sent to Holmes while he was staying at Mackellar's Hotel in London, are omitted.

rest, it was developed some time in the 18th century by some one who had much leisure, but I have no doubt that it preserves medieval elements.

Our speculative fellowship founded by Lyall[2] & ourselves at the Athenaeum (Sidgwick[3] being the first recusant) has done nothing yet, but I have some fit persons in mind when I can catch them. Suppose you associate your wife (whom I know to be qualified, and hereby do propose), then she and you together can co-opt any one on your side whom you judge desirable. You remember the only rule we made was that, regular meetings being improbable, any two of us might from time to time choose a new one.

We had a pleasant month on the Norman coast at a tiny watering place: Dreyfus troubled us little, and Fashoda was not yet.[4]

My new edition of Spinoza is beginning to get into type, and the *Harv. Law Rev.* will shortly publish an instalment of a short history of English law[5] which may take final shape some years hence if I live long enough.

Yours ever,
F. POLLOCK

BOSTON, December 9, 1898

Dear Pollock:

For months (as against your *weeks*) I have been meaning to write you or Lady Pollock but the infirmities of age and the high pressure of work have hindered me. I brought home from Ireland a little case of the shingles — an ignominious but painful disease, as the C. J.[1] remarked to me — and my shoulder

---

[2] Sir Alfred Comyn Lyall (1835–1911); Anglo-Indian Administrator and writer.

[3] Henry Sidgwick (1838–1900). See Pollock's memoir of Sidgwick, in 2 *Pilot* 325 (Sept. 15, 1900).

[4] In July 1898 a French expedition, under Captain Marchand, had occupied Fashoda, in Egyptian Sudan. A British force under Lord Kitchener arrived at Fashoda on September 19, and, as a result of negotiations between the French and British, actual hostilities were averted.

[5] "The King's Justice in the Early Middle Ages," 12 *Harv. L. Rev.* 227 (November 1898). See also "The King's Peace in the Middle Ages," 13 *Harv. L. Rev.* 177 (November 1899).

---

[1] Walbridge Abner Field.

still aches and the small of my back does the like. Meantime I have been busy with cases and for a few days with an address to the N. Y. State Bar Association for next January. Your letter comes first as I was thinking to myself that I must get and read your *Spinoza* which by some chance I never did. I shall wait for the 2d edition to appear. The same things which have kept me from writing have kept me from reading — except a little law before I start forth of a morning. I read Thayer's *Preliminary Treatise on Evidence* the other day — admirable piece of work. He has not genius but he is one of the few illustrations which I know of the worth and possible success of industry (an old fellow I lunch with who has made a great fortune says, "I went to school with many industrious boys. They all died poor. I sat round & did nothing and when I saw a chance, took it."). You feel sure that Thayer has examined *everything* he can lay his hands on & has not trusted to intuition. He prints in an Appendix a paper by V. Hawkins [2] on Legal Interpretation which I think poor stuff, or rather think not to be the last word. I agree with Wigram [3] and Lord Wensleydale [4] that we don't care a damn for the meaning of the writer and that the only question is the meaning of the words but as words are not mathematic figures the question becomes what do those words mean in the mouth of the normal English speaker — our old friend the prudent man in a special garb — & therefore we let in evidence of circumstances. When we let in direct evidence of intent on the question of who or what is meant by a proper name, I still stick to my old explanation that by the *theory of speech* the proper name means only one person or thing though it may *idem sonans* with another proper name, & you let in intent not to find out what the speaker meant but what he said. Instead of being an anomaly it was an instinctive right judgment that led to the exceptional rule.[5] Do remember me most affectionately to Lady Pollock and the children. I am much

[2] F. Vaughan Hawkins, "On the Principles of Legal Interpretation," originally published in 2 *Juridical Society Papers* (1860) 298.

[3] Sir James Wigram (1793–1866); *Examination of the Rules of Law Respecting the Admission of Extrinsic Evidence in Aid of the Interpretation of Wills* (1st ed., 1831).

[4] In Doe v. Gwillim, 5 B. & Ad. 122, 129 (1833) and Grey v. Pearson, 6 H. L. Cas. 61, 106 (1857).

[5] Holmes developed this thesis in his short article "The Theory of Legal Interpretation," 12 *Harv. L. Rev.* 417 (January 1899); reprinted, *C. L. P.*, p. 203.

pleased at your notion of a short history of English Law. I wish you would do it. . . . Dicey has been here and has been much liked. The Tavern Club gave him a dinner at which a lot of us turned out and made speeches. I think it was the best after dinner speaking I ever heard. I mean taking the average.

Yours ever,
O. W. H.

LONDON, Feb. 22, 1899

My dear Holmes:

This is a specially interesting number of the *Harvard Law Review*. I don't feel competent to discuss the Constitution of the U. S. in its possible application to Salvage Yles beyond seas [1] (men sain that thei ben in the partes of Lamarye, and right foul folk dwellen ther, but I have not sen hem) — but I have no doubt that Langdell's view is right in point of policy and will have to be made so in law. [2]

On the true method of interpretation I am with you. [3] If the actual intent were the criterion, no reason can be given against admitting proof that the testator used every word in the language in a non-natural sense peculiar to himself. Short of that, we can only fall back on the objectively reasonable meaning of what the testator has said: though we cannot, as in the case of contract, say that the question is not what was in the parties' minds, but what they have given one another the right to expect. Vaughan Hawkins's mind is too fussy and elaborate: that is one of the things that spoilt his career. I think we talked of him when you were here in the summer.

Some time next month I am to be delivered of a serious and a frivolous work — the second edition of Spinoza (not that I have put much new work into it), and the *Etchingham Letters*, written jointly with Mrs. Fuller Maitland. I hope this may

[1] Presumably this refers to an article by Simeon E. Baldwin, "The Constitutional Questions Incident to the Acquisition and Government by the United States of Island Territory," 12 *Harv. L. Rev.* 393 (1899).

[2] Langdell, "The Status of our New Territories," *id.*, p. 365.

[3] Holmes, "The Theory of Legal Interpretation," *id.*, p. 417; *C. L. P.*, p. 203.

not lead the bibliographer of the future to strange confusions with Pollock & Maitland, *History of English Law*, also that the fates may contrive a decent interval of a week or ten days between the forthcoming of the two works.

The charming lady (an invalid, more's the pity) who had the idea of writing a book in really exchanged letters, and did me the honour of choosing me as the partner, is not related to our learned friend of Cambridge, England, who is now doing himself much good in Grand Canary. It is well the war was over — you might have been tempted to send a gunboat and carry him off to your Cambridge as a distress then and there found, at the risk of a plea of *vee de nam*.

Yours ever,
F. Pollock

London, March 15, 1899

My dear Holmes:

Your paper in *Harv. L. Rev.* is most interesting.[1] It suggests more questions than one can make up one's mind on offhand. From pp. 457-460 I gather that you are oppressed by your statutory sharpenings of the line between the functions of judge and jury. As law and practice here go, there is not and never has been any hard rule either that juries are the judges of all questions of fact, or that they are judges of nothing else. A good judge and a good jury (have you special juries by the way?) work together so that one can hardly separate their contributions to the result. It is true I have seen nothing of juries for many years, except one day last year when I was for my sins an unwilling witness in a foolish action, but I remember something of what I learnt as old Willes's marshal.

I am not prepared to admit that there is more anomaly in the jury passing on the question of negligence than in their power to find a general verdict in any other kind of case: and I think it would be a serious burden for the Court to take judicial notice of what a reasonable man's conduct would be in every

---

[1] "Law in Science and Science in Law," 12 *Harv. L. Rev.* 443 (1899); *C. L. P.*, p. 210.

variety of circumstances. But this must wait for our next meeting. . . .

Gertrude Bell and I have been worrying out Persian prosody (different enough from Greek or Latin to puzzle the mere classical scholar) at odd times. She is one of the most remarkable people I know. Did I ever tell you to read Browne's *Year amongst the Persians?*

Accounts of Maitland are as good as possible.

Yours ever,
F. POLLOCK

BOSTON, April 6, 1899

Dear F. P.:

I can only dash off a line of thanks for your *Spinoza*. I have read about half and am reading it for a few minutes of a morning before envisaging the cruel world. I can't tell you how much I like it, or what varied and extraordinary talent it shows on your part. Your devilish readiness for any idea in any language, as well mathematical or metaphysical as Dutch or Persian, is the despair of other men. The clearness and interest of the exposition and the sober good sense of your own fundamental judgments strike me as equally admirable. In short my friend I think you have made a little masterpiece and I congratulate you.

Yours always,
O. W. HOLMES

LONDON, July 5, 1899

My dear Holmes:

We lost my mother last week. She had been feeble for some time, and rapidly failing for about a month before. One cannot complain of people dying at fourscore, but it is a closing of one of the doors of the memory. Life roughly divides itself into compartments, and one shifts on from one to another like the nautilus, with a more or less watertight partition at the back.

And the distinct finding that we are ourselves the older generation is such a move. You hardly knew my mother, I think — I wish she could have crossed the Atlantic: she would have thoroughly enjoyed both the voyage and the other side. But my father was an indifferent sailor and hated long journeys of any kind.

Enclosed is a note from my very learned friend Elphinstone.[1] I suspect the differences between you all would turn out on full discussion to be not very substantial.

Thanks for the fresh copy of the Boston Address.[2] I am a little bit disappointed that you only say Austin did not know *enough* law.

The truth is that his law is thoroughly amateurish — his Roman law almost worse than his English — and this is why he has a reputation among half-educated publicists. I do think he scored one point in working out the distinction of political from legal science, *viz.* that a lawyer, as such, is not bound to have any theory of politics at all, or one kind of theory more than another; but he [*sic*] doubt if he ever knew it, for he wastes many pages on dogmatic utilitarianism.

I am meditating a course of lectures on the Law of Nature.[3] The present calls of executorship business don't help my meditation — the whole mass of my father's papers which my mother had never touched, to sort out somehow. If I can find you some little remembrance I will.

Yours ever,

F. POLLOCK

Maitland is all the better for his winter in the Canaries, but I fear not quite right yet. He is taking to the wheel. Is the

---

[1] Sir Howard Warburton Elphinstone (1830–1917). In his letter to Pollock, Sir Howard wrote: "I have read Holmes' article. I think that he has entirely forgotten that the ordinary man intends his writing to be understood by others, and that for that reason he employs language that they will understand. . . . So far as I am aware no serious writer on interpretation has ever stated that the problem is to ascertain *the intention* of the writer, on the other hand the careful writer states the problem as that of ascertaining the *expressed intention* of the writer which may be something very different."

[2] Holmes, "The Path of the Law," 10 *Harv. L. Rev.* 457, 475 (1897); *C. L. P.*, at p. 197.

[3] See Pollock, *The Expansion of the Common Law* (1904), p. 107.

'free wheel' seducing you in New England? I don't feel clear about it — but I have never ridden one.

My family are out at Hind Head. About August 10 we go to Bayreuth to slay the thrice slain worm: and shall be back at Hind Head in September.

BEVERLY FARMS, July 16, 1899

My dear Pollock:

You have my affectionate sympathy. I imagine that in your case as in mine the loss is mitigated by the fact of some previous loss of powers, but the death of one's mother always must be one of the great events of life. Perhaps because I have no children I have not been so conscious of that step into the front rank but everyone feels it more or less. I remember my old partner Shattuck speaking of it very strongly. This morning I read in the paper the death of our Chief Justice (Field). Poor man he had suffered a great deal. ... He had not what Choate said John Quincy Adams had, the instinct for the jugular,[1] but he had a fertile suggestive mind, good sense in the main, and the sweetest of tempers.

Apropos of the Law of Nature do you know Ahrens' book?[2] I dare say it is an old story nowadays, but I remember when I was much younger thinking very well of it.

As to Elphinstone's note, I think it must be inspired by a desire to differ — at least I can't see any indication that he and I do not think alike. I am surprised at his thinking I showed forgetfulness that writing is intended to be understood by others. But he does not know what has been written if he thinks that no serious writer ever stated that the problem is to ascertain the intention of the writer. If that had been the fact I should not have printed. I did print what in substance I had written to Thayer, at his suggestion and request because my theoretic form of expression differed from him and from Hawkins. I agreed and suggested that in practice it does not much matter whether you say discover the intent of the writer so far

[1] See Samuel Gilman Brown, *The Life of Rufus Choate* (1870), p. 417.
[2] Heinrich Ahrens, *Cours de droit naturel ou de philosophie du droit* (1838).

as the words permit or discover the meaning of the words. But theory is none the less interesting when it is outside the limits of possible proof or refutation. . . . My vacation has begun, and I have worked so hard that I think I shall keep my mind empty, bike in a pottering way of an afternoon, play solitaire and read little, not bothering about improving my mind. I am reading Carlyle's *Past & Present*. Curious how stirring and searching his preachment is even while one believes to the bottom of his reason that the man's philosophy of life is hardly worth serious consideration. His literary genius is so great. It illustrates anew the fundamental opposition of poet and philosopher. The man who feels and the man who explains. No man is both in spite of your Goethes. If Carlyle had not spent so much energy in posing as a prophet his ultimate influence and abiding charm would not have been less. The opening part of the book disgusted me and seemed to have no significance except as possibly a vague precursor of the *Book of Snobs*. Give my love to the Lady, the boy and the girl.

Ever yours,
O. W. HOLMES

BEVERLY FARMS, July 27, 1899

Dear F. P.:
   This is just a line to say that the Governor has nominated me for Chief Justice. The nomination has to be confirmed by the Governor's Council, but I don't suppose there is any doubt that they will confirm it as it seems to have been generally expected and to be approved.[1] I am sure of your friendly interest.

   I am idling playing solitaire and sleeping — not much even of *belles lettres*. I suppose it is a sort of automatic insistence of one's mind upon rest. . . . Do you know Verhaeren's poems? I have sent for them being much impressed by some translations by Alma Strettell. I am sad with the sense of the transitoriness of things brought home to me by the C. J.'s death & my appointment. But Spinoza was wise in teaching us to think

[1] The nomination was confirmed by the Governor's Council on August 2, 1899.

of life. So *semble per* Kaneko,[2] a former student of mine now a great man, the Japanese who leave the next world to look out for itself and try to do their best in this. He said to me that they had had the advantage of not being hampered by religion. Give my love to Lady Pollock and the children.

Yours always,
O. W. HOLMES

LONDON, August 9, 1899

My dear Holmes:

We send our best congratulations on your advancement to the chief seat in your Court, though we could wish the incidents of it included some relief from the ordinary routine work, as we fear it does not. Tomorrow my family come up from Hind Head, and on Friday night we set forth to the Wagner plays at Bayreuth. . . .

These last few weeks I have had a thorough search of my parents' house. It is hardly credible that people with any sense of business or of literature (my father had a good deal of both of these, and my mother of one) should leave such a chaotic mass of documents as I found. . . .

Our ancestors are thought by many to have had more leisure than we. I don't believe it. They muddled away many hours in doing small things with futile elaboration, and when they were not doing that they took commonplace books and wrote out, as the case might be, extracts from perfectly well known and accessible works, or anecdotes barely worth preserving at all. Women continued this practice longer than men, I think.

Preserving ms. which has gone into print is a thing one should abstain from in mercy to one's executors.

I have not read Verhaeren, though I have heard him praised. Carlyle's plunge into the Middle Ages — of which I believe he knew nothing — in *Past & Present* was, if I remember right, more free from blunders than might have been expected. He made Jocelyn of Brakeland talk of "viscounts"; but Travers

---

[2] Viscount Kentaro Kaneko (1853–   ); Harvard Law School, 1876–78; author of works on Japan and Japanese history.

Twiss, with far less excuse, did the same by Bracton. I am much interested in the Continental history of law of nature & Social Contract as expounded by Gierke in his *Johannes Althusius*. I ought to have known it long before.

Yours ever,
F. P.

BOSTON, December 1, 1899

Dear F. P.:

I just have time to send my love to you and Lady Pollock not omitting the children and to enclose a somewhat garbled and wretchedly printed copy of what I said about my predecessor last Saturday.[1]

I sent you a little *Fables in Slang*[2] a while ago, thinking it might make you smile, as it did me. "She was short on Intellect, but long on Shape" seemed to me large. You know the broker's lingo.

I thus far have had more to do than ever, partly from temporary causes partly from my own fault in assigning perhaps rather a lion's share to myself. I anxiously wish you a speedy success in your war.[3]

Yours ever,
O. W. HOLMES

[1] Enclosed with this letter was a newspaper clipping containing an account of Holmes's answer to resolutions of the Boston Bar, November 25, 1899, on the death of Chief Justice Field. See *Speeches*, p. 75.

[2] By George Ade; published in 1899.

[3] The Boer War had commenced in October 1899.

III

1901-1907

Dear Lady Pollock:

I do not remember whether or when I have sent you a written reminder of my affection, but as in the moments of leisure I have found myself sending off discourses to various new acquaintances it has struck me that there has been a disproportionate silence between us. The whirl begins again tomorrow and at any moment may become continuous, but accident has given me two empty weeks since I have been at home [2] — voids which were filled at once pretty full with private affairs. . . . I am in flourishing condition. Weigh more, I guess, than when I came to London, and have something of the ease of mind that comes with fat. I have read a little — *The Odyssey* with a refreshed appreciation of forgotten and unexpected excellencies, coupled with the pleasure which the unsimple modern feels at the first intentions characteristic of classic literature. I used to say that it was a pleasure to deal with an honest man, he could be humbugged more easily. In like manner one agreeably patronizes the simplicity of the ancients. The last day or two I have taken up Marcus Aurelius again. *The Golden Treasury* translation is very good reading, not monotonous, not giving the impression of an old man who after the day's work was done went home and wrote down a platitude — but an august and lonely figure. The translation seems to be very good from one or two crucial comparisons with the Greek. Also some mystical works [3] of men seeking to lift themselves by

---

[1] A letter from Holmes to Lady Pollock, dated April 12, 1901, and two short notes from Pollock to Holmes, dated May 8 and July 22, 1901, are omitted.

[2] Holmes had been in England in the summer of 1901.

[3] Among the books appearing in Holmes's Journal for 1901 are Édouard Récéjac, *Essay on the Bases of Mystic Knowledge* (Sara C. Upton, tr., 1899), and Charles Ferguson, *The Religion of Democracy* (1900).

the slack of their own breeches, and demanding that the final compulsions under which we reason, love, etc., should be admitted as of cosmic validity. I stop short of that. All I mean by truth is the road I can't help travelling. What the worth of that *can't help* may be I have no means of knowing. Perhaps the universe, if there is one, has no truth outside of the finiteness of man. "To what a height my spirit is ascending." To come down, let me recommend *Japanese Plays & Playfellows* by O. Edwards as a very pretty and clever and interesting book, with some insights in it. The Japanese attitude, so far as I can picture it, on moral questions seems to me sounder than ours; with us morality tends to become a branch of Oxford exquisiteness, like Burne-Jones's pictures. And exquisiteness is a doubtful good, needing much battle and sudden death to justify it. My uncle John Holmes always had to smoke 5 cent cigars for fear that his taste should become too refined. . . . From the time I went aboard ship until recently it seemed as if death were striking all about among my acquaintances, but the slaughter seems to have paused. I wonder where H. James is. I sent him a photograph, to Rye, which he has not acknowledged. Economy not vanity makes me wonder whether I have spent my cash in vain (this is not a message to him). I must put in a legal line to the young Frederick.[4] You know my affection and how much happiness I always owe to you in my English visits.

Affly Yours,
O. W. HOLMES

BEVERLY FARMS, July 31, 1902

Dear Lady Pollock:

I wrote last, but now it is vacation and I am not in the preoccupied and uncommunicating state which is the blight of winter letters. Today however promises to be busy. I am going over to Ipswich, a town about an hour's drive from here, where they are going to unveil some Memorial Tablets, and as two ancestors of mine, Governor Dudley and Ann Bradstreet, a

---

4 Any such letter is missing.

poetess of the 17th Century whom I fear you never heard of, although she was called the 10th muse in her day, lived in Ipswich once, I am in for a little speech. [1] Would 'twere done. However it is a beautiful day and if I can remember what I have written I think I can make them wiggle. I have been reading philosophy which I don't believe by Wm. James and Royce and which I do by Tarde [2] — and which I don't feel bound to take too seriously by Nietzsche,[3] although the last named gent said some things worth remembering. On the whole I am on the side of the unregenerate who affirm the worth of life as an end in itself as against the saints who deny it. I may whisper in your ear that the male saints whom I have seen near to have been flats. Now I am idling and mean to read some books. I even should not mind one or two that would call a blush to the cheek of my innocence.

Aug 1. The show is over. Everything went off with success; luncheon at a charming farm then drove over to a church on the site of the original one of 1630–40 where a pretty little girl descendant of one [of] the early settlers who has kept the old land from the beginning (where we lunched) unveiled a tablet, and I unveiled one to Ann Bradstreet in front of what seems to be or to contain part of her original house, etc. Then to the church where there was a little country audience and some simple discourses including a little horn blast from me — made nonsense of in the papers this morning — and a church tea and a visit to a house preserved by the historical society with I think the finest oak beams I ever saw here or in England in a private house, and home in the afternoon. All beautiful with every innocent and peaceful charm. The sand of the Ispwich beaches is white and as you catch glimpses of them driving in the distance have the look of magic. At the same time they are dangerous: years ago they noticed on a farm a little stream of sand blown inward. The tide flowed on and now the farm is a

---

[1] See *Speeches*, p. 92.

[2] William James, *Varieties of Religious Experience* (1901); Josiah Royce, *The World and the Individual* (2 vols., 1900, 1901); and G. Tarde, *La Psychologie économique* (1901), according to Holmes's Journal.

[3] In Holmes's Journal it appears that he had recently read volumes x and xi of Nietzsche's Collected Works, including his *Case of Wagner*, his *Anti-Christ*, his *Genealogy of Morals*, and his *Poems*.

waste and the dead trees are all that is left to show what once was. My wife said I ought to put them in so I wound up thus: "And to many a gallant spirit two hundred years from now as two hundred years ago the white sands of Ipswich, terrible as engulfing graves, lovely as the opal flash of fairy walls, will gleam in the horizon, the image of man's mysterious goal" — which I thought rather a pretty figure. Now I am free — no more speeches thank the Lord, and I mean to read Flaubert's *L'Éducation Sentimentale* if I don't find that I have already because I saw it referred to the other day by a clever chap as the French *Odyssey*. I am afraid that I never have realized that there was anything particular in Flaubert's style, although he makes so much row about style in his letters and is praised correspondingly. The writer to whom I refer as mentioning him (Remy de Gourmont in the *Mercure de France*) distinguishes between those who put their passion into their phrase and those who put it into their life, as antithetical, to the disadvantage of A. de Musset's writing. I am afraid I never have got so far as to find him hollow and so I want to find out whether I can see the point. I haven't read him for many years.

Hope that Fred is having a vacation and is well. There are many things that turn up on which I wish that I could talk with him but they pass and other questions take their places and it would take too long to write. Perhaps next year if all goes well I shall get over and have another chance to "parcourure the universe" — as a girl once said to me. Give my love to him and the young people. I am one of the few who stick to the bicycle as a pleasure and an exercise. I hope that F. hasn't given it up? Fashion, as I long have said, is a law of life, and I suppose as soon as the odious automobiles get cheap the rich will give them to their servants, as Mr. Dooley said the other day. However I should like to see them replace horses altogether in the cities. I am adding not to my stature but to my weight — my clothes are all becoming instruments of torture. But I have not grown out of recognition and fat has not invaded my affection for you.

Affly yours,
O. W. HOLMES

HIND HEAD COPSE
HASLEMERE, SURREY
July 21, 1902

My dear Holmes:

Do you think that in any conceivable circumstances a fraudulent obtaining of "constructive delivery" of goods by transfer in a warehouseman's books, without any handling of the goods themselves, can be larceny at common law? Lord Halsbury does. See his *dicta* in *Farquharson and Co.* v. *King*, forthcoming in August number of L.R., and a humble editorial note thereon.[1] He says it is mere quibbling to talk of asportation. Luckily this is quite immaterial for the decision. . . .

My son has been feasting — lucky boy — with George Meredith, who is as vigorous as ever in mind though weak in body.

Yours ever,
F. POLLOCK

BEVERLY FARMS, August 13, 1902

Dear Pollock:

. . . The legal question I hang up until I can look at Lord Halsbury's *dicta*. Of course the decisions that fraudulent possession in any case can be a basis of larceny historically is an enlargement or departure or whatever eu- or dyslogistic epitaph one may choose to apply. I should think that any stopping place was arbitrary until embezzlement was swallowed up in larceny newly defined (by statute). I have had one or two touches at the matter in cases which I can't cite here. My news you perhaps will have heard before this reaches you. The President has offered me a place on the U. S. Supreme Court which I shall accept — subject to confirmation by the Senate. There have been powerful influences against me, because some at least of the money powers think me dangerous, wherein they are wrong. The N. Y. *Evening Post* I see says that I have not been a great Judge, being brilliant rather than sound.[1] But

---

[1] [1902] A. C. 325, noted by Pollock in 18 *L. Q. Rev.* 333 (1902).

[1] See the editorial entitled "Remaking the Supreme Court," New York *Evening Post*, Aug. 12, 1902, p. 4. The editorial stated that Holmes "has been more of a 'liter-

that paper and *The Nation* always have treated me and my father before me with reservations — most of its criticism has been pointedly incompetent — and I say this with perfect confidence notwithstanding my personal interest. On the whole the nomination seems to be very warmly received notwithstanding the occasional note of anxiety. But the incompetence and inadequacy of the ordinary talk while expected is annoying, whether praise, as it generally is, or blame. I shall go on with my work here until the Senate acts and shall not vacate my place except by taking the new one — following Gray's example [2] — unless something turns up to show that I ought to do otherwise. I envy your boy for his visit to Meredith. I have not been able to see him for many years, much to my regret. I have to cut this short because I have a stack of letters already to answer and they are pouring in. The news only came yesterday morning. The President had offered the place to me [3] but I was not at liberty to say anything until he made it public.

Affly yours,
O. W. Holmes

Beverly Farms, September 6, 1902

Dear Lady Pollock:

This is just to thank you and Fred. for your kind words.[1] I shall keep on here as C. J. until I am confirmed by the Senate, which I suppose will be in December if nothing unforeseen happens. . . .

I read *L'Éducation Sentimentale* as a study in style and because I saw it spoken of as the French *Odyssey*. I pity the French for their Odysseus. It is all very well to give us a care-

ary feller' than one often finds on the bench, and he has a strong tendency to be 'brilliant' rather than sound."

[2] Horace Gray (1828–1902); Associate Justice of the Supreme Judicial Court, 1864–73; Chief Justice, 1873–81; Associate Justice of the Supreme Court of the United States, 1881–1902.

[3] In Holmes's Journal there appears the following entry: "July 24. Presdt offered me Judgeship."

[1] The letters referred to are missing.

fully visualized picture, but a picture of a squalid and worthless life is a kind of art in which I take little pleasure.

I took much more in reading a book which describes unspeakable practises on the part of the heroine. One's jaw drops with amazement to find it assumed that two women can't be alone in a room together without exciting sinister suspicions — suspicions that in the particular case are supposed to be true. And yet, incredible, you like the woman (*Claudine En Ménage*).[2] And there is humor, of a sort not usual in French books. Well, to be civilized is to be potentially master of all possible ideas, and that means that one has got beyond being shocked, although one preserves one's own moral and aesthetic preferences. I regard the latter, however, as more or less arbitrary, although none the less dogmatic on that account. Do you like sugar in your coffee or don't you? You admit the possibility of difference and yet are categorical in your own way, and even instinctively condemn those who do not agree. So as to truth. We tacitly postulate that if others were as intelligent and well educated as we they would be compelled to agree with us — but that is a mere ideal, not an actuality. They don't agree in fact. The fact is that each has his more or less differing system; whether there is an objective reality in which is to be found the unity of our several compulsions or whether our taste in truth is as arbitrary as our taste in coffee and there is no objective truth at all, I leave to philosophers by profession. I think the law is a better calling — though I used not to. The president's choice of me has been received in a way that I think I may regard as a triumph, although at first by perversity of temperament I was very blue — after the first joy of the way in which he put his wishes to me, which was a reward for much hard work. Love to Fred.

Affly Yours,
O. W. HOLMES

[2] Collette Willy; *Claudine en Ménage* (1901).

BOSTON, Feb. [September ?] 23, 1902

Dear Fred:

I am just back from this week's circuit and must vent a line of unreasoning — rage I was going to say — dissatisfaction is nearer. There have been stacks of notices of me all over the country and the immense majority of them seem to me hopelessly devoid of personal discrimination or courage. They are so favorable that they make my nomination a popular success but they have the flabbiness of American ignorance. I had to get appreciation for my book in England before they dared say anything here except in one or two quarters. There were one or two notable exceptions. And now as to my judicial career they don't know much more than that I took the labor side in *Vegelahn* v. *Guntner* [1] and as that frightened some money interests, and such interests count for a good deal as soon as one gets out of the cloister, it is easy to suggest that the Judge has partial views, is brilliant but not very sound, has talent but is not great, etc., etc. It makes one sick when he has broken his heart in trying to make every word living and real to see a lot of duffers, generally I think not even lawyers, talking with the sanctity of print in a way that at once discloses to the knowing eye that literally they don't know anything about it.

Believe me I am not exaggerating.

The legal periodicals are generally in vacation. I hope some one of them may have an intelligent word, but you can understand how at a moment of ostensible triumph I have been for the most part in a desert — when I hoped to see that they understood what I meant, enough not to bully me with Shaw, Marshall and the rest. If I haven't done my share in the way of putting in new and remodeling old thought for the last 20 years then I delude myself. Occasionally some one has a glimpse — but in the main damn the lot of them. This is a confidential ebullition of spleen to an intimate which will do me good. I ought to be doing other things but first stopped for a moment to unpack my heart.

Yours,

O. W. H.

---

[1] 167 Mass. 92, 104 (1896). See *supra*, p. 81.

LONDON, October 3, 1902

My dear Holmes:

$$\mu\epsilon\tau\grave{\alpha} \; \kappa\grave{\alpha} \; \tau\acute{o}\delta\epsilon \; \tauο\hat{ι}σι \; \gamma\epsilon\nu\acute{\epsilon}σθω$$

said that much-enduring Odysseus. How should the lay gentry, or even the average lawyer, understand the development of the Common Law, or the work that men such as you and Bowen put into it? I name Bowen as the English judge of our time whose judicial mind seems to me to have been most like yours: and your work and his have both been thought, at times, by fairly competent persons to be a little too finely edged for cutting the blocks of common business. A crude lay version of this line of criticism seems to have found its way into your newspaper cuttings, though the notion that what is brilliant cannot be sound is dear to our friend the reasonable man, who in the flesh is a Philistine pig, on the general principles of his pig-piety.

Wherefore, disquiet not thyself with what he saith, but leave him to worship his god Dagon and divers, to wit, thirty thousand cartloads of other devils, and if he ever gets a soul, the Lord have mercy on it.

Concerning Flaubert — do you know the volume called *Trois Contes* wherein Hérodias is, I think, his masterpiece of workmanship? He tells you the story of John the Baptist so that you see the whole thing and never think for a moment whether the story-teller may be Jew, Christian or pagan — only a feeling in the air that something greater than John *is* coming, which, after all, is bare historical fact. The end is consummate, no moralizing, no epithets; just two of John's disciples receding into the desert, carrying his head between them.

L'Éducation Sentimentale is a little long — very fine satire, though, and the Revolution of '48 much truer, I should guess, than any historian has yet made it.

The only book of his I can't read is *Salammbô*: the dictionary of antiquities chokes me, though I have no doubt he took immense pains with it and got it all or nearly all right. . . .

Cast your eye, if you have time, on my discourse of the Monroe Doctrine *The Nineteenth-Twentieth Century* [1] (which of

---

[1] 52 *Nineteenth Century* 533 (October 1902).

course we all call *Nineteenth Century* still). I rather hope you will like it. Anyhow the history has never been properly told here before.

Yours ever,

F. POLLOCK

BOSTON, October 24, 1902

Dear Lady Pollock:

. . . I have just taken 3 or 4 days off with some qualms to go to Chicago — it seemed an enormous undertaking, more than to go to London — for the purpose primarily of pleasing Wigmore, Dean of the North Western University Law School, and giving him a puff. I think him a very deserving and quite superior man in what I have read and seen of him. He generally has pitched into me — the young fellows are apt to try their swords in that way — but his implications are flattering and his work good. The Chicago Bar united in his invitation by offering me a banquet, and so for two days and a half I was in alternate crowds of College Presidents (there was a new president to be inaugurated)[1] and of Judges and leaders of the bar, so I was a howling swell for a time and they seemed to like it and I did. I got back last night. I made two speeches[2] which were two more than I felt up to, but they also seemed to please. Indeed, as I soaped the Dean I was sure of having one hearer in my favor. But I said no more than I meant. The next pleasantest thing to being intelligently cracked up oneself is to give a boost to a younger man who seems to deserve it, and who has not yet had much public recognition. Fred I think, will know his name and will correct me if I am wrong, as I have read him only in a fragmentary way. As usual after four days absence I find no end of letters to answer and odds and ends to attend to, but my cases are done until Monday when Circuit begins again, so while I am bothered with a lot of little things I have

---

[1] Edmund Janes James (1855–1925), President of Northwestern University, 1902–04.

[2] Holmes's address at the dedication of the Northwestern University Law School building, October 20, 1902, is printed in *C. L. P.*, p. 272. His other speech is printed at least in part in 17 Chi. Law Rev. 733 (1902).

not big ones on my hand, except the inconvenient move to Washington. Lord how I tremble at the thought of that. . . .

On my way to and from Chicago I reread *Tristram Shandy* with a cold and inadequate preface by Saintsbury. I always say that our 19th, 20th Century literary genealogy is *Hamlet — Tristram Shandy — Faust*: the looking glass at each end of the room instead of the first intention and *naïveté* of the classics. How little pungent, how flat, are the great authors of the past before the time when men saw themselves seeing. How odious a virtue the much praised simplicity. The only simplicity for which I would give a straw is that which is on the other side of the complex — not that which never has divined it. With which remark I shut up. Only adding that I am simply and affectionately yours — with love to all.

O. W. HOLMES

SUPREME COURT OF THE UNITED STATES
WASHINGTON, D. C.
December 28, 1902

Dear Pollock:

Yes — here I am [1] — and more absorbed, interested and impressed than ever I had dreamed I might be. The work of the past seems a finished book — locked up far away, and a new and solemn volume opens. The variety and novelty to me of the questions, the remote spaces from which they come, the amount of work they require, all help the effect. I have written on the constitutionality of part of the Constitution of California,[2] on the powers of the Railroad Commissioners of Arkansas,[3] on the question whether a law of Wisconsin impairs the obligation of the plaintiff's contract.[4] I have to consider a question between a grant of the U.S. in aid of a military road and an Indian reservation on the Pacific coast.[5] I have heard

[1] Holmes took his seat on the Supreme Court of the United States on December 8, 1902.
[2] Otis v. Parker, 187 U. S. 606 (1903).
[3] Hanley v. Kansas City Southern Railway Co., *id.* 617 (1903).
[4] Diamond Glue Company v. United States Glue Company, *id.* 611 (1903).
[5] This case has not been identified.

conflicting mining claims in Arizona [6] and whether a granite quarry is "Minerals" within an exception in a Railway land grant [7] and fifty other things as remote from each other as these.

As to the matter you write about,[8] as you know, my mind is made up, subject to a few outlying questions, in accord with an article I wrote in the *Harv. Law Rev.*, on "Privilege, Malice and Intent." [9] I think that in some cases which should be approached from the point of view of privilege — the temporal damage being foreseen and even intended — the nature of the motive may make all the difference, and the fact that motive makes no difference as to land, has absolutely no bearing on the case of giving a character to a servant or destroying a man's business. The last Mass. case (after *Vegelahn v. Guntner*), *Plant v. Woods*,[10] followed the line of thought in my article although I dissented on a difference of degree.

You give me a pang when you tell me you are giving up your professorship at Oxford.[11] Why do you? No doubt you have good reasons but I don't know them; I don't know either about your American lectures. Tell me. . . .

Yours ever,

O. W. H.

---

[6] Perhaps Kennedy Co. v. Argonaut Co., 189 U. S. 1 (argued, Dec. 10, 11, 1902; decided, March 9, 1903), though the claims were in California, not in Arizona.

[7] Northern Pacific Railway v. Soderberg, 188 U. S. 526 (1903).

[8] The letter referred to is missing.

[9] 8 *Harv. L. Rev.* 1 (1894); *C. L. P.*, p. 117.

[10] 176 Mass. 492 (1900). The majority of the Court in this case, in an opinion by Hammond, J., held that an injunction had been properly issued against the officers and members of a labor union who, in an effort to increase union membership, had threatened the employers of rival union labor with strikes and boycotts if they did not either induce their employees to join the defendants' union or have them discharged. It thus apparently held that a strike for a closed shop was illegal. In a dissenting opinion, Holmes, believing the purpose of the threatened strikes and boycotts to be legitimate, urged that no injunction should have been issued. See note, 45 *Harv. L. Rev* 1227 (1932).

[11] The last five-year term for which Pollock had been elected Corpus Professor of Jurisprudence expired on February 1, 1903, and he did not seek re-election. See 19 *L. Q. Rev.* 1 (1903).

LONDON, January 17, 1903

My dear Holmes:

I am glad you like your new work, as I thought you would. . . .

I see by the *Columbia Law Review* [1] that a Federal judge has held that an inhabitant of Puerto Rico, though owing allegiance to the U.S., is an alien for some purposes until Congress has defined his status: [2] *quod miram.* The only parallel I can think of is the position assigned, in defiance of treaties, to the Jews in Roumania, against which the U.S. has been protesting. [3]

The Secretary of the Franco-Scottish Association in Edinburgh has sent me a wonderful mare's nest about a supposed right of Scotsmen to be naturalized in France under some ordinance of the 16th century, to which there was a corresponding Scottish Act. I pointed out that (*inter alia*) the first experience of a Scot who claimed to be naturalized in France would be a liability to military service. As to the Scottish statute it is presumably abrogated by desuetude, which is recognized in Scots law though not by the Common Law as a real and effectual mode of repeal. If the statutes had been in execution of a treaty (which does not appear) I conceive the treaty would have been abrogated by the total change of the political conditions on James VI. of Scotland becoming James I. of England. But you may yet have to sit in judgment on some thing quite as odd from the Philippines.

Maitland is sunning himself with Year Book mss. in the Canaries. . . .

Jack is going in for a Socialist phase; that seems to be the tendency of the clever young men at our Cambridge just now. Anyhow it is better than the hard-shelled and philosophically unsound individualism of the old utilitarian school.

I am writing a farewell lecture for Oxford on the history of comparative jurisprudence, [4] not with much pleasure, as I really

---

[1] Coudert, "Our New Peoples: Citizens, Subjects, Nationals or Aliens," 3 *Columbia L. Rev.* 13 (1903).

[2] *In re* Gonzalez, 118 Fed. 941 (1902), Lacombe, J.

[3] In July and August 1902, John Hay, the American Secretary of State, made vigorous protest against anti-Semitic legislation of the Roumanian Parliament.

[4] See Pollock, *Essays in the Law* (1922), p. 1.

have little to put into it that is either new or important. When
that is done I must think of American law schools for the summer.[5] I fancy the Expansion of the Common Law, a study of
our assimilation of foreign and cosmopolitan elements,[6] might
serve.

Yours ever,

F. POLLOCK

LONDON, March 25, 1903

My dear Holmes:

I perceive that the New York *Sun*, being presumably interested in lottery tickets, is very angry with the decision of the
Supreme court that Congress has power to stop their transit
by mail from one state to another[1] — at least so I understand,
not having seen the decision itself — and also thinks it is in
some way peculiarly wicked of you to be one of the majority.
It seems about in the manner of our extreme Trade Unionist
leaders' comments on the *Taff Vale* decision.[2] The very last
thing that occurs to the lay commentator is that any court
should really try to determine cases according to law.

For my October lectures I want to take up a thesis I threw
out in a sentence or two in my Harvard address[3] — the eminent
vitality of the Common Law as shown by its power of assimi-
lating foreign elements. It ought to come to something worth
putting together, but I feel very short of time for doing it
properly. . . .

[5] During the late summer and fall Pollock made a lecture tour of American law
schools, appearing at Yale, Michigan, Toronto, Chicago, Iowa, Harvard, and Columbia, and also attending the meeting of the American Bar Association at Hot Springs,
Virginia, in August. His address to the American Bar Association on English Law
Reporting is reprinted in his *Essays in the Law* (1922), p. 242.

[6] These lectures were subsequently printed in his volume *The Expansion of the Common Law* (1904), p. 25 *et seq.*

[1] Lottery Case (Champion v. Ames), 188 U. S. 321 (1903). The majority opinion
was written by Harlan, J. Fuller, C. J., Brewer, Shiras, and Peckham, JJ., dissented.

[2] Taff Vale Railway v. Amalgamated Society of Railway Servants, [1901] A. C. 426.
In this case it was held by the House of Lords that a trade union might be sued in its
registered name, and therefore that union funds might be applied to the satisfaction of
the plaintiff's judgments.

[3] "The Vocation of the Common Law," printed in *The Expansion of the Common
Law* (1904), p. 1. See *supra*, p. 57.

I have just been to a meeting of the British Academy. Meetings are more and more abominations to me, but I had to go to make a quorum of a sectional committee. We shall justify our existence, I trust; and meanwhile we are really a fairly distinguished company.

Yours ever,
F. POLLOCK

HIND HEAD COPSE
HASLEMERE, SURREY
July 6, 1903 [1]

My dear Holmes:

... In view of a new edition of Pollock on *Torts* being called for next winter I want to know whether *Derry* v. *Peek* [2] is generally approved of in America or not. I have seen rather conflicting statements, and as to Mass. in particular can't reconcile the later with the earlier decision. My own view is that, on principle, making an assertion as of fact, for my neighbour to act upon, without any reasonable ground for believing it, is no better than making it without any belief at all, and that this is good common law without recourse to any peculiar doctrine of equity. But the House of Lords as you know decided otherwise.

Then, is there any tendency to a definite doctrine on the various questions raised by *Quinn* v. *Leathem*? [3] I have no difficulty in accepting that decision or in finding it quite consistent with *Allen* v. *Flood*: but the variety of the reasons given is quite bewildering. The Court of Appeal is giving judgment today, I believe, on the extent of the justifications or excuses admissible in an action for procuring breach of contract. [4] But

---

[1] Holmes was in England when this letter was written. A brief note and a postal card, each from Pollock, and dated respectively July 1 and July 2, 1903, are omitted.

[2] 14 App. Cas. 337 (1889).

[3] [1901] A. C. 495. The House of Lords, distinguishing Allen v. Flood (see *supra*, p. 77), held that it was proper to award damages in favor of an employer against the officers of a trade union who, in an effort to unionize the plaintiff's shop, had, as the jury found, wrongfully and maliciously conspired to induce the plaintiff's employees and customers not to deal with the plaintiff. Separate opinions were written by the Earl of Halsbury, Lord Macnaghten, Lord Shand, Lord Brampton, Lord Robertson, and Lord Lindley.

[4] Glamorgan Coal Company v. Miners Federation, [1903] 2 K. B. 545.

I don't think our Court of Appeal is very enlightening at present. Romer's [5] judgments are usually the best. Vaughan Williams [6] is terribly diffuse and slipshod, though he is a very clever man. Stirling [7] is sometimes very good, but I think unequal. . . .

Yours ever,
F. POLLOCK

I don't know whether Conflict of Laws interests you — or the specially vexed question of *renvoi*. There is a curious case in the June *Law Reports* [8] which Dicey thinks wrong but I venture to think right.

WASHINGTON, January 2, 1904

My dear Bart.:

A happy New Year to you and thanks for your letter.[1] I will keep my eye peeled for your remarks on Restraint of Trade.[2] Of course I will not speak about the case before us at present.[3] *Hilton v. Eckersley* [4] in your book on contracts sounds like the *U. S. v. Trans Missouri Freight Association*, 166 U. S. 290,[5]

---

5 Sir Robert Romer (1814–1918); Judge of the High Court of Justice, Chancery Division, 1890–99; Lord Justice of Appeal, 1899–1906.

6 Sir Ronald Bowdler Vaughan Williams (1838–1916); Judge of the High Court of Justice, Queen's Bench Division, 1890–97; Lord Justice of Appeal, 1897–1914.

7 Sir James Stirling (1836–1916); Judge of the High Court of Justice, Chancery Division, 1886–1900; Lord Justice of Appeal, 1900–06.

8 *In re* Johnson, [1903] 1 Ch. 821. The case was noted by Dicey and Pollock in 19 L. Q. Rev. 243–247 (1903).

---

1 The letter referred to is missing.

2 Presumably Pollock's article "The Merger Case and Restraint of Trade," 17 *Harv. L. Rev.* 150 (January 1904), discussing the issues raised by the Northern Securities case in the Circuit Court, United States v. Northern Securities Co., 120 Fed. 721 (1903).

3 Northern Securities Co. v. United States, 193 U. S. 197 (1904). The case had been argued December 14 and 15, 1903, and was decided March 14, 1904. A majority of the Supreme Court held that the formation of the Northern Securities Company with the purpose of holding the stock of competing interstate railroads was a violation of the Sherman Anti-Trust Act. Holmes wrote a dissenting opinion. *Id.*, p. 400.

4 6 E. &. B. 47, 66 (1855–56). "An agreement between several master manufacturers to regulate their wages and hours of work, the suspending of work partially or altogether, and the discipline and management of their establishments, by the decision of a majority of their members, is in general restraint of trade as depriving each one of them of the control of his own business, and is therefore not enforceable." Pollock, *Principles of Contract* (7th ed., 1902), p. 356.

5 This case held that the Sherman Anti-Trust Act of 1890 was applicable to combinations among transportation companies.

which is one of the great reliances of the Government in the present case. Brown [6] wrote the *Saratoga Vichy case* [7] very much along the line of your thought about it when you heard it, *i.e.* on the effect of time. For myself I can't for the life of me see that any right of the plaintiff ever would have been infringed by the use of the word Vichy with the word Saratoga prefixed in letters of equal size. But that case is far in the past and we are in fresh fields and pastures new now.

The pressure here is very constant, and I find that even this week with my cases all written I have been kept so occupied that I have had no time to read — or almost none. I did read a pamphlet young Amos [8] sent me from Egypt on *Personalité Morale.* [9] Perhaps it is because I am growing older (but I don't think so) that I fail to find in these discourses about corporations, partnerships, charitable foundations, etc., seeking profound underthoughts, much except mares' nests. I don't see why the prevailing points of view are not adequate and intelligent. . . .

I have heard an echo or two of you and Lady Pollock in letters. I hope you both are fully recovered from the fatigue your journey must have been. [10]

Please give her my love.

Yours ever,
O. W. HOLMES

WASHINGTON, January 10, 1904

Beloved Lady:

As usual I have about a minute and a half before doing something else. But it is ever thus. I love seeing your dear

---

[6] Henry Billings Brown (1836–1913); Associate Justice, Supreme Court of the United States, 1890–1906.

[7] The French Republic v. Saratoga Vichy Company, 191 U. S. 427 (1903). The French Republic, together with its lessee of the springs at Vichy, was, in this case, denied an injunction against the defendant's use of the word "Vichy" in connection with Saratoga spring waters bottled by the defendant and sold as "Saratoga Vichy Water." Brown, J., for the Court, denied relief principally because of the twenty-five-year delay of the plaintiffs in starting suit, but partly because the defendant, by use of the word "Saratoga" in connection with the water, prevented any deception of the public.

[8] Sir Maurice Sheldon Amos, Judge of the Cairo Native Court of First Instance.

[9] Léon Michoud, *La théorie de personalité morale* (1906–09).

[10] Sir Frederick and Lady Pollock had been in the United States in the fall of 1903.

handwriting again — and, of course, I am always your dear Judge. In formal converse we are always Justice but I should hate to have you change. . . .

I still read nothing, and at times like other people I feel discouraged. My mode of thinking and doing things sometimes seems to me academic to the point of unreality, but after all it is not my own shortcomings alone of which I am conscious. I find people pleasant — I will change the order and say I find pleasant people here as elsewhere, and am amused with the dining out which now is pretty constant. I don't twang the tremolo very much — hardly at all — but there is a good deal of a kind of pleasantness which one can appreciate before the final collapse. When people wish to be polite they express the hope that I still have 10 or more years of activity ahead, which is accurate but sounds short. We always exempt ourselves from the common laws. When I was a boy and the dentist pulled out a second tooth I thought to myself that I would grow a third if I needed it. Experience discouraged this prophecy. Goodnight my dear friend. I hope you have recovered from the fatigues of the voyage etc., and should like to be sure of it. My love to Fred.

Always affectionately yours,
O. W. Holmes

It seems to me that we did nothing for you when you were here and yet we wanted to do so much. You must take affection for deeds and have faith.

Postal Card, Pollock to Holmes

London, February 24, 1904.

I don't think you differ with the ingenious G. E. M.[1] so much as you suppose. He does not set up an absolute good: on the contrary he says that the predicate "good" in our various judgments of what is "good" is *sui generis* and unanalysable,

---

[1] In Holmes's Journal there appears among the volumes read in the early part of 1904, George Edward Moore, *Principia Ethica* (1903). The letter concerning the book, which he had apparently written to Pollock, is missing.

and *therefore* no universal external criterion of goodness can be assigned — such as pleasure-giving quality, utility however defined, or conformity to any one ideal. In short, so far as we know there is not one good but very many goods with apparently nothing in common but just being good. And the question — what *ought* we to judge good? — seems on this view to be rational only in the sense: By preferring what sort of 'goods' do men and nations succeed? Not much catching the tail of the Cosmos there. I don't say that I agree with this view myself, but I think it at least worth going through.

F. P.

A great deal of the detailed criticism — on utilitarians *e.g.* — seems to me quite excellent.

Postal Card, Pollock to Holmes

LONDON, May 11, 1904

Thanks for the judgments in *Northern Securities* case.[1] I entirely agree with your reasons. In my opinion the agreement by which the Northern Securities Company was formed was probably in restraint of trade so far as not to be enforceable between the parties to it, but was not on the face of it a violation of the Act, and was not shown to have any violation of it as an intended or probable consequence. A *quia timet* injunction to restrain the doing of something which may possibly lead to the commission of an offense in the future is a new kind of equity. John C. Gray in *Harv. Law Rev.* is also good.[2]

F. P.

BEVERLY FARMS,
September 24, 1904

Dear Pollock & Lady Pollock:

. . . Mrs. J. R. Green [1] has been stopping with us for a few days, leaving today. She is a witty clever creature with a pretty

---

[1] 193 U. S. 197 (1904).
[2] "The Merger Case," 17 *Harv. L. Rev.* 474 (1904).

---

[1] Alice Stopford Green (Mrs. John Richard Green, 1848–1929); historian.

accurate eye for personal appreciations, and, of course, is full
of Ireland and Irish things. I hope she has not found it dull,
but she has not seen much of the world with us. People, or at
least those we thought of getting, are leaving — we start for
Washington Oct. 6. We have enjoyed our talks with our guest
very much. They have interrupted my reading for the time.
The last book I have read is Patten, *The Development of English
Thought* (Macmillan), which I can recommend if you want
something that has a surprise in every package, abounding in
rather whimsical, original thoughts which you don't feel bound
to take too seriously but which always stimulate and suggest.
The trouble with all explanations of historic causes is the absence of quantification: you never can say *how much* of the
given cause was necessary to provide how much effect, or how
much of the cause there was. I regard this as the source of the
most subtle fallacies. But such exercitations always are amusing and tickling if new. I never know any facts about anything
and always am gravelled when your countrymen ask some informal intelligent question about our institutions or the state
of politics or anything else. My intellectual furniture consists
of an assortment of general propositions which grow fewer and
more general as I grow older. I always say that the chief end
of man is to frame them and that no general proposition is
worth a damn. You see that I am still in an idle frame of mind.
I alternate between that and being a law machine that turns
out answers when you put questions into the hopper. But the
reading of a certain number of products of the past, the contents of which generally are either platitudes or exploded, re-
stores one to a normal feeling and sends one back with a few
new ideas, suggested *by* but not *in* the ancient words. . . . Mrs.
Green handed me L. Stephen's *Hobbes*, of which I read about
half. What a pleasant writer L. S. became.[2] He did not start
so. I think he was much superior to his brother [3] to whom he
used to look up with great reverence. Well, this is just a vacant
ramble to send you all my love. I shall welcome the *Torts*. It
has given you much reputation and I am very proud to be

[2] Sir Leslie Stephen had died on February 22, 1904. His book on Hobbes was published posthumously in the same year.
[3] Sir James Fitzjames Stephen (1829–1894).

named in it.[4] We lunched with the Bryces the other day. He seems to be shrinking to an interrogation point, but I always have an affectionate feeling for him. H. James is in the country but I haven't heard from him and don't know whether I shall see him.

Affly yours,
O. W. H.

Washington, October 8, 1904

Dear F. P.:

Just arrived here and joyful to be back with my books about me and work soon to begin.

7th Ed. *Torts* welcomed me. I am very much pleased with the look of it glancing through it here & there. I fear me we are not at one on the limit of damages in contract.[1] I adhere to my old tendencies, *The Common Law,* and highly approve of Willes in *British Columbia Saw Mills Co.* v. *Nettleship.*[2] I had a chance to fire off my mouth in *Globe Refining Co.* v. *Landa Cotton Oil Co.,* 190 U. S. 540, & *I done it.*[3]

Love to the lady and the children.

Yours ever,
O. W. Holmes

[4] The seventh edition (1904) of Pollock's *Law of Torts,* like the sixth (1901), was dedicated to Holmes and James Shaw Willes. The prefatory letter to Holmes which had appeared in the first five editions was, however, omitted. In a postal card dated May 8, 1901, Pollock explained that "the old epistle dedicatory is omitted as being out of date, and I lump you in with the late Willes, J. — which I hope you will think good company."

[1] In the seventh edition (1904), of his *Law of Torts,* Pollock discussed the question of the amount of damages recoverable in contract actions and expressed the opinion that the damages, as in tort, are properly to be measured by the reasonably predictable consequences of the defendant's conduct. He said further that "a contracting party's liability to pay damages for a breach is not imposed by his agreement to be liable, but is imposed by law." *Cf. supra,* p. 80.

[2] L. R. 3 C. P. 499 (1868). In his opinion Mr. Justice Willes, at p. 508, used language suggesting that damages for breach of contract were recoverable because the defendant had agreed that they should be.

[3] "When a man commits a tort he incurs by force of the law a liability to damages, measured by certain rules. When a man makes a contract he incurs by force of the law a liability to damages, unless a certain promised event comes to pass. But unlike the case of torts, as the contract is by mutual consent, the parties themselves, expressly or by implication, fix the rule by which the damages are to be measured." 190 U. S. at 543. Pollock, in the eighth edition (1908) of his *Law of Torts,* p. 558, ft. g, referred to this case. See *supra,* pp. 21, 79–80.

LONDON, October 25, 1904

My dear Holmes:
    . . . I fear we shall not agree about the theory of special damage. The contract-theory (seemingly started in Mayne's book)[1] seems to me a superfluous fiction. A man is answerable for such consequences as would appear probable to a reasonable man in his place: and consequences made probable by knowledge of special facts which he happens to possess are probable enough to *him* (*sicut per dominationem vestram, Commonwealth* v. *Pierce*).[2] There *may*, no doubt, be an express term of the contract about damages: if so, it must be proved. Of course, if you put the *whole* liability to pay damages on contract, as suggested in *The Common Law*, you get a consistent doctrine, though I don't agree with it any more for that.

Yours ever,

F. P.

LONDON, July 15, 1905

My dear Holmes:
    I am sending you my note on *Lochner* v. *State of New York*,[1] also a sample of what I am doing with Maine's *Ancient Law*.[2] I have just come to the end of it, and I suppose the new edition with commentary will be out early in the autumn.

    Dabbling in primitive marriage & such like for the note on the Patriarchal Theory has not increased my respect for the average common sense of professed anthropologists. Maine's

---

    [1] John D. Mayne, *Law of Damages* (1st ed., 1856). Holmes had cited this work in his opinion in Globe Refining Co. v. Landa Cotton Oil Co., 190 U. S. 540, 544, 547 (1903).
    [2] 138 Mass. 165 (1884). See *supra*, p. 26.

    [1] 198 U. S. 45 (decided, April 17, 1905). A majority of the Court, in an opinion written by Peckham, J., held that a New York statute forbidding the employment of persons in bakeries for more than ten hours a day was unconstitutional under the fourteenth amendment. Holmes wrote a dissenting opinion, *id.*, p. 74. The case was noted by Pollock in 21 *L. Q. Rev.* 211 (July 1905). In a post-card dated May 27, 1905, Pollock wrote to Holmes: "Many thanks for the judgments. I like yours very much." Probably the judgments referred to were those in the Lochner case.
    [2] Portions of Pollock's Notes to a new edition (1906) of Maine's *Ancient Law* appeared in 21 *L. Q. Rev.* 165, 274 (1905).

imperfect materials, 40 odd years ago, led him to see many processes as shorter and simpler than they are, and he did not escape quite odd mistakes in detail. But his larger views and instincts are almost always sound — more than once right *against* what seemed then the best information.

Towards the middle of September I leave these shores to spend a month in Canada and find out, if I can, how people really feel there about organizing the British empire. Incidentally I hope to see the Pacific. On the way back, about the end of October, I must put in some days in New England: I fear you will have gone to Washington and I shall have no time to go South. . . .

Yours ever,
F. POLLOCK

Postal Card, Pollock to Holmes

LONDON, November 15, 1905

Certainly I believe you are as real as I am,[1] but, as you are *ejusdem generis* with me, that does not make you a *Ding an sich* in the Kantian sense: whether there is to be postulated a *Ding an sich* behind you & me — or distinct ones for each of us — is a further question which I answer in the negative. I rather think I believe in the independent existence of things chiefly because they are common to you and me — *i.e.* believe in other people first and things afterwards: but I don't know how far this could be dialectically justified. If Berkeley's assumption that the Ego is simple and immediately known were tenable, I should be a Berkeleian: but Hume and Kant showed conclusively that it is not. This however does not affect the position that 'unknowable reality' is a combination of terms without meaning and of no use. *Unknown x's*, of course, are plentiful everywhere, but I have nothing to say to the *unknowable* $\sqrt{-1} \cdot x$ of Kantian orthodoxy. Such are my fundamentals as I laid them about 30 years ago. The partly logical partly metaphysical problems of predication, universal propositions,

---

[1] The letter from Holmes to which this postal card is responsive is missing.

necessary truth, etc., seem to me different again: on some of them I sympathize with Wm. James's 'Humanism.'

F. P.

WASHINGTON, November 23, 1905

Dear F.:

A word in reply to your card. I have just finished (having a day or two of leisure) K. Pearson's *Grammar of Science*, which hits my way of thinking better than books of philosophy. I have not studied W. James's Humanism but it seemed to me on the way to my formula of truth — as merely my *can't help*, which has validity for my world — but which I can't assert concerning *the* world if there is one. But K. Pearson, you & also everyone who writes a book for or a letter to his neighbor, admits a somewhat independent of his consciousness and that's what *I* mean by a *ding an sich*. I quite agree that when we decide that our brother is not our dream it is his agreement with us as to chair, table, etc., that makes us surmise that they also are not only our dream — and I add that if I admit my brother I don't see why I should not admit the world. Yet as I can't get outside my dream I admit something I don't know. I put it as a mere bet. I give it no predicates of any kind except to say that in some sense, I know not what, I bet that I came out of an I know not whatness, and that *I know what* is not exhaustive. Hence I cannot assume my limits to be cosmic limits. I am just turning to Santayana's last two volumes of *The Life of Reason* which I like better than any philosophy I have read — or nearly so. Do you know it? Shall I send it to you? I should be glad to. But more and more I am inclined to belittle the doings of the philosophers while I think philosophy the end of life.

Ever yours,
O. W. H.

WASHINGTON, May 25, 1906

Dear Pollock:

Your pleasant letter has just come.[1] I have finished my (presumably) last case and am free to answer at once. Brooks Adams sent me the book you mention and Bigelow also wrote to me about it.[2] I acknowledged it at once with necessary excuses but read it later and felt the same enbarrassment that you do. Bigelow is a good and most creditable creature, but you must have noticed before now that he never hits the first rate and that at times he assumes an air of significance hardly warranted by the facts. I couldn't see that he had anything important to say. Brooks Adams I still find it hard to formulate with confidence of justice. I have known him from boyhood. I have found him more suggestive than almost anyone, generally with propositions which I don't believe, and yet I still don't quite know what to say or think. He will hand you out a statement with an august air, and you can't tell whether it is the result of ten years study or a fellow told it to him just before he met you — or for the matter of that whether you didn't tell it to him yourself within half an hour. Whatever matter he is interested in, generally a question of property, a brief history of the world winds up with his solution. I imagine that dissatisfaction with the treatment of Spokane, where he had land, has stirred him up on the rate bill, and you hear the echo of his grievances in his first chapter.[3] This of course can't be said. I thought his customary picture of a class gradually rising through self protection to knocking the one previously dominant in the head was amusing and not without stimulating power. On the other hand I think his talk about the world being slaves to the man who commands the necessaries of life, rot. If Jim Hill (the great railroad man) does not follow the economically necessary course he comes to grief. I remember what a very able man who made a fortune on the Stock Ex-

---

[1] The letter referred to is missing.

[2] In Holmes's Journal for 1906 appears, "*Centralization and the Law* [1906] (Melville M. Bigelow, Brooks Adams *et al*)." A brief account of Adams's early association with Holmes and Bigelow may be found in Adams's "Melville M. Bigelow," 1 *B. U. L. Rev.* 168 (1921).

[3] The first of the two lectures by Adams was entitled "Nature of Law: Methods and Aim of Legal Education."

change once said to me. "They talk about our leading the procession — we only *follow it ahead* like little boys. If we turn down a side street it doesn't." Under modern conditions the crowd presents the inevitable to itself as the fiat of some great man, and hates him, but it is very silly. Brooks at present is in a great stir and thinks a world crisis is at hand, for us among others, and that our Court may have a last word as to who shall be master in the great battle between the many and the few. I think this notion is exaggerated and half cracked. But I don't read the papers or otherwise feel the pulse of the machine. I merely speculate. My hobby is to consider the stream of products, to omit all talk about ownership and just to consider who eats the wheat, wears the clothes, uses the railroads and lives in the houses. I think the crowd now has substantially all there is, that the luxuries of the few are a drop in the bucket, and that unless you make war on moderate comfort there is no general economic question. I agree however that there are great wastes in competition, due to advertisement, superfluous reduplication of establishments, etc.. But those are the very things the trusts get rid of. But I am wandering far afield. I think I should damn with faint praise — recognizing the streak of suggestiveness in B. A. and the unpretentious virtues of Harriman (who is original in his book on Contract) and Haines.[4] I still have not read your notes to Maine, because since they arrived I have been constantly loaded with work. I have read a part with the expected pleasure and profit, and ever recurring wonder at your acomplishments. . . . We adjourn next Monday. Dinner to Brown,[5] who retires, on the 31st & then freedom and Beverly Farms as soon as we like — one of the first days in June. . . . It has been a satisfactory year, although I have had comparatively few cases that had a very general interest. There is always the fun of untying a knot and trying to do it in good compact form. By the by — I ought to tell you that in *Commonwealth* v. *Pierce*,[6] cited on p. 432 of *Torts*, 7th Ed., I struck out "personal equation or" to please some one or more

---

[4] Edward A. Harriman's lecture was entitled "Law as an Applied Science"; the paper by H. S. Haines, "An Object-Lesson in Extension; Rate Making," was the final lecture in the volume.

[5] Henry Billings Brown.

[6] 138 Mass. 165, 176 (1884).

of my brethren, before the case went into the reports,[7] although it was printed with the words in some of the periodicals, I think *Amer. Law Register, e.g.* I got them in however in *The Germanic*, 196 U.S. 589, 596.[8] One of time's revenges. . . .

Yours ever,
O. W. HOLMES

LONDON, June 13, 1906

My dear Holmes:

Thanks for your letter. I have managed to write a notice of Brooks Adams, Bigelow & Co. which I think will explain my point of view without hurting their feelings.[1]

As for predicting a world-crisis, the only successful case I know is that of Young[2] and the French Revolution. I am sure you are not going to have a French Revolution, nor we neither, and I doubt whether Brooks Adams is up to Young's mark.

A little while ago I looked at one volume of Santayana. I am curious to know what part of his work has impressed you most, so I shall be very glad to receive that part from you.

Also thanks for judgments in *Haddock* v. *Haddock*:[3] your too polite clerk of the Court put them up with a covering letter, the too formalist postmaster at Washington apparently fastened

[7] At the page to which Holmes refers, Pollock had quoted from Holmes's opinion in *Commonwealth* v. *Pierce*: "If a man's conduct is such as would be reckless in a man of ordinary prudence, it is reckless in him. Unless he can bring himself within some broadly defined exception to general rules, the law deliberately leaves his *personal equation or* idiosyncrasies out of account, and peremptorily assumes that he has as much capacity to judge and foresee consequences as a man of ordinary prudence would have in the same situation." (Italics added.)

[8] In discussing negligence in *The Germanic*, Holmes, for the Court, said, "The standard of conduct, whether left to the jury or laid down by the court, is an external standard, and takes no account of the personal equation of the man concerned."

[1] 22 *L. Q. Rev.* 320 (1906).
[2] Arthur Young (1741–1821), *Travels in France* (1792).
[3] 201 U. S. 562 (1906). It was held in this case that the New York courts were not bound by the full faith and credit clause of the constitution to recognize as valid a divorce decree entered in Connecticut in a husband's favor when his wife, retaining her New York domicile, was served with process in New York and did not appear in the Connecticut proceedings. The majority opinion was written by Mr. Justice White. Holmes and Mr. Justice Brown wrote dissenting opinions in each of which Harlan and Brewer, JJ., concurred.

or as children say "licked up" the flap, *per quod* the packet became not printed matter but "in the nature of a letter," and the British and U. S. Postal revenues will divide, in proportions to this deponent unknown, an ill gotten half-dollar collected here for extra postage. So far I have looked only at your dissenting judgment: it seems to me that it ought to be right if it isn't. . . .

I have lumped in with Brooks Adams & Co. a learned Frenchman,[4] who seems to think there is some magical virtue in the word *Sociologie*, and shall probably lump in a little tract by a learned Austrian [5] whom I think the best of the lot. . . .

Yours ever,
F. POLLOCK

BEVERLY FARMS, June 23, 1906

Dear F. P.:

I write to Little Brown & Co. to send you Santayana — 4 vols — but not big ones. My wife says that the critics are not so warm as I in praise of it. I liked it because the premises are so much like my own. I always start my cosmic salad by saying that all I mean by truth is what I *can't help* thinking and that I have no means of deciding whether my can't helps have any cosmic worth. They clearly don't in many cases. I think the philosophers usually are too arrogant in their attitude. I accept the existence of a universe, in some unpredicable sense, just as I accept yours — by an act of faith — or by another can't help, perhaps. But I think the chances are much against man's being at the centre of things or knowing anything more than how to arrange *his* universe — according to his own necessary order. I dare say you will think Santayana something of an *improvisatore*, and say that he talks too much. But to my mind he talks like a civilized man, and with a good deal of charm of speech, though that also may weary, after you have caught his rhythm and trick. At all events his book was one which seemed to me to express the world as I should express it,

---

[4] Raoul de la Grassiere, *Les Principes Sociologiques du droit civil* (1906).
[5] Eugen Ehrlich, *Sociologie und Jurisprudenz* (1906), reviewed, *id.*

more nearly than often befalls. I am reading, or have been, some sociological books [1] — which also have hit me where I live — apart from the desirability that one who administers constitutional law should multiply his scepticisms to avoid reading into vague words like "liberty" his private convictions or prejudices of his class — but in doing so, like others, simply confirm what I already believe. I have sent for a translation of the *Nicomachean Ethics*. To my shame I have read but little of Aristotle and I am now old enough to read more. I think it a humbug to bother boys with the great men of the past. I think one should begin with books which have our own emphasis and that it takes preparation to read any others. I have no doubt that most of us miss a good deal even of Shakespeare's meaning, and the classics are a good deal worse. Their poetry is as first intentioned as the bark of a dog, and we are subtle (relatively). I might run on — but good-bye.

Ever yours,
O. W. H.

LONDON, July 6, 1906

My dear Holmes:

Many thanks for Santayana: it makes a pleasant humanist link for us. I guess he is rather a philosophical humanist than a professional philosopher. I shall take him to Hind Head next month. Curiously enough I had some talk of philosophy with Shadworth Hodgson the very day I got your letter. He is a strenuous thinker, unfortunately without the gift of agreeable exposition and quite unknown to the general public, but he has done and is still doing good work. His view is really not unlike yours: he frankly renounces having a complete explanation of the Universe and aims only at analysing experience as we find it, though he does not adventure so far as William James

---

[1] In Holmes's Journal the following books, among others, are listed as having been read in 1906: Edward Alsworth Ross, *Social Control* (1901), Edward Alsworth Ross, *The Foundations of Sociology* (1905); Karl Marx, *Capital*; W. J. Ghent, *Our Benevolent Feudalism* (1902); Jane Addams, *Democracy and Social Ethics* (1902); Lester Frank Ward, *Outlines of Sociology* (1898); Richard Theodore Ely, *Monopolies and Trusts* (1906).

and some of our younger men in maintaining that our world is what we choose to make it. . . .

Touching Aristotle don't forget the *Politics*, which are almost better than the *Ethics* and really quite modern in the main ideas. Weddon [*sic*],[1] a trustworthy scholar, has translated both. if you think the classical poets are wanting in subtilty, read Verrall on Euripides; about two thirds paradox to my mind but always brilliant.

The judgment of your majority in *Haddock's Case* is amazing, anyhow it has amazed Dicey, Beale of Harvard [2] (and with him, if I read him aright, very many of the learned) and myself. You will see what Dicey says in the July *Law Quarterly Review*.[3]

Bigelow is in London, so perhaps I shall have it out with him about Brooks Adams. . . .

It is our first real hot night, whereby I am sleepy and stupid and for the moment indolently averse to attending to small things: tomorrow I am going to see two charming Americans who make one forget them, Mrs. Erskine Childers[4] of your State, with whom I am reading Dante's *Purgatory* in such times as we can steal, and Elizabeth Robins of Kentucky: a good balance of North and South. Mrs. E. C. is a modern marriage by capture—her husband went to Boston with the Hon. Artillery Company and brought her home. They are devoted to sailing a small boat (she can steer a course) and their baby rising some six months is known as the Admiral.

Yours ever,

F. POLLOCK

BEVERLY FARMS, Sunday, July 15, 1906

Dear Pollock:

A few words in answer to yours. I didn't know Shadworth Hodgson was still going. Years ago I read his *Time & Space*

---

[1] Presumably J. E. C. Welldon, whose translations of the *Ethics* and the *Politics* were published in 1892 and 1883 respectively.

[2] See, Joseph H. Beale, Jr., "Constitutional Protection of Decrees for Divorce," 19 *Harv. L. Rev.* 586 (1906).

[3] 22 *L. Q. Rev.* 237 (1906).

[4] Margaret Osgood Childers, whose husband, Erskine Childers (1870–1922), author of *The Riddle of the Sands* (1915), was executed by the Irish Free State at the close of the Irish civil war, 1922.

and *Theory of Practice* with much profit, although I could not recite a line now. I thought him a very able man. I read Aristotle's *Politics* a summer or two ago, with your opinion of them. At this moment my serious reading is Rabelais, whom I have alleviated by McKechnie's *Magna Carta* which strikes me as an excellent book, not so much for novelty as for careful lucid exposition. I was glad to go through it. Incidentally it was interesting to set his account of the origin of the assises against Brooks Adams. B. A., I think, has no first hand knowledge, but reads compendiums and jumps to conclusions. I don't see that his notion of the ultimate meaning of the substitution of the recognition for the duel gets much backing from the facts when you look at them closely, but indeed I never bother to inquire whether he is right or wrong as I take his speculations rather as amusing and suggestive might-bes. In speaking of McKechnie I do not forget any more than he does Pollock and Maitland, *History*, but I like to take the document and go through it — moreover I do not remember the details. It is so long since I read that great work. . . . I was on the verge of writing to you to say that I have just read his [Jack's] *Popish Plot* [1] with much pleasure. I guess his very judicious talk about the judges and trials of the time must have owed a good deal to his father. I can't conceive that a lad could have got so far into the spirit of the time without guidance. I was delighted to hear a good word for Scroggs.[2] My only first hand notion about him was that when I lectured on Agency in the Law School I found a sentence in Modern by him which was the original and only authority for an acute proposition,[3] I forget what. So I always have hoped to hear some good of him. I

[1] John Pollock's book, *The Popish Plot*, was published in 1903.
[2] Sir William Scroggs (1623–1683); Justice of the Court of Common Pleas, 1676–78; Lord Chief Justice of England, 1678–81.
[3] In Mires v. Solebay, 2 Mod. 243, it was held that trover would not lie against a servant for an unlawful interference with the goods of the plaintiff when the servant acted at the command of his master. "And this rule Justice Scroggs said would extend to all cases where the master's command was not to do an apparent wrong; for if the master's case depended upon a title, be it true or not, it is enough to exeuse the servant: for otherwise it would be a mischevious thing, if the servant upon all occasions must be satisfied with his master's title and right before he obeys his commands; and it is very requisite that he should be satisfied, if an action should lie against him for what he doth in obedience to his master." The case, and the language of Scroggs, was referred to by Holmes in his article on Agency, *C.L.P.*, p. 49, at 79.

read in connection with Jack one or two of the state trials and
thought the C. J. appeared to advantage. I am interested at
what you say about *Haddock* v. *Haddock*. Of course the discussion in my dissent was narrowed by the assumption of the
majority that our previous decisions, especially *Atherton* v.
Atherton,[4] were not overruled; and I think my task was easy
on that assumption, as White's [5] reasoning had no tendency to
show a distinction but only to show that *A.* v. *A.* was wrong.
His mode of exposition rarely strikes me as felicitous or as at
all doing justice to his great ability. I rather wish now that I
had gone into a justification of *Atherton* v. *Atherton*. At the
time it seemed to me an impertinence, and also my dissent was
written not as a dissent but as a memorandum which I hoped
might modify opinion, or at least White's mode of putting the
case. I fear it only succeeded in irritating him. He is a great
friend of mine, but I gathered from something he said that he
felt some kind of resentment. If so he has forgotten it by this
time. I was not conscious of anything that might give offense.

Yours ever,
O. W. HOLMES

My love to Lady Pollock and the children.

BEVERLY FARMS, August 13, 1906

Dear Pollock:

I am always being indebted to you for suggestions. I read
Verall on your mention,[1] and then some Euripides. V. has the
merit of realizing that you must realize that the incredible has
been believed, but I don't think he quite succeeds himself in
getting into the Euripidean frame of mind. I don't believe E.
thought it unnatural that the husband should accept the sacri-

---

[4] 181 U. S. 155 (1901). It had been held in this case that the New York courts were
compelled by the full faith and credit clause of the constitution to recognize the validity
of a divorce granted to the husband in Kentucky, the last matrimonial domicil of the
parties, though the wife was not served with process in Kentucky, had moved to New
York, and had entered no appearance in the Kentucky proceedings.

[5] Edward Douglass White (1845–1921); Associate Justice of the Supreme Court of
the United States, 1894–1910; Chief Justice, 1910–21.

---

[1] A. W. Verrall, *Euripides the Rationalist* (1895).

fice of Alcestis. How would it be even now in the case of the President? Thanks again to you — *i.e.* to your excellent notes on Maine, I sent for Girard's *Manuel de droit Romain*,[2] and now am reading that with satisfaction. The other day I finished a difficult task and worked myself into despair over *The King's English*.[3] Some of its dogmas I declined to accept, and I felt pleasure in thinking it ill written. Still it gave me what I blush to say I never had before and don't more than three quarters accept now, an intelligible theory of the relations of *that* & *which*, and it made me miserable over my own legal style. When one is going free, especially in the empassioned language of a speech, it is a different matter. But in an opinion, where you are subject to the dominion of the thesis, when details must be dovetailed together, and when the whole is technical, I think it a heart breaking task to give an impression of freedom elegance and variety. At times I have felt that I succeeded, but after reading *The King's English*, it seemed to me that my sentences read as if they had been written by a schoolboy on a slate. There is a big book out on the theory of Legal Liability (3 vols)[4] which I was notified had been sent to me and which I glanced at in the Law Library (my copy went to Washington). From a glance it seemed to me on the one hand a thing that would have been a boon 40 years ago, but under present conditions rather a padded piece of work. I discovered no penetration or personal power — and without that a writer on such themes rather irritates one and makes one wish to snub him, as one would snub the young gentlemen of the *Harvard Law Rev.* for their cocky notes, if the latter were not a legitimate part of their youth. But I may be all wrong about the book. Please give my love to Lady Pollock and the children.

Yours ever,
O. W. H.

Some day when you are in a second hand bookseller's shop, would you inquire what Bodin, *De Republica* costs, and if they

---

[2] Paul Frédéric Girard, *Manuel Élementaire de Droit Romain* (1st ed., 1896). Pollock had cited this work in his "Notes on Maine's Ancient Law," 22 *L. Q. Rev.* 73, *passim*.

[3] By H. W. and F. G. Fowler (1906).

[4] Thomas Atkins Street, *The Foundations of Legal Liability* (1906).

have it for not more than one pound, say, ask them to send it
to me with the bill. If it would not arrive before Oct 1, then to
Washington, its ultimate destination. It is more probable
that you would only get information, I suppose. I know nothing about editions, etc., hardly even the names. I once spent a
day to get sight of a copy & to verify a citation.

HIND HEAD COPSE
HASLEMERE, SURREY
August 28, 1906

My dear Holmes:
I fear no prompt return can be made to your inquiry for
Bodin, *De Republica*. It is not a common book — whether
really scarce or not I can't say here — and I should think worth
more than £1 when it turns up. Also I can't remember whether
the Latin or the French text has the author's last hand (see my
little book on the *Science of Politics*, which does not seem to
be here). . . .
If I were you I should not trouble myself much about *The
King's English*. I understand it is better than most books of
the kind, but after all there is no rule in English but the usage
of good writers, and I suspect you and I know as much of that
as the ingenious authors of *The King's English* and their like.
Some licences once current are obsolete, no doubt, such as the
constant use of a singular verb, in a dependent sentence with
a plural antecedent, by the Elizabethan poets: and probably
others not now generally allowed will in turn prevail. Anyhow
logical consistency is not the test. No Indo-European tongue
worth its salt has a logical grammar: certainly not Attic Greek.
I suppose modern French is more nearly logical than most —
not without having paid for it.
I don't see what you want any theory of *that* and *which* for.
Which is an intruder or *déclassé* — being (hwilc) originally
qualis, not *qui*. *That* is the old Anglo-Saxon relative (neuter
form). They wrote þæt, and I believe pronounced it exactly as
we do. It is now archaic to use *which* after a personal antecedent not being a noun of multitude, or, more roughly, it is not

synonymous with *who*. Otherwise, whether you say *which* or *that* is a matter of taste and ear. In the 18th century *that* all but drove out *which* for a time. Now it tends to be unduly neglected.

As for legal style — in technical writing one has to be clear at all costs, but I have always thought yours particularly good.

That big book on *Legal Liability* came in just before I left London. If it is not a work of genius I shall not be much disappointed.[1]

BEVERLY FARMS, September 6, 1906

Dear F. P.:

I have just extracted from the past a delightful letter to which I reply at once. In October my work begins and there is little letter writing then. . . . Business may begin again to-morrow for I am sitting for my portrait for some collection of the Justices in Philadelphia[1] but today I am free. You are consoling as to English and I quite agree, of course, that the Dixonary gents and the like are simply registers of your and my practise, but one can't be *plus fin que tous les autres*, and one gets or may get wrinkles from many sources. Your notion as to the usefulness of an unoriginal summary of modern intelligent notions on Legal Liability is one to which I fully agree. Only there is an aggravation in seeing an unauthoritative person adopt the semi dogmatic judicial tone about his betters — something of what I feel when by chance I see the comments of the youth in the *Harv. Law Rev.* Argument is all right: everyone has a right to use it and no one is free from the need of being ready to answer it. But not everyone is entitled to speak *ex cathedra*. You talk well also as to Santayana, except that what you rightly call the exotic quality in his style charmed and bullied me until I thought that I saw the trick and began to be slightly bored at the recurrence of the device. Let me not fail to thank you for having put me on to Girard (*Droit Romain*). I have read it, notes and all, with profit and satisfaction. I think

---

[1] The rest of this letter is missing.

[1] Presumably the collection painted by Albert Rosenthal (1863–1939).

it the best book for the whole subject I ever read. I was so
delighted with it that I wrote to him but then let my letter
stand on my table as I don't know how a Mossoo would take
that sort of thing. There it is likely to remain until I go to
Washington and it goes to the fire. I have had a very happy
quiet time trying to fill some of the grosser gaps in my knowledge, but this week and last I seem to have accomplished nothing, not even frivolities. I had a new book by Willy which I
hoped was indecent but which so threatens to be tedious that
I have let it lie,[2] and have been reading Shakespeare and Browning aloud. Whenever I read S. I am struck with the reflection
how a few golden sentences will float a lot of quibble and drool
for centuries, *e.g.* Benedick & Beatrice.

Goodbye dear lad. I am a little blue. I don't quite know
why and feel older, but tomorrow or next day it will be the
other way. I think it is only because of the accidental futility
of the last ten days.

Please give my love to Lady Pollock.

Yours ever,
O. W. H.

LONDON, October 19, 1906

My dear Holmes:

By all means send your letter to Girard — explaining who
you are, for he is not likely to be versed in the literature of the
Common Law. That sort of tribute from unexpected quarters
is just what a learned Frenchman is sure to like. . . .

My wife and I had a fine time in Tuscany and Umbria but
came home with particularly bad colds. . . . We are going to
Rye to clear out the remains of them, and hope there to see Henry
James and his chameleon — a chameleon that walked in from
a neighbour's garden and has settled in H. J.'s greenhouse. It
seems somehow an appropriate creature for him, and having
lately been at Assisi I imagine an extra chapter of the Fioretti.
*Chome [sic] un agniolo di Dio apparve a frate Ziacomo con forma
di chameleone, ed egli ebbene grandissima consolazione.*

---

[2] In Holmes's Journal for 1906 appears an entry: "Willy, *Jeux de Prince.*"

I have begun to look into that big law-book and think it sound work, not without ingenious ideas, tho' the learned Mr. Street — is that his name? — rather overrates their novelty and importance. But what I want to see is a rational exposition of the *modern* Common Law with the history kept apart. I have tried to do it for Contract, very concise, in the *Encyclopedia of the Laws of England.*[1] For some topics, such as Real Property, this is and for some time will be impossible.

Bigelow does not much like my review of the Boston University Law School lectures in *L. Q. R.* I didn't think he would. He says it is all part of a grand social movement against the monopolists, which I partly understand: and that the historic school he objects to wants to reduce all causes (of social phenomena) to an approximate equality, which I don't understand the least bit, and have told him so.

Look out for Maitland's *Life of Leslie Stephen* in about three weeks. It will be published in America as well as here. M. has had much trouble with it and professes not to be satisfied with his work, but it is sure to be good.

Yours ever,

F. POLLOCK

HIND HEAD COPSE
HASLEMERE, SURREY
December 28, 1906

My dear Holmes:

My New Year's card to you was hardly posted when the bad news of Maitland's death came.[1] He had a wintry voyage to the Canaries, and it seems got pneumonia just on starting, and there was no reserve of strength to resist anything acute. I want something good said about him from your side. If you know enough of his work, some words from you, however few, would be most welcome.[2] Very few scholars of our time have been so completely open-minded. He was just to all sorts and conditions of men and opinions. Such men should not be put

---

[1] *3 Encyclopedia of the Laws of England* 335 (1897).

[1] Frederic William Maitland died on December 19, 1906.
[2] See 23 *L. Q. Rev.* 137 (1907); reprinted, *C. L. P.*, p. 283.

to serve the tables of university routine: but there is nothing else to give them.

And so you are to have Bryce at Washington.[3] He will like it much better than Dublin Castle [4] — but how will Ireland like his successor (as yet unknown)? On that score I don't feel quite easy. . . .

You will like Maitland's *Life of Leslie Stephen* — his last work, it is good that he lived to finish it and see it appreciated by the right people: and if you can get hold of Oliver Elton's memoir of York Powell there are lots of good things in it: the biographer is to my mind a shade too apologetic.

We have a real snowy and frosty Christmastide, with plenty of sunshine, and are glad to be out of London.

Yours ever,

F. POLLOCK

WASHINGTON, January 5, 1907

Dear Pollock:

. . . The adjournment of the last two weeks draws to an end. Conference this morning and arguments again on Monday. We have had some very important cases. One pretty important one as to the validity of a New York tax on sales of stock I shall fire off on Monday.[1] But one that one hardly can help worring [*sic*] over (although I always say that a sense of responsibility is a confession of weakness — it means that you are not keeping all your thoughts and energy for the problem —) is a fight in our Court between Kansas and Colorado over the Arkansas River.[2] Colorado depends on irrigation, Kansas says it is drying up the river: the question concerns about $\frac{1}{3}$ of the United States. I think I sent you a case I wrote last term in which Missouri tried to stop the drainage of Chicago,[3] in which I gave a light

---

[3] In December James Bryce was named British Ambassador to the United States to succeed Sir Mortimer Durand.

[4] In 1905 Bryce had been named Secretary for Ireland.

---

[1] New York, *ex rel.* Hatch v. Reardon, 204 U. S. 152 (1907).

[2] Kansas v. Colorado, 206 U. S. 46 (argued, Dec. 17-20, 1906; decided, May 13, 1907).

[3] Missouri v. Illinois, 200 U. S. 496 (1906).

touch to fundamentals. I was truly sorry to hear of Mait-land's death. It is a great loss. I regret that I never had any talk with him except a few words at a dinner you gave. I have been working like a beaver ever since I have been here, turn-ing out about one written opinion a week in addition to sitting most of the time, and with rather an interesting average. We have a new Judge,[4] another Mass. man whom I think well of. At least there is not that certainty of the second rate which I felt as to many names mentioned. I hope for better than that in his case. I must stop, for as usual I have many things to do. Remember me specially to Lady Pollock.

Ever sincerely yours,
O. W. HOLMES

[4] William Henry Moody (1853–1917), who had been Attorney General since 1904, was appointed Associate Justice of the Supreme Court, December 17, 1906. He resigned in 1910.

IV

1908-1914

Postal Card, Pollock to Holmes

May 29, 1908 [1]

... At Oxford last Sunday we had a sight of William James, who seems to be enjoying himself. He has an ardent follower there, as you may know, indeed one might say a little school. But, as the man at his lecture said, "What *is* pragmatism?"

We went cruising in the Mediterranean at Easter time and had a hurried but pleasing view of the Sicilian and South Italian coasts.

F. P.

What is the nationality, if any, of a child of Filipino parents born on board a French ship in the harbour of Port Said? Fact, I am told.

BEVERLY FARMS, June 17, 1908

Dear F. P.:
... We are settled here (Bev. Farms, Mass.) now for the summer and I am expecting and more or less beginning to rest. However I have to sit in the Circuit Court of Appeals tomorrow and may have a few days, only a few days, work. *I* think

[1] Between Holmes's letter to Pollock of January 5, 1907, and this postal card from Pollock, all letters which either may have written to the other are missing, with the exception of three brief postal cards dated January 16, 1907, May 15, 1907, and February 5, 1908, and one short letter dated January 25, 1907 — all from Pollock. In August 1907 Pollock had attended the meeting of the American Bar Association in Portland, Maine, and from June to September, Holmes had been in England and Ireland.

pragmatism an amusing humbug — like most of William James's speculations, as distinguished from his admirable and well written Irish perceptions of life. They all of them seem to me of the type of his answer to prayer in the subliminal consciousness — the spiritualist's promise of a miracle if you will turn down the gas. As I have said so often, all I mean by truth is what I can't help thinking. And I don't see why the appeal to the will to believe, etc., doesn't postulate that there is something on which I have *got* to agree with the writer — and that is the only part I call true. It postulates that I must agree with him in what he thinks desirable — which, by the by, I probably should not. W. J.'s argument for free will, to give another example written many years ago, seemed to me just like the one I have mentioned, and fitted to please free thinking Unitarian parsons and the ladies. I always think of a remark of Brooks Adams that the philosophers were hired by the comfortable class to prove that everything is all right. I think it *is* all right, but on very different grounds. However, I must turn from you to affairs. With regard to your question of nationality did not Sir A. Cockburn point out the possible conflicts of the principles of parentage and place of birth? Such would be my recollection. I rather think I referred to it in my notes to Kent.[1] (Kent in the Commentaries Caesar writ.) I heard the other day that you can tell a Bostonian anywhere, but you can't tell him much — which I thought good. My love to Lady Pollock and the children.

Yours ever,
O. W. H.

London, June 26, 1908

Postal Card, Pollock to Holmes

. . . I never know whether Wm. James & Co. are uttering what one knew before or wild paradox: he seems to me to confuse deliberately "truth" of fact (what you *find* so) with "truth" of concept or formula (what you *make* to tie up your

---

[1] 2 Kent, *Commentaries* (12th ed., 1873), p. 49.

facts so far as known), but professions of extreme liberalism always come to [sic] round to holding that of course every right-minded person will freely come to *my* conclusions. . . .

F. P.

BEVERLY FARMS, July 6, 1908

Dear Pollock:

. . . As to pragmatism an interview in the paper the other day gave me some light. W. J. suggested that instead of *truth* it would be better to say *truthfulness*. He postulated that a certain reality exists, but "we don't pry into the question of the nature or constitution of that reality." The truthfulness of our ideas consists in the fact that they will work, etc. And I now see, as I have seen in his other books that I have read, that the aim and end of the whole business is religious. I spoke of his free will and his answer to prayer the other day; the wind up of this (*in cauda venenum*) is that just as an automatic sweetheart wouldn't work (the illustration is his) an automatic universe won't — or not so well as one that has a warm God behind it, that loves and admires us. But for that conclusion I don't believe we ever should have heard from him on the subject, taking that as the significance of the whole business I make it my bow. W. J. speaks for his own temperament and nature, and as usual there are fundamental differences that make one man's truth another man's falsehood. I think the reasoning humbug so far as the conclusion goes — as to the rest I agree with you.

I saw an alarmist article in a paper about India.[1] I do hope that it was excessive and that you are not going to have much trouble there? I have finished my work and begun a little reading. I finished Langdell's *Equity Jurisdiction* yesterday (a collection printed by the *Harv. Law Rev.* after his death). It has his acumen and patient discussion of detail, but I think brings out the narrow side of his mind, his feebleness in philosophising, and hints at his rudimentary historical knowledge. I think he was somewhat wanting in horse sense, but for inten-

---

[1] During the years 1907 and 1908 Indian affairs were marked by terrorism, bombings, and assassinations directed against the British.

sity of thought it seems to me to compare favorably with a book by a lot of Columbia pragmatists dedicated to W. James that also I am reading.[2] However, I haven't finished that and it is by different hands. I still keep Balzac on hand, as when I wrote to Lady Pollock, but I get little pleasure from him. What I mainly am doing is taking a rest.

Yours,

O. W. H.

August 10, 1908

Dear Pollock:

I add a line to my letter of the other day [1] to say that having finished *The Wheel of Wealth* [2] I qualify my enthusiasm a little. I think the author still is in the bonds of darkness on certain themes. I think he does not appreciate the originality, the courage, the insight shown by the great masters of combinations. He thinks they can be summed up as tricksters, and thinks he knows the inside history of Standard Oil, I presume from the young woman's tale that has been printed.[3] He only appreciates the more obvious contributions of professional inventors and the like. Also I think before he howls over world follies he would get a clearer view if he would take my picture of the stream of products, forget ownership and money and think only of the questions what are the products, who consume them, what changes would you make. I believe that the crowd now has substantially all there is and that the luxuries of the few, in this country at least, are a drop in bucket. But he is an original man and has given me much pleasure.

Of course I did not mean to criticise the *tone* of Ames's recent article.[4] He always is civil in these days, but one would think that he saw nothing but error.

Yours,

O. W. H.

---

[2] *Essays Philosophical and Psychological in Honor of William James* (1908).

---

[1] This letter is missing.   [2] By John Beattie Crozier (1906).
[3] Ida M. Tarbell, *History of the Standard Oil Company* (2 vols., 1904).
[4] James Barr Ames, "The Origin of Uses and Trusts," 21 *Harv. L. Rev.* 261 (1908). In this article Ames had criticized views which Holmes had developed in his essay "Early English Equity," 1 *L. Q. Rev.* 162 (1885); *C. L.P.I.*

My dear Holmes:

Your outlook on things in general is much after my own heart — you might even be more emphatic on the point that the business of ideals is to devour formulas.[1] Dante, *Purgatorio*, XXVII, *ad fin.* has the sum of this, and contains the truth which Nietzsche supposed to be new. This also is the thing signified by the antinomian language of the great mystics. Here what Jalālu 'ddīn Rūmī who is called the Maulānā-i-Rūm (doctor Asiaticus) saith: "The man of God is beyond infidelity and religion." And again he saith: "To dwell in the soul is his task, to shatter penitence (*tauba* — the whole business of 'conviction of sin,' repentance, ceremonial expiation) is his task."

Sed non omnis capit hoc verbum; the natural man is not happy till he has cut up any ideal he gets hold of into formulas and put them in locked glass cases. Thus Bigelow is drunk with Brooks Adams, and his new edition of his otherwise meritorious book on *Torts*[2] is disfigured by a lot of talk about "social forces" and "direction of economic energies." It isn't so easy as he thinks to see which way the world is going. Besides I reserve the right of saying, when I choose, that the world's way is wrong. Cato may yet come to his own, and likewise your dissenting judgment in *Vegelahn* v. *Gunter*, which M. M. B. regards as fighting against the stars in their courses.[3]

Why do you think the habit of not answering letters with no business in them is peculiarly British? It may be common here, but in my experience it is universal on the Continent of Europe. There, however, the new year's card keeps the account open, being understood to say, "All right, I am here when you want me": whereas, for want of any such convention, we risk drifting into oblivion.

I want to send a dutiful address to H. M. the King of Bulgaria with an exordium in the words or to the effect following:

---

[1] If Holmes had written to Pollock on this subject the letter is missing.

[2] Melville M. Bigelow, *The Law of Torts* (8th ed., 1907).

[3] In a footnote, p. 251, Bigelow described Holmes's dissent in Vegelahn v. Guntner (see *supra*, p. 82) as "an opinion of great logical power but against the direction of economic energy."

"Sire:

For centuries the very name of your gallant people has been among the great nations of the West a synonym of manly valour combined with independence of thought. . . ." [4]

Do you know what the Paulician heretics did profess to think? I don't. Anyhow a little showing of the British flag in the Aegean may do their descendants good: and incidentally we shall stand all the better with the Mahometans of India.

Yours ever,

F. POLLOCK

WASHINGTON, October 18, 1908

Dear F. P.:

You certainly are the cleverest creature going and manage to allude to more things that I don't know, on a sheet of paper than I can find in the Bible. I am delighted that you are on to Bigelow's intoxication. I truly esteem him but he is a wooly headed gent and *inter alia* is a sort of toady of your country in little ways that rile me, *e.g.* he once published some verses "by a *Barrister.*" [1]   We don't call ourselves barristers in these parts. Yesterday I received a book from another of that class, not at all, I think, as deserving of respect as Bigelow is — Hannis Taylor, *The Science of Jurisprudence.* I don't believe he has anything whatever to say except to repeat what is well known. But he swaggers and poses, and if he loses a case before us, I believe that he writes articles pitching into the Court, or has been known to. One former book of his *The Rise & Growth of the English Constitution* [2] I thought as far as I read it to be a mere echo of Freeman [3] & Stubbs. The present volume I acknowledged at once in a polite letter but from a rapid glance

---

[4] On October 7, 1908, Prince Ferdinand declared that Bulgaria was independent of Turkey, thus repudiating provisions of the Treaty of Berlin. The British government made prompt objections.

---

[1] *Rhymes of a Barrister* (1884).
[2] *Origin and Growth of the English Constitution* (1905).
[3] Edward A. Freeman (1823–1892); author, *inter alia,* of *The Growth of the English Constitution* (1872) and *History of the Norman Conquest of England* (6 vols., 1867–79).

should suppose to be of the same sort. But he flatters you people and has managed to receive degrees, I gather from the title page, from Edinburgh & Dublin. He is a pushing man. Of course, as far as I know, his honors may have been the spontaneous outpouring of grateful Scotch and Irish. Are your Paulician Heretics Gibbon's Paulicians, Vol X, Chapter 54? I am up to my elbows in details of one sort and another. We are sitting. As yet I have but one easy case to write that I dare say I shall polish off tomorrow before and after the Court. Before I left Boston I bought for a Xmas present to my wife an original set of Cruikshank's Comic almanacs at rather a high price. I have been converted by her to a very high appreciation of his originality and variety. Are you an admirer of his? Don't say anything about it on a postal card as she might see it. When I get from the binder half a dozen vols. of my father's Ms. in addition to four that I have here now I shall feel that I have done all that I can to preserve his remains with filial respect. I am tucking in ends of this sort and I suppose when everything is all right it will be about time to die — for which at present I have no desire, as I am enjoying life to the full. I must stop as I have several things that I must do before I make my Sunday call on the Chief.[4] Please give my love to Lady Pollock and the children.

Yours ever,
O. W. H.

LONDON, October 16, 1908

My dear Holmes:

I have read Ames on Uses in *Harv. Law Rev.* for February [1] . . . and compared your article in *L. Q. R.*, i., 162.[2] Ames's controversial attitude seems to me quite superfluous. There is really no conflict between his work and yours. You showed where the feoffee to uses came from, and how he was possible

---

[4] Melville Weston Fuller (1833–1910); Chief Justice, 1888–1910.

[1] "The Origin of Uses and Trusts," 21 *Harv. L. Rev.* 261 (1908).
[2] "Early English Equity," reprinted, *C.L.P.*, p. 1.

in medieval England: whereas Ames wants to trace the process by which uses became enforceable in equity jurisdiction, a wholly different question. I don't think his exposition very clear and am not sure what he means to be the capital point, but I enclose some pencil notes I made in reading it. I see no difficulty in believing that *cestuis que use* were content to do without any judicial protection for a considerable time. Much property here is held on secret unenforceable trusts for Roman Catholic uses to this day. You know the curious Indian parallel of Benāmi conveyances.

Certainly I do not believe that a devise of land was ever administered by a spiritual court, but I cannot find that you ever said it was. On the other hand Ames's evident desire to squeeze the ecclesiastical courts and the canonists out of the story is incompatible with the manifest pressure of their competition in matters of *fidei laesio* (Pollock on *Contracts*, 7th ed., 170, note) and also with the important part played by men of religion, notably the Franciscans, in the practical development of gifts *ad opus*: Pollock and Maitland, *History of English Law*, ii, 233 (231), to which you may add, though not to the present purpose, that the phrase *al oes* occurs in the *Chanson de Roland*, now believed to have been written in England. Compare too Vinogradoff in the *L. Q. R.* just published.[3] Paul Vinogradoff however seems to me (not being an English lawyer) hardly to realize that when St. Germain[4] wrote, the action of assumpsit was already pretty well established, and his object in stating the canonist doctrine of promises was not to supply the common lawyers with a theory but to show that Canon and Common law (whatever the theory of the latter might be) did not lead to very dissimilar results.

Mansfield's later and partially successful endeavours to bring in modern civilian (*i.e.* practically canonist) doctrine about founding a promise on precedent moral obligation, etc., were due, I take it, to a quite new and distinct movement of cosmopolitan rationalism starting from Grotius and his immediate

[3] Paul Vinogradoff, "Reason and Conscience in Sixteenth Century Jurisprudence," 24 *L. Q. Rev.* 373 (1908).

[4] Christopher St. Germain (1460 ca. — 1540); author of *Two Dialogues between the Doctor and Student* (1523, 1530).

successors. If one found anything like them in 16th–17th centuries the canonist influence would be proved.

"Rely at your peril" — but do you? What about specific performance?

Have you ever found any *logical* reason why mutual promises are sufficient consideration for one another (like the two lean horses of a Calcutta hack who can only just stand together)? I have not.

Yours ever,

F. P.

[The following penciled note was enclosed with this letter.]

Equity acts upon the person not because it has a higher ethical standard but because there is no other way it can act: but no doubt it always stood for a "higher law": the king's justice reserved for extraordinary needs.

As to the titles in Abridgments, the case of Assumpsit is quite parallel to that of Uses. There is no such heading and you have to look under Trespass.[5]

It cannot be assumed that equity was *following* common law whenever they agreed, any more than the converse.

LONDON, October 21, 1908

My dear Holmes:

Now comes a second vol. of *Essays in Anglo-American Legal History*, and there are you and Ames all but cheek by jowl with only some pages of L. O. Pike to keep the peace between you.[1] This gives me a peg to hang some remarks on in the *L. Q. R.* if I think fit:[2] but if so they will have to be very short. What I like in Ames's paper is the other part of it — *Tyrrel's*

---

[5] Ames in his article "The Origin of Uses and Trusts," *supra*, note 1, at p. 266, had said: "It is significant that in the oldest and second oldest abridgments there is no title of 'Uses' or 'Feffements al uses'."

---

[1] Luke Owen Pike, "Common Law and Conscience in the Ancient Court of Chancery," 2 *Select Essays in Anglo-American Legal History* (1908), p. 722. Pike's article was preceded by a reprint of Holmes's "Early English Equity" (p. 705) and was followed by Ames's "The Origin of Uses and Trusts" (p. 737).

[2] See 25 *L. Q. Rev.* 94 (1908).

case.[3] There I think he has succeeded — like Sir Howard Elphinstone with the rule in *Shelley's case* — in exploding a venerable and hollow mystery by showing that the doctrine appears quite natural in its contemporary frame. . . .

Yours ever,
F. POLLOCK

WASHINGTON, February 21, 1909

Dear Lady Pollock:

This is just a line of greeting and farewell. We are drawing to the close of a 3 weeks adjournment in which I have written five decisions,[1] a concurring opinion,[2] and a dissent,[3] and with other matters have not had much time for culture books. I did read Fred's article or address on Government by Commission,[4] and as always was edified and improved by his discourse. He is a frightfully clever devil — please give him my love. Mephistopheles is improperly treated by the crowd. The intellect that is not to be humbugged by phrases keeps the green scum off the pool. Though, by the by, I learned in a great case that I wrote (between Missouri and Chicago)[5] that the stagnant pool is the safe place, because then the harmless bacilli simply stifle and wipe out the typhoid fellers. Clear water is the thing to be afraid of! Micro Mania, the terror of the infinitesimal, seems to have displaced the older forms of insanity. The town is full of preparations for Taft.[6] The present incumbents are

---

[3] Dyer, 155 (1557). The second part of Ames's article was concerned with this decision.

---

[1] F. L. Grant Shoe Co. v. Laird, 212 U. S. 445; Cariño v. Insular Government, *id.*, 449; Santos v. Roman Catholic Church, *id.*, 463; The Eugene F. Moran, *id.*, 466; Bagley v. General Fire Extinguisher Co., *id.*, 477. All of these cases were decided on February 23, 1909.

[2] Perhaps Hurley v. Atchison, Topeka and Santa Fe Ry., 213 U. S. 126 (decided April 5, 1909, Holmes concurring in the result, without publishing an opinion).

[3] Probably Atchison, Topeka and Santa Fe Ry. v. Sowers, 213 U. S. 55, 71 (decided March 1, 1909).

[4] "Government by Committees in England," a paper by Pollock read at the International Historical Congress at Berlin, August 1908, and printed in 25 *L. Q. Rev.* 53 (1909); reprinted in *Essays in the Law* (1922), p. 110.

[5] Missouri v. Illinois, 200 U. S. 496 (1906).

[6] The inauguration of William Howard Taft as President, succeeding Theodore Roosevelt, took place on March 4, 1909.

very sad, I think. I shall miss them personally a good deal, but I can't help thinking it is well for the country to have a change. I wish I didn't have to assist at the ceremony and sit on a wind swept platform where the old are killed every year by pneumonia and what not — neither do I hanker for the ball. We are dining out pretty much all the time these last weeks. It is a pleasant change after a day's hard work. One meets many agreeable acquaintances (and very few intimates). Most of my life is in this house and the Capitol. I have one case to fire off for which I really care. I shall be tempted to send it to Fred, though it is off his beat I am afraid.[7]

Well, as I said, this was just to say how-de-do and good bye. I must go and call on the Chief anon. My love to the children also and a lot to you.

Affectionately yours,
O. W. Holmes

London, February 24, 1909

My dear Holmes:

This is from a man wondering when he will he allowed to shave himself again, and acquiescing meanwhile in the mowing-machine which your honoured father praised at least as much as it deserved when some one made him a present of one for his voyage to Europe.[1] But how have I lost the autoxyric franchise of a lawful man? That is part of the price for the luxury of convalescing from a real first-class illness. I have been fighting with Influenza and Pneumonia, foul fiends both, and the latter "a full felonous beast" as the pseudo-Mandeville says of the three-horned creature which "chaseth and sleeth the olifant." I thought I knew something about the influenza fiend from sundry former brushes, but this was a real attack in force, repelled with the latest g. f. artillery of the medical art, to wit an oxygen cylinder. And so now, in the third week of my imprisonment, I am eating and drinking for all I am worth, sitting up for

---

[7] See Holmes's letter of March 7, 1909, suggesting that the case here referred to was Cariño v. Insular Government, 212 U. S. 449 (1909).

---

[1] In *Our Hundred Days in Europe* (1887), Chapter 1.

several hours in the afternoon and able to see select friends, and hoping to follow my wife into the country in about a week. She has been depressed for many days by a queer form of neuritis and has at last got off today.

Moreover our cat — an imposing though not beautiful animal with a real personal affection for the housemaid — has been assaulted by a dog unknown and is only just recovered. So we have had a houseful of casualties. My son happily is well and vigorous and has been doing much for us.

You have spoken much and well of the External Standard in law: have you considered how the human microcosm depends on exact maintenance of the internal standard of temperature? Let it stray 3° or 4° beyond the reasonable norm, and the microcosm is out of joint and the values wherewith it traffics with the macrocosm all awry. Notably the little world of one's sleep is transformed. Instead of the innocent incoherence of lawful or normal dreams, one's sensations (mostly unpleasing) get somehow detached from oneself as objects (that is the only way I can express it, whether it is good psychology or not) and spread out against the background of a mysterious Plan — of which, if one had the key, one would learn everything — connected in fact by the most wildly nonsensical pseudo-logical links. Then the Plan reveals itself in partial concrete visions. One floats in ether like the Spirits in Hardy's *Dynasts* (a mighty fine book, as I think I have already told you) looking on secular developments. Once I seemed thus to be aware of London growing through the centuries and then to sit, somewhere near the Duke of York's column, with sages whom I wondered at not having known before, making grandiose designs for its future. Somehow all these things pass in a monochrome atmosphere, gray or pale moonlight for the most part.

One night I had a scene of a showy festival given by some Yeomanry regiment under the Regency, and the tone of that, rather appropriately, was copper-coloured. Such have my fever dreams been (of course I am not without experience of having a temperature on former occasions of sorts, but it is many years since I have had so much). They were never terrible or disgusting, but there was the consciousness all the time of being in an abnormal world even as dreams go, and of one's own bellows to mend being somehow intimately mixed up all through it. Then there occur inventions which seem excellent, but waking memory judges inexorably that there was no point in them, not even a bad one. What think you of a revelation that the appointed seat for the future Grand Court of the English-speaking nations is the Scilly Islands? — partly because of the ease of excluding reporters! I wonder if that Antietam bullet didn't give you in its time some queer views of things in general.

In waking hours I have read a lot of mixed literature, ranging from the classic Izaak Walton — a little bit overrated I think — and more than classic Charles Lamb to Maurice Donnay's serious or frivolous plays. Almost all French plays are good enough to read, if written by any one who counts at all. And I have in reserve what is said to be the greatest of modern detective stories, *Le mystère de la chambre jaune*,[2] with a sequel.[3]

I have been trying Wilkie Collins's stories of adventure which fascinated the people of 1850–70 or thereabouts. The construction is to modern eyes marvelously crude and inartificial, and the less said about style the better. Yet there is a story-telling power which breaks through the clumsy machinery. But how childish is the Anglo-American workmanship of that period compared to R. L. Stevenson's, not to speak of any modern Frenchman who knows his trade! (I am not sure whether or not Hawthorne can be excepted, having indeed not read much of him. But I think he stands outside the novel of adventure.) Lamb's letters are a perennial joy. Now and then I mumble over a chapter of Montaigne: an author who has for a lazy reader one great merit, that it is no matter where one takes him up.

My drink is changed from champagne to claret, a good vintage sold off to its members by the Hon. Society of Lincoln's Inn. I take this to be step towards resuming the serious business of life. Meanwhile, adore Dionysos with me, for he will surely survive all the tribe of Carrie Nation.

Yours ever,

F. POLLOCK

[2] By Gaston Leroux; published in 1908.
[3] *Le Parfum de la dame en noir* (1909).

LONDON, February 27, 1909

My dear Holmes:

P.S. That adjective ought, I believe, to be autoxyristic, but my Greek books are in my study down two pair of still forbidden stairs, and seem as far off as Patagonia.

I find in Lamb's letters a pretty bit of testimony to the reputation of that starched and pedantic person James Alan Park, J. among intelligent laymen "as empty as Judge Park's wig when the head is in it." Do you know the story of Park and Holroyd, JJ. and the Chinese witness? I think I must have told it you. "He be d—d, he's no more a Christian than I am," *per* Holroyd, J.

If you want to sample a new English novelist you will find Galsworthy worth trying. I read a volume of his yesterday, *Fraternity*: extremely clever writing, but the people seemed to me to be types or "characters" in the old fashioned sense rather than individuals. This, however, is only an offhand impression.

Yours ever,

F. P.

WASHINGTON, March 7, 1909

My beloved Frederick:

You wring my heart by the account of your illness of which I had heard no hint before your letters came. However, you are out of it and as it has been the occasion of a damn good letter I will not spend time in regrets now. I don't see why autoxyric wasn't right, but I revere the power to use any forms of the word without looking it out. I am up to my ears in work as usual; just now reading the evidence to see whether we shall punish some alleged murderers and connivers at murder for — contempt of court in so doing! A negro convicted of rape and sentenced to be hung had asked for a *habeas corpus* and had taken an appeal to our Court on the ground that his trial was a tragic farce. Whereupon he was taken out of jail and lynched. The State to which punishment of the murder belongs will do nothing but we had to take steps to deal with the contempt of our authority — which we have done, in your chancery's delightful phrase, with all deliberate speed.[1] I sent you a Philippine case [2] in which I took pleasure in opening some broad considerations. It was argued wholly on the Spanish law, in the ordinary technical manner of lawyers. I don't often send you opinions, but having gone so far I will put an older one into the post as, though unlike anything that you are likely to come across, the diversities there taken may interest you. They seem to me plain as the primer, but they didn't appear so to counsel who argued the case and I have noticed that the statements of it, e.g. in *Harv. Law Rev.* are lamentably stupid.[3] Tomorrow I shall be 68 — wind fair and ship going well. We have got in our new president, and I have avoided the risk I feared of your trouble by his delivering his inaugural in the Senate Chamber. We have to sit and listen to it, which on a wind swept platform in the open air is not fun. He seems to be speaking frankly and truthfully. Otherwise the address did not seem to me remarkable — though I am told that Mr. Roosevelt called it the best since Lincoln, no doubt because it promised to pursue the reforms of "my distinguished predecessor." As I am rather sceptical about the reforms I was less impressed. My friends grow few, so do take care of yourself. . . . I have no time to read, but I have lying by me S. Reinach's 3d vol. *Cultes, Mythes, et Religions* which is delightful to take up — all sorts of short essays on classic and archeological themes. He is an admirer of Fraser's *Golden Bough*, and a whole hogger on universal preliminary totemism, as to which I don't know; but he is most learned and acute and entertaining, with many grave side lights on our holy religion — thrown with latent malice I fear — but good sport to read. I don't know better volumes to have on hand in weary moments. Now I must make my Sunday call on the Chief Justice. Love to all.

Affly yours,
O. W. H.

---

[1] United States v. Shipp, 203 U. S. 563 (1906); 214 U. S. 386 (1909).
[2] Cariño v. Insular Government, 212 U. S. 449 (1909).
[3] Probably Old Dominion Copper Company v. Lewisohn, 210 U. S. 206 (1908); critically noted, 22 *Harv. L. Rev.* 48 (1908).

March 7, 1909

Dear F. P.

P.S. This is not an imitation of you but absolutely *bona fide*. As I sat at luncheon just now it came over me, that you need the *ist* to signify the activity of the razor*er*. 'Autoxyric franchise' were your words. I suppose that would mean 'purely razorly franchise' instead of self razoring franchise as you intended. *Inter leges silent Graecae* — (*sc. literae*).

Yours,
O. W. H.

THE STEPS, PLAYDEN, SUSSEX
March 19, 1909

My dear Holmes:

Many thanks for your letter and the prints of judgments. In the case of the Filipino possessory title I am sure our Judicial Committee, if properly guided by Macnaghten, would have given the like judgment and for much the same reasons. The other one is less in my line but I will read it shortly.

Is it not the part of a wise President succeeding Roosevelt to make his first address *not* remarkable? "Murder may be contempt of Court" would make a good old-fashioned head-note.

I am glad you have got hold of *Cultes, Mythes & Religions*. My copy is in London, so I am not sure whether "La Curiosité de Tibère" is in the volume before you. Reinach has got to the point of gravely doubting whether there was so much as a Crucifixion, and I am by no means sure that he is wrong. For if it was not an extraordinary and irregular case, the whole Gospel story evaporates: and if it was, how did it fail to be notorious or to be reported to Rome? But see the learned S. R. at large. He has also produced a wonderful little book called *Orpheus*, a pocket history of universal religion from Totemism to Modernism, so good in everything I know a little about that I feel safe in taking the rest on trust, for the facts at any rate. I have a great mind to send it to you. . . .

We think there is not to be a European war, but news from the Balkans continues to be pretty confused.

Yours ever,

F. POLLOCK

WASHINGTON, April 4, 1909

Dear Pollock:

I am so much obliged to you for *Orpheus*. I looked through the list of S. Reinach's works and don't find it and concluded that you meant an essay bearing that title. I am delighted to have this little book and shall read it at once. It came this morning. I have had a pleasant week of nearer leisure than I often get down here, and have read law (a book on the Interstate Commerce Act [1] & some articles on mining problems),[2] "Municipal Problems,"[3] S. Reinach, etc., have dined out, and have driven in the park watching the spring, and the monkeys tigers and birds in the Zoo. *Mem.*: Tigers and wolves dislike either me or a tall hat, which is the exception in these parts. A tigress spit at me as long as I was in sight and the wolves seemed both to fear and hate. Tomorrow an early conference and then the wheel begins to go round again. I hope you are all right again, now. It was a shock to hear that you had been ill. . . . I find that there is a little work that I must do before tomorrow. They have a way here of frequently asking for rehearings and filing briefs that simply reargue the case. I think it an abuse. I suppose it comes from the habit in some states. Latterly I have escaped except in cases where a crank was sure to ask it if the case was decided against him. At first a good many such applications were made in my cases — the fact that the decision was written at once being regarded as evidence of inadequate consideration. Such humbugs prevail! If a man keeps a case six months it is supposed to be decided on "great consideration." It seems to me that intensity is the only thing. A day's impact is better than a month of dead pull. Meantime

[1] Henry S. Drinker, Jr., *The Interstate Commerce Act* (3 vols., 1909–10). Holmes has read one volume, according to his Journal.
[2] H. N. Arnold, "Lode Locations," 22 *Harv. L. Rev.*, 266, 339 (1909).
[3] L. S. Rowe, *Problems of City Government* (1908).

there is a pile of applications to be looked over in other men's decisions. So after going to make my usual Sunday call on the Chief I must fall to work.

Ever yours,
O. W. H.

London, November 29, 1909 [1]

My dear Holmes:

I am sending you *The Cornhill Magazine* with some lines of mine [2] which you will surely understand if any man does, seeing you have fought in the wars of the Lord with David and sit on the judgment seat of Solomon, or the nearest thing thereto that the western world can show.

Yours ever,
F. Pollock

Washington, December 11, 1909

Dear F. P.:

. . . Your poem has arrived and for the many'th time impresses me with your gifts. I humble mine eyes expecting the season decreed, but hardly expecting the illumination of which Solomon is confident. It is a moving thing and I thank you for it. I am in the usual tempest of work now, turning out a decision each week in the intervals of sitting and having a lot of outside reading of submitted cases, applications for certiorari, etc. to do. At odd minutes I am doing what I never expected or intended to do until the *3rd* eternity. The first I expect to devote to mathematics, the second, unless it is too late and the ground adequately covered, to my great work on anthropology and the 3rd to picking up neglected *belles lettres*. But to my

[1] Holmes had been in England in the summer of 1909 and had received the degree D.C.L. at Oxford. In August Pollock had attended the meeting of the American Bar Association in Detroit, Michigan. His remarks at that meeting are printed in 34 A. B. A. Reports, 832 (1909).

[2] Pollock's poem "King Solomon's Vigil" was printed in 27 *Cornhill Magazine* (New 3rd Series) 778 (November 1909) and later reprinted in his volume *Outside the Law* (1927), p. 26.

surprise I am reading Dante. I don't know Italian, but with Latin and a translation I find it very easy. And it is absurd to be afraid of any book, as it is to be so of any case. I long have said there is no such thing as a hard case. I am frightened weekly but always when you walk up to the lion and lay hold the hide comes off and the same old donkey of a question of law is underneath. But there are two that I must be able to recite on in an hour so I must stop with this hurried word.

My love to Lady Pollock and the children.

Ever yours,
O. W. H.

LONDON, December 23, 1909

My dear Holmes:

We are just off for ten days in Paris. You are quite right not to be afraid of Dante. There are really no linguistic difficulties to speak of: not a dozen places in the whole *Commedia*, I should say, that give any trouble to construe — a few constructions are harsh and some ambiguous. The real trouble is that he assumes you have read Thomas Aquinas and also to know all the gossip of North Italy — the latter of these conditions already made many allusions as obscure to 14th century commentators as they are to us. By the way Benvenuto da Imola's commentary (Latin, printed only in 1887) would amuse you if you can get hold of it, and is often as instructive as any other. Warren Vernon's notes are the most comprehensive in English. I would suggest jumping on to *Purgatory* after the introductory cantos of *Inferno*: it is far more human and interesting. Archaic Italian is for us easier than modern, but after a while you will have no trouble with a modern Italian Commentary. Some, *e.g.* Casini, are very good.

Yours ever,
F. P.

The Lords have affirmed Artemus Jones's case.[1] I still think it wrong: professional opinion is much divided.

---

[1] Hulton & Co. v. Jones, [1910] A. C. 20. Noted, presumably by Pollock, in 26

Dear F.:

Before your letter came I had finished the *Inferno* and begun the *Purgatorio*, but just now what with law by day and
dinners by night I have few chances to tuck in a canto. I agree
with you in preferring the *Purgatorio*. The *Inferno* postulates
that sin is a fundamental reality, that men by their free will
choose it, that God hates them and that we are quite right in
spitting on them and lying to them. As one doesn't look at
things in quite that way one reads with a dilettante appreciation only, as the alternative to loathing — but I love his holy,
bright, clear colored medieval pictures. Longfellow's translation seems to me really a *tour de force* of accuracy and Charles
Norton's prose seems to me much indebted to it, and adding
but little. I note your references; whether I shall have a chance
to use them rests with the future. We just got through the arguments in the *Tobacco Trust Case* [1] yesterday and with that and
several other complications have enough to think about. I
have just dissented in a case where 4 JJ. to 3 have decided that
the U.S. Courts were not bound to follow a State decision as
[to] the effect of a deed of coal in the State.[2] They follow an established though very fishy principle started by Story, that in
general commercial law the U.S. Courts would follow their own
judgment, *non obstant* decisions of the State as to transactions
within it.[3] This has been extended to general law, while as to
state statutes & constitutions the rule is the other way. They
say we must use our independent judgment. I reply, as to what?
The State law. But the State judges and the State legislatures
make the State law — we don't — and I refer to decisions and
John Gray's recent book [4] to show that we have had to recognize in other cases the law-making functions of the judges. I

L. Q. Rev. 103 (1910). It was held in this case that the plaintiff, Artemus Jones, in an
action for libel, could recover the damages which he suffered as a result of the defendant's publication of a defamatory article concerning one Artemus Jones, whom the
defendant believed to be a fictitious character.

[1] United States v. American Tobacco Co., 221 U. S. 106 (argued, Jan. 3-6, 1910;
reargued, Jan. 9-12, 1911; decided, May 29, 1911).
[2] Kuhn v. Fairmont Coal Co., 215 U. S. 349, 370 (1910).
[3] Swift v. Tyson, 16 Pet. 1 (1842).
[4] *The Nature and Sources of the Law* (1909).

think I punched a hole in their bottom, though a very keen man might require a little further analysis than I thought expedient to go into as against old Harlan who simply rolled off the cases. Adieu — a Happy New Year. I must go to work.

Yours ever,

O. W. H.

LONDON, January 20, 1910

My dear Holmes:

. . . Tonight I go to Glasgow to see my barely possible Constituents, the Graduates of Glasgow and (on Saturday) Aberdeen. Finding myself a candidate in a general election is a most unexpected experience.[1] But a Committee of the free-trading Scots graduates invited me and I thought it right not to refuse.

You know enough of Scotland to be aware that this does *not* entail ordering a kilt or learning the Kailyard dialect.

The chance is strictly, so far as I can guess, what is called sporting. My wife is very keen for Free Trade and agin the Lords, and our car runs to and fro to help Liberal candidates: so far it has been on the losing side every time.

The forecast is for a considerably diminished Liberal majority though probably a working one.

Yours ever,

F. POLLOCK

LONDON, February 23, 1910

My dear Holmes:

As I expected, I did not succeed in overcoming the academic conservatism of Glasgow and Aberdeen.[1] It is curious that the Scottish universities and London University have become almost as Tory as Oxford and Cambridge. In Scotland

[1] The Universities of Glasgow and Aberdeen by the Redistribution of Seats Act, 1885 (48 & 49 Vict. c. 23), had one seat in the House of Commons. The first Parliament of George V was elected in January and February, 1910.

[1] The Conservative candidate, Sir Henry Craik, defeated Pollock in the election by a majority of 1468 votes out of a total of 8390 votes cast.

the clerical element is Presbyterian (the Episcopal Church is in that kingdom an insignificant dissenting body), but that seems to make no difference: and the general tendency of the medical profession is also conservative. . . .

I agree with your objection [2] to the undeveloped land tax, which however is only a minor point in the Budget.[3] The intention was to discourage the speculative holding up of building land, not to penalize the preservation of open spaces. But the drafting of these new land clauses was not happy, in this and other places, in making the intention clear. There was little or no economic heresy: it is a daring attempt to execute that which economists have commonly held for the last thirty or forty years to be sound in principle but almost impossible to put in practice. As put forward, the scheme has many and complicated exceptions. I think it ought to have been laid before the House and the country, and withdrawn to be brought up in a better form in 1910. But the besetting fault of Liberal Ministries is to be in a hurry to do too much at once. The Lords' contention that they were justified in throwing out the Budget, as amounting to a political revolution disguised as finance, did not seem to me tenable. For myself, my Liberal friends think the better of me for having put up a fight, my Unionist ones no worse, and I have had a quite interesting experience.

What text of Dante are you using? there are wide differences of merit in the editions. I have seen by chance a pamphlet by some kind of Polish Jew maintaining that the *Commedia* is a ciphered panegyric of Judaism and Beatrice an allegory of the *Talmud*. This is one better than the Bacon-Shakespeare craze.

My wife is off to Egypt next week . . . to get a good sunning. I don't think she will trouble herself much about the Pharaohs. A month hence I hope to go to Rome for the Easter vacation — it will be seven years since I was there: and perhaps Jack will go with me.

Send me any of your judgments that are of general interest.

---

[2] No letter in which Holmes expressed such objections has been found.

[3] The Budget, adopted by Parliament in November 1909, imposed, with certain exceptions, new taxes on owners of land including a duty of ½ *d.* in the pound on the site value of land not built on or used in any industry other than agriculture.

We are beginning to contemplate a written Constitution here, and many learned persons favour the Referendum in some form.

Yours ever,

F. POLLOCK

WASHINGTON, April 1, 1910

Dear Pollock:

I have been rather hindered in writing by work, but in the fortnight's adjournment just coming to an end I have had some leisure, rather sadly broken by Brewer's death.[1] I had a dreadful fear that we should all have to make a flying journey to Leavenworth, Kansas and back, which, in view of a blizzard that has been raging, would have meant serious danger to the Chief if not to all, and as it would have cut into our final sitting this month and interfered with public business we decided not to go. Mrs. Brewer behaved like a heroine, saying she knew the state of business in the Court and how upset we should be if a single Judge were disabled, and begged us not to do it. I was glad of his death on his own account, as well as otherwise, for I had become convinced that his activities were failing and dreadfully feared what happened with his uncle, Field,[2] that he might remain after his mind had gone. He came of a strong blood and had been a man of great power, I believe, although I have not very definite knowledge of his earlier work. He was a very pleasant man in private, but he had the itch for public speaking and writing and made me shudder many times. I had to remind myself that one should not allow taste to blind one to great qualities, as it is apt to. I have heard him speak in public with a curious bitterness about some of the decisions of his brethren that he disagreed with. Altogether I think he was rather an *enfant terrible*. However, it is fair to remember that I believe a part of his outside discourse was to make a little money for his wife. I finished Dante on my first leisure days. I have had no chance to look at any Commentaries. The edition

[1] David Josiah Brewer, Associate Justice of the Supreme Court of the United States, died on March 28, 1910.

[2] Stephen Johnson Field (1816–1899), Associate Justice of the Supreme Court, 1863–97.

I used was published by G. Barbèra, Florence, '84. The text seems to vary slightly once in a while from that implied by Norton's translation, but it answered all my purposes. I doubt if I ever got such a sensation from literature (not including philosophy). And I quite agree with you in preferring the *Purgatory* and *Paradise* to the *Inferno*. The holy rapture that he embodies is one of the emotions of a life time. I could discourse at length but won't. Also I read Chesterton's *Tremendous Trifles* and *Orthodoxy*. I thought at first I had found a man I should like to talk with. He *is* a clever dog, with an occasional glimpse of the profound, but it seems to me only an occasional glimpse, and I think it would not be very difficult to outsubtilize his subtilties in *Orthodoxy*. I doubt if he knows much of the history of human thought, and in his dealing with materialists he does not seem to get beyond that blunt type that thinks it knows what matter is. I don't see why a man should despair because he doesn't see a beard on his Cosmos. If he believes that he is inside of it, not it inside of him, he knows that consciousness, purpose, significance and ideals are among its possibilities, and if he surmises *in vacuo* that those are all finite expressions inadequate to the unimaginable I see no more ground for despair than when a Catholic says that he does not know the thoughts and purposes of God. It is a fallacy, I think to look to any theory for motives — we get our motives from our spontaneity — and the business of Philosophy is to show that we are not fools for doing what we want to do. All of which no doubt I have said twenty times before. Love to all yours.

Yours ever,
O. W. HOLMES

LONDON, April 13, 1910

My dear Holmes:

I wish you all joy of your *Standard Oil*, which I see is to be re-argued[1] after the good old fashion of the 16th–17th cent. (*The Reports, passim*).

---

[1] Standard Oil Co. v. United States, 221 U. S. 1 (argued, March 14–16, 1910;

Only a few days ago I came back from Rome, where I learnt authentically from a live Cardinal who speaks English like a native, being half Irish, that there is to be a new *Corpus Juris Canonici*: also saw the Villa Albani for the second time, which is better for a man before God, as Littleton saith, than canon law or anything popish or most (not all) things medieval. It is an Italian prince's palatial collection of antiques with a remarkable percentage of really fine works and a few unique masterpieces: one can see it only by favour, and I had the luck to be of a favoured party. . . . It is an odd result of history that the best places on the whole to study Greek art are London and Rome.

Your way of taking the *Divina Commedia* with a rush, and no more commenting than absolutely required to know what Dante is talking about, which Norton gives you, is certainly the best for a first reading. Next you will have to read the *Vita Nuova* — not at all difficult Italian, in fact much easier than modern books, also translated by Norton (and many others, but his will be as good as any) and the poems. And the *De Monarchia* lets one more inside the medieval way of looking at politics than any other book of comparable length. It is very nice medieval Latin, not affecting classicism like John of Salisbury whom a learned clerk of Oxford has been elaborately editing.[2] There is a curious little link between the said John and Dante, which I will tell you some other time.

Chesterton *is* a clever dog: that is absolutely the right word: not very wise nor well informed: rather spoilt I think by popularity following on (I suspect) a longish period of obscure journalism: now he can get pay for writing whatever comes into his head, and thinks he is a prophet.

Certainly the people who make theories make them to justify the motives they have already. The trouble is that the theories may have much influence over other people's motives for generations, by no means always for good.

My wife will be back from Egypt by the end of the week. She doesn't take much stock in Pharaohs and mummies and

restored to docket for reargument, April 11, 1910; reargued, Jan. 12, 13, 16, 17, 1911; decided, May 15, 1911).

[2] Clement Charles Julian Webb's edition of John of Salisbury was published in 1909.

enormous temples, and from the humanist point of view I guess
she is right.

Yours ever,
F. P.

WASHINGTON, April 23, 1910

Dear F. P.:

I am just too late to get the return mail in answer to yours
but I hasten to reply, partly because I have just received a
semi-request to send you the accompanying paper.[1] I know the
writer only by correspondence. He seems to me half crank, and
yet I am told that he has done things in former days in connection with news, and he seems to me to have ideas. My
trouble is that while he has been sending in things for two or
three years I don't seem to get any forrader with what he has
to say. He thinks himself that he has done more than Darwin.
His contempt for government interference with rates etc., and
his belief in the validity of the outside organizations I confess I
share to a great extent. Of course I enforce whatever constitutional laws Congress or anybody else sees fit to pass — and do
it in good faith to the best of my ability — but I don't disguise
my belief that the Sherman Act is a humbug based on economic
ignorance and incompetence, and my disbelief that the Interstate Commerce Commission is a fit body to be entrusted with
rate-making, even in the qualified way in which it is entrusted.
The Commission naturally is always trying to extend its power
and I have written some decisions limiting it (by construction
of statutes only). However I am so sceptical as to our knowledge about the goodness or badness of laws that I have no
practical criticism except what the crowd wants. Personally
I bet that the crowd if it knew more wouldn't want what it
does — but that is immaterial. I have been working madly to
keep my cases written as soon as given to me, but my share
this year has not been of remarkable interest. The term draws
to a close — one week more of argument and final adjournment

---

[1] Enclosed with this letter was a four-page bulletin, *The News Office*, Franklin Ford,
Director (New York City, April 20, 1910).

as usual at the end of May. Now I must rush to a Conference. My love to Lady Pollock to whom I will write soon.

Yours ever,

O. W. H.

LONDON, May 12, 1910

My dear Holmes:

Mr. Franklin Ford's paper is obscure to me because I don't know exactly what he is driving at. . . .

I thought the Sherman Act a queer piece of drafting when I looked into it some years ago in connexion with the *Northwestern* [sic] *Securities case*: beyond that I cannot profess to have an opinion: except that if the Fathers had foreseen the growth of inter-state and international business they would have made some things in the Constitution more explicit.

Our constitutional controversy [1] here is in abeyance — probably for several months — by the demise of the Crown [2] and the obvious necessity of letting George V. have time to look around.

Is not Roosevelt's quasi-royal progress extraordinary? [3] William hit it rather neatly when he pointed out to R. that he was the first private citizen who had ever reviewed German troops. I have secured the Nobel address for the *L. Q. R.*,[4] not that there is very much law in it, but for the law of nations it is legal enough to pass muster. . . .

Yours ever,

F. P.

Last Saturday I saw a manor court (for several manors together) held for the first time. It was delightfully casual and informal. So far as I could see the only business done was that a tenant of a manor strolled in and gave the steward sixpence. . . .

---

[1] The question whether the House of Lords had the right to reject a money bill adopted by the House of Commons. See Pollock to Holmes, *supra*, p. 159.

[2] King Edward VII died May 6, 1910.

[3] From March to June, 1910, after returning from his hunting trip in Africa, Theodore Roosevelt made an extensive tour of the European countries.

[4] Roosevelt's speech, "The Promotion of Peace," delivered before the Nobel Prize Commission at Christiania, May 5, 1910, was printed in 26 *L. Q. Rev.* 199 (1910).

PLAYDEN COTTAGE
PLAYDEN, SUSSEX
August 23, 1910

My dear Holmes:

. . . Since I came here I have been reading, mostly, neither
tragedians nor comedians, but the proofs of the marvellously
ill written reports of a certain Kentish Eyre which the Selden
Society will publish some time this winter [1] after annoying delay caused by the first editor having died suddenly when his
materials were not quite ready for printing.[2] The date is 1312–
13 [sic], and I don't yet make out what kind of scribes wrote
French so ignorantly and corruptly when it was still the living
language of the courts and polite society. One is reduced to
conjecture in many places in both the French and the Latin.
However, I have run through Oscar Wilde's plays which are in
the house. He was immensely clever, almost a charlatan and
almost a literary genius, and produced one really good though
conventional comedy (not a disparaging epithet, for all art is
really conventional and so called realism is only the discovery
of new conventions by means of a more or less fresh point of
view), some very clever farce, and some full-flavoured Wardour
Street Elizabethan tragedy, and the *tour de force* of *Salome* is
quite good French, a sort of *variations sérieuses* on the Maeterlinck trick. As for Aristophanes I rather agree with you,[3] but
much depends on the translator. B. B. Rogers, a scholarly
lawyer now retired from practice, with whom Maitland read
thirty odd years ago, is about the best. Aristophanes could be
a real poet when he chose (much of *The Birds* and some of *The
Frogs*). Gross buffoonery has to be discounted, after all, even
in Shakespeare, and much more in the other Elizabethans: and
even the polite Gray talks of a special edition of his letters on
the finest soft brown paper for the use of the curious.
Last Christmas time I got hold of Bergson's work [4] in Paris

---

[1] *The Eyre of Kent, 6 & 7 Edward II*, 1313–1314 (vol. 1, 1910), being vol. 24 of the
Selden Society Publications.

[2] Leveson William Vernon Harcourt, 1872–1909.

[3] The letter referred to is missing. In Holmes's Journal it appears that at approxi-
mately this time he read *Acharnians, Knights*, and *Birds*.

[4] It appears in Holmes's Journal that he had recently read Bergson's *Le Rire, Essai
sur les données immédiates de la conscience, Matière et mémoire, Évolution créatrice*.

and also Poincaré's. In my mind Poincaré is the stronger man and I think you would like him better. But I don't think Bergson wants to bolster up any system of irrational beliefs, unless it is irrational to hold (as you do) that ultimately you have to come to betting on certain events. So long as you know you are betting there is no shuffling with reason. . . .

Truly I should like to see you at the head of your Court, but I suppose the inevitable balance between different States and sections is in the way.[5] If there are any other reasons I think they must be bad. . . .

Medieval justice was a quaint thing. When you missed the right criminal you found reasons for fining jurymen and suitors all round and consoled yourself by thinking that anyhow you had collected a little revenue for the King. Counsel were quite as persistent in taking every possible point, and a few not possible, as they are now.

I must stop if I am to make sure of this being in time for tomorrow's mail.

Yours ever,
F. POLLOCK

BEVERLY FARMS, September 1, 1910

Dear Fred:

I don't quite know where to send this, but I must answer your most pleasant letter at once before leaving a card on the President — must — because you make me long to talk with you. I have read a book or two of Poincaré, as to whom I agree with you. I was bothered by his mathematics, but I said to myself that if the premises and conclusion are above the table and you accept both it doesn't matter so much by what particular wheels underneath the writer brings out the result. After finishing the dramatists (Greek)[1] I turned to *Highways of Progress* by James J. Hill the great railroad man, reinforcing

---

[5] Chief Justice Fuller died on July 4, 1910. His successor was not appointed until December 12, 1910.

[1] Holmes's Journal indicates that in addition to the play of Aristophanes which he had recently read he read Aeschylus, Sophocles, and Euripides.

my own beliefs in a striking way. Then I combined my reflections like the gent in Pickwick when he wrote on Chinese Metaphysics. I regard a man like Hill as representing one of the
greatest forms of human power, an immense mastery of economic details, an equal grasp of general principles, and ability
and courage to put his conclusions into practice with brilliant
success when all the knowing ones said he would fail. Yet the
intense external activity that calls for such powers does not
especially delight me. Barring the intellectual flowering of the
last fifty years, most of the great things have been done with
a thinner population. If civilization keeps on, and we don't
discover a new source of energy before the coal is exhausted, the
population must thin out, but perhaps we shall have time to
produce beauty and still to philosophize. If we are destined to
drop from Jim Hill to Aeschylus there are compensations. This
thought makes me less unhappy at my duty of enforcing laws
that I believe to embody economic mistakes. Now I am going
to try to drop improvement and read novels. . . . Wm. James's
death [2] cuts a root for me that went far into the past, but of
late, indeed for many years, we had seen little of each other and
had little communication except as he occasionally sent me a
book. Distance, other circumstances and latterly my little
sympathy with his demi spiritualism and pragmatism, were
sufficient cause. His reason made him sceptical and his wishes
led him to turn down the lights so as to give miracle a chance.
In connection with the Greeks I read *Six Greek Sculptors* [3] and
a short history of art by S. Reinach, *Apollo*, having his usual
power to penetrate and to interest. But in spite of feeling as
keen an interest in life as ever, the shadows begin to lengthen.
I am more lonely as my old friends die off. I reflect on the mistake that I have seen it to be in others to remain on the bench
after seventy. (I *must* remain till after I am 71 to get my pension.) In short, once in a while as today I succeed in feeling sad
without a pose — without an effort to reflect rationally on
probabilities which my health and temperament seem to defy.
I suppose it is good for one. And as recognition gradually comes
one should take it as a warning that the end is near. However,

[2] August 26, 1910.
[3] By E. A. Gardner; published in 1910.

I don't do it to excess, I can swear. This vacation has gone by on wings, and I hardly have enough to show for it, even enough idleness. Oh — have you seen a book published in India by G. F. Arnold, *Psychology Applied to Legal Evidence*? A Florida Judge [4] sent me an opinion in which he referred to it. There is a chapter on The Normal Man, pitching into our views. I thought it drool. I thought the introduction and that chapter, which were all I read, showed the arrogance of an outsider who thought no lawyers knew anything about philosophy and a complete failure to understand the purpose of the law to fix a line of minimum social conduct required of men at their peril. Perhaps I should have read more, but the Florida gent, an admirer of Will James and Pragmatism, seemed to me one of the not unfamiliar type of people with nothing to say, who dilate with futile fervor when they read a new and clever book — or even a new one. A most excellent and worthy little deaf man he seemed when he called, but I didn't get no nourishment out of him. Now I am off for the President. My love to Lady Pollock and the children.

Yours ever,
O. W. H.

PLAYDEN COTTAGE
PLAYDEN, SUSSEX
September 16, 1910

My dear Holmes:
That book of Mr. Arnold's came to the *L. Q. R.* in due course, two or three years ago I think, and was duly sat upon by a learned contributor.[1] From my own cursory inspection I diagnosed an acute but uninteresting case of œdematous encephalitic paranoia—*Anglice*, a d—d conceited ass with a swelled head who had read a little law in books without understanding it and thought he could teach lawyers their own business.

Columbia University has made me a splendid offer to give an address for the opening of its new Law School at the end of

---

[4] Thomas Mitchell Shackleford, Associate Justice of the Supreme Court of Florida.

[1] 23 *L. Q. Rev.* 113 (1907).

October, which I have unwillingly refused, as the first half of November will be just about my busiest time at home, organizing a Commission of Public Records [2] besides the regular work on *Law Reports*, etc. and supervising a Selden Society edition of a singularly difficult and corrupt 14th century Anglo-French text.

They also asked for a course of lectures on anything I pleased. It would have been a rush to invent them even if I could have stolen the time. But people seem to think one has one's pocket full of ready-made lectures: as perhaps some learned friends have.

Yours ever,
F. P.

N.B. Œdicephalitis runs in the tribe of Arnolds more or less. You know they are of the chosen people by origin.

BEVERLY FARMS, September 24, 1910

Dear Fred:

Your letter is a great consolation to me. As I believe I said, Arnold's book struck me wholly as it did you, but I read only the introduction and one chapter on the normal man, but as it was cracked up by the Florida Judge with the air of preciocity and of knowing higher, holier things than the run, I desired your confirmation, although the worthy judge seemed to me also to have nothing to say. He was an admirer and friend of W. James and one of his pallbearers. What W. J. thought of him I can only guess, but we all are kind to those who think us great men. . . . Deaths did not stop with my letter of last week to Lady Pollock. My dear old friend of fifty years, nearly, Capt. Magnitzky, was buried this week. He was my first sergeant, then promoted and finally Captain in the regular army. He was bookkeeper and general boss for Shattuck Holmes & Munroe and since then made out my accounts as Trustee under my sister's will. A quiet steady effective man,

---

[2] In October Pollock was officially named Chairman of the Royal Commission on Public Records.

distinguished in bearing and in soul — as I said in a little notice of him.[1] The vacation has been interrupted and saddened by these recurring deaths and I am content to make a new start from Washington. The President said he meant to send for me and talk about the new appointments.[2] I know of no one whom I so want to see on our Bench as much as I did the late Solicitor General.[3] As to the Chief Justiceship I am rather at a loss. I should bet he will appoint Hughes,[4] who has given up a chance of being Republican nominee for the Presidency, but I know nothing. I think White who is next in Seniority to Harlan (too old, etc.) the ablest man likely to be thought of. I don't know whether his being a Catholic would interfere. I always have assumed absolutely that I should not be regarded as possible — they don't appoint side Judges as a rule, it would be embarrassing to skip my Seniors, and I am too old. I think I should be a better administrator than White, but he would be more politic. Also the President's inclination so far as I can judge seems to me towards a type for which I have but a limited admiration. I am afraid White has about as little chance as I. I really don't care much who is appointed, if only he is a man who can dispose of the little daily questions with promptitude and decision. Apart from that and the honor of being figurehead, the C. J. like the rest of us must depend on his intellectual power. I know of no first rate man except White. His writing leaves much to be desired, but his thinking is profound, especially in the legislative direction which we don't recognize as a judicial requirement but which is so, especially in our Court, nevertheless. I am sorry we shall not see you here, but I should not suppose that you could come, and I don't doubt you share my unwillingness to do anything that time does not permit to be your best. By the by, I praise the scientific terms you have coined for your Arnold diagnosis. I have read very

---

[1] *Boston Evening Transcript*, September 20, 1910; reprinted in Bent, *Justice Oliver Holmes* (1932), pp. 118–119.

[2] Justice Moody, owing to illness, was known to be contemplating retirement, for which Congress had already made special provision, and Chief Justice Fuller had died on July 4, 1910.

[3] Lloyd Wheaton Bowers, appointed Solicitor General of the United States, April 1, 1909; died September 9, 1910.

[4] Charles Evans Hughes was appointed an Associate Justice by President Taft on April 25, 1910, and took his seat on October 10, 1910.

little lately. *Why I am a Socialist*, by a newspaper man,[5] seems to think the argument by dramatic contrast (the man in the mine, mill, engine — Vanderbilt's yacht, somebody's palace) conclusive. It never considers the question of relative amounts. What per cent is withdrawn for the luxuries of the few? Not one per cent, I should guess. But the public reasons by pictures, not by statistics, and the rich in this country seem to me foolish in failing to bear that fact in mind. I think public display of private splendor a stupidly antisocial thing here, although I have almost greater objection to Carnegie's and Rockefeller's charitable gifts. I think charitable gifts on a large scale are *prima facie* the worst abuse of private ownership — from the economic point of view. My love to Lady Pollock & the children.

Yours ever,

O. W. H.

London, December 17, 1910

My dear Holmes:

I am sending you for your vacation reading a book called *The Pursuit of Reason* by C. F. Keary, an old Cambridge friend of mine. He is a scholar with plenty of literary knowledge (especially French) and artistic taste, but somehow lacks driving power and has been very near hitting off something all his life, including elaborate novels in the modern French manner which have every merit except being readable. This is an excursion into things in general — far from conclusive, but as you don't expect philosophers to be conclusive you will hardly count that a fault: and though I find some difficulty in seeing what Keary really thinks he is after, it is full of clever things and fine observation. When he gets on politics and practical affairs he seems to me mostly to talk nonsense due to imperfect acquaintance with the facts of life: one can't be solitary and fastidious without paying for it. Still it's the clever sort of nonsense that might be sense in some other world, and is never dull.

---

[5] Charles Edward Russell.

It would please me better if you were C. J.,[1] and so thinks my learned young friend Hazeltine [2] the Reader in English Law at our Cambridge. But from what you have already written to me I take it you are content with White's appointment. . . .

Yours ever,
F. POLLOCK

WASHINGTON, December 18, 1910

Dear F. P.:

A Merry Xmas to you and yours, and thanks for your letter.[1] I shall be more than glad to get the new edition of the *History of the Science of Politics* and trust your judgment about the Contracts. As I remember it Ames had an absurd theory on mutual promises; but Ames with all his merits wanted actuality. I quite agree with what I believe is your view, that it is a case of jumping in — call one binding and both are. It is more convenient to say both bind than that neither does, therefore *voilà vous êtes.* . . .

Misfortune, and deaths among my friends have marked this year — I suppose it is the concomitant of growing old. (I shall be seventy March 8.) White, I suppose, will be sworn in tomorrow. It took everyone by surprise but I think he was the best man in sight, who could be thought of. He is about five years younger than I am, though many years my Senior on this Bench. So he has a fair chance of a reasonable term of service. It soon will be time for me to resolve whether I will leave when I have done my ten years (Dec. 8, 1912) but not quite yet. Meantime I seem to be in good condition and find the work alarmingly easy. When a pen writes best it is nearly worn out. . . . I am like the devil in a gale of wind, *e.g.* I have written two decisions requiring thought, this last week, and have sat

---

[1] Justice White was appointed Chief Justice on December 12, 1910.
[2] Harold Dexter Hazeltine (1871–   ); American-born lawyer, graduate of the Harvard Law School, 1898; University Reader in English Law at Cambridge University, 1907–19; Downing Professor of the Laws of England, Cambridge University, 1919 to date.

---

[1] The letter referred to is missing.

in Court all the week, which means a lot of other outside work. I must stop as a chap is coming to luncheon and after that I must work on the status of some Indians under the 14th amendment.

Ever yours,
O. W. H.

WASHINGTON, January 27, 1911

Dear F. P.:

This is just a line to say that I am deep in Keary's book and am reading it with the greatest pleasure and interest. I always know when you send me a book, whether by yourself or another, that I shall have good cause to be grateful and this is no exception. K. is a very keen chap and while I think, as no doubt you do, that he falls into occasional fallacies (*e.g.*, I think he makes his judgment of existence in the case of the Gods go beyond the phenomenon to accompanying hypothetical explanations) he abounds in vivid *aperçus*, and frequently expresses views which though familiar to you and me are not commonly accepted and are, as I think, profoundly true. Altogether I am having a bully time with him when I get an hour, and I hasten to tell you so. We have just finished *Virginia* v. *West Virginia*[1] for a division of the old debt and today take up Gompers's case and that of John Mitchell[2] (the two labor leaders), and after finishing them on Monday adjourn to try to digest them and Tobacco[3] and Standard Oil.[4] Love to all yours.

Yours ever,
O. W. H.

[1] 220 U. S. 1 (argued Jan. 20, 23–26, 1911; decided March 6, 1911).

[2] Gompers v. Bucks Stove and Range Co., 221 U. S. 418 (argued Jan. 27, 30, 1911; decided May 15, 1911). Mitchell was one of the defendants in this suit.

[3] United States v. American Tobacco Co., 221 U. S. 106 (argued Jan. 3–6, 1910; restored to docket for reargument April 11, 1910; reargued Jan. 9–12, 1911; decided, May 29, 1911).

Standard Oil Co. v. United States, 221 U. S. 1 (1911).

WASHINGTON, February 15, 1911

Dear Pollock:

Many thanks for the *Sonderabdruck*.[1] I have read it with my usual interest in your writing though I never have realized the Corporation entity question as a very burning one. So far as I know I was the first to make Ultra Vires a special topic (5 *Am. Law Rev.*, Jan. 1871) and then it seemed to me to be plain that as when corporations "escape liability for acts beyond their powers, it is not on this ground that such acts are not to be attributed to them, but that they are illegal or at least unauthorized and void, as acts of natural persons would have been under the same circumstances."[2] The expression left something to be desired, but the tendency seems to have been right. I see that in 140 Mass. 494, 501,[3] I did say that the existence of a corporation was a fiction, but that inaccurate phrase was only by way of preface to a proposition that would-be realists sometimes forget: "but the very meaning of that fiction is that the liabilities of the members shall be determined as if the fiction were true." I have this moment distributed an opinion in one of our damned great cases,[4] which I think will be agreed to and I rest from my labor till next Monday. I am pretty tired and mean to get a sleep before the C. J. and others come here to dine tonight.

Let me repeat with what continued pleasure I read Keary to the end, finding so many *aperçus* with which I agreed, that I didn't mind my disagreements.

Since that almost nothing — but old Mosby, the famous guerilla man on the Southern side in and about the Valley (Shenandoah) sent me his book on *Stuart's Cavalry in the Gettysburg Campaign*, which is interesting and instructive as far as I have got. I do not usually as willingly read on those themes.

. . . Love to all.

Yours ever,
O. W. H.

[1] "Has the Common Law Received the Fiction Theory of Corporations?" in *Festschrift Otto Gierke* (1911), p. 105; reprinted in 27 *L. Q. Rev.* 219 (1911), and in *Essays in the Law* (1922), p. 151.
[2] "Ultra Vires: How Far are Corporations Liable for Acts not Authorized by their Charters?" 5 Am. L. Rev. 272, at p. 278.
[3] E. Remington & Sons v. Samana Bay Co. (1886).
[4] Probably Virginia v. West Virginia, 220 U. S. 1 (decided March 6, 1911).

WASHINGTON, February 26, 1911

Dear Pollock:

Leonhard sent me his essay.[1] He translated my book into German but found trouble in getting a publisher. I believe he has lectured on it. But I have not done more than glance at his discourse as I don't read German as easily as you do. I wrote to you apropos of your contribution. The few odd minutes I have had to spare I have given to Plato, recurring to his *Symposium* after fifty years; with a translation alongside I find the Greek easy. My successive reflections have been these: How natural the talk. But it is the "first intention" common to the classics. They have not a looking glass at each end of their room, and their simplicity is the bark of a dog, not the simplicity of art. But they seem to say things that no human being really would say and think. But that criticism shows how small a part of the field of human possibilities any one man realizes. On the other hand, platitudes. But is not this simply an illustration of the flatness of an original work when it has wrought its effects and been followed by centuries — millenia — of development, so that we take for granted what it took a man of genius to say? More specifically, just as Christianity is taken to have brought a new note of love into the world, was not Plato the first to make articulate the high idealizing that we recognize as the best thing in man? No doubt the divine gossip — Aristophanes hindered from discoursing by the hiccups — and Alcibiades more or less drunk describing Socrates — have done much toward floating the dialogue down to us, but is there not a more portentous significance in it, of the kind I mention? I am not quite sure. When I have finished it I may reach conviction.

If I didn't believe that socialism rested on dramatic contrasts and not on a serious consideration of what changes it could be expected to make in the nature or distribution of the stream of products, I should listen to it with more respect. But the argument never gets much farther than look at the big house and

---

[1] Presumably, Rudolf Leonhard, "Ein Amerikanisches Urteil über die Deutsche Besitzlehre," in *Festschrift Otto Gierke* (1911), p. 19. The essay was concerned with Holmes's discussion of possession in his *Common Law*. Pollock apparently had mentioned that essay and other matters in a letter which is missing.

the little one. It never becomes quantitative, asking how much does the tax levied by the rich for the pleasures of the few amount to. Also it never proposes to begin by taking life in hand, which seems to me the only possible starting point for an attempt at social renovation. κ.τ.λ. . . .

Yours ever,
O. W. H.

I shall be 70 March 8! but I probably have said it more than once as it impresses one.

London, March 11, 1911

My dear Holmes:

It is about a thousand years since I looked at the *Symposium*. We should appreciate Plato better if we knew exactly how far the Sophists had got. Meanwhile we know that logic was not yet born: also that (as Thompson [1] used to point out) Plato was a great humourist. Certainly nobody ever talked like his *Dialogues*: nor like Berkeley's and Hume's: nor does anyone really talk like any modern dramatic dialogue, not even Ibsen's. There is no simplicity about P.'s literary art, though his Greek as you truly say is not difficult apart from the difficulty of following what he is thinking about — which Westerns also find in modern Eastern tongues, and modern scholars in medieval studies. Attic talk *ca.* 450–400 B.C. must I think have been rather like the best living French conversation, which differs far less than ours from the language of good books. So you are *aequalis* of Gierke within a few months: I wish you could meet him: he too is a war veteran and still upright and alert.[2] Won't you come to the Historical Congress here in 1913? The *Green Bag*, which I don't much esteem generally, has published a rather good group portrait of your Hon. Court.[3]

Yours ever,
F. P.

---

[1] William Hepworth Thompson (1810–1886), Master of Trinity College, Cambridge, and editor of the *Phaedrus* (1868) and the *Gorgias* (1871).
[2] Pollock had participated in the celebration of Otto von Gierke's seventieth birthday in January, 1911.
[3] 23 *Green Bag* 55 (1911).

WASHINGTON, March 12, 1911

Dear F. P.:

Contracts is here and many thanks for it. It arrived as a birthday present, just after I had turned the great corner of seventy. I see no answer to what you say as to mutual promises. Ames's notion that the act of speaking (utterance), was the consideration struck me as absurd, and you dispose of it. According to a phrase that I sometimes have used it is not the conventional inducement of the counter promise.[1] I stick to my paradox as to what a contract was at common law: not a *promise* to pay damages or, etc., but an act imposing a liability to damages *nisi*.[2] You commit a tort & are liable. You commit a contract and are liable *unless* the event agreed upon, over which you may have no, and never have absolute, control, comes to pass. Were it not so I don't see why Bramwell's suggestion that notice of special consequences before breach, though after the contract was made, is enough would not be sound.[3] However I don't mean to refight the old battle. I had some pleasant things and letters on my birthday though we don't make much of such anniversaries as the Germans do. A day or two before (*i.e.*, last Monday), I fired off a decision in one of our so-called great cases[4] — small enough from the point of view of legal theory, except as reemphasizing our peculiar position in the matter, to which I believe I was the first to call attention in a fight between Missouri and Illinois.[5] We have cases like this one, in which Congress couldn't legislate and so our decision may embody principles that could be changed only by overruling it or a change in the Constitution or a compact between the States concerned with an assent by Congress. The case is *Virginia* v. *West Virginia*. I will send it — not as specially interesting. I put in a summary of bill and answer to satisfy

[1] See Wisconsin & Michigan Ry. Co. v. Powers, 191 U. S. 379, 386 (1903).
[2] In the eighth edition of Pollock's *Contracts* (1911), p. 192, footnote κ, he said: "Mr. Justice Holmes . . . suggests that every legal promise is really in the alternative to perform or to pay damages: which can only be regarded as a brilliant paradox. It is inconsistent not only with the existence of equitable remedies, but with the modern common law doctrine that premature refusal to perform may be treated at once as a breach."
[3] Gee v. Lancashire and Yorkshire Ry. Co., 6 H. & N. 211, 218 (1860).
[4] Virginia v. West Virginia, 220 U. S. 1 (1911).
[5] Missouri v. Illinois, 200 U. S. 496 (1906).

the wish of the C. J. for superfluous longwindedness — the abiding desire of many in these parts.

Give my love to Lady Pollock. Tell her the old man swept round the last post to the home stretch going strong.

Yours ever,
O. W. H.

LONDON, May 3, 1911

My dear Holmes:

Either your dissenting opinion in the *Miles Medical Co.'s case*[1] is right or much of our recent authority here is wrong. In the *National Phonograph Co.'s case*,[2] where very similar agreements were before the Court of Appeal, nobody said a word about holding them bad for restraint of trade. A mutual agreement among the retail dealers to keep up the price would no doubt be in restraint of trade at Common Law. But that, again, was not in the case at bar: nor had you any doubt (as our Court of Appeal had on part of the case in National Phonograph Co.) who the parties to the agreement really were.

It seems to me that the majority of your Honourable Court are being led into an archaic reaction by their anti-monopolist zeal: and I cannot think that any sound doctrine of public policy requires you to favour the cheapening of Dr. Miles's medicines to the citizens of the United States.

The rule that you can't make a covenant run with goods has obviously nothing to do with the case, but seems to have introduced some confusion.

We have read about as much of *Jean Christophe* as you have. It is far above the common run of novels, but the author might have had more regard for the limitations of human life: it must be two or three times as long as Tolstoy's *War and Peace*, and that is surely long enough.

[1] Dr. Miles Medical Co. v. Park and Sons Co., 220 U. S. 373, 409 (1911). The majority of the Court, in an opinion by Hughes, J., held that contracts for price maintenance between the manufacturer of a medicine, made by a secret process, and retail dealers were in restraint of trade and illegal at common law and under the Sherman Act. Holmes wrote a dissenting opinion.

[2] National Phonograph Co. v. Edison Bell Co., [1908] 1 Ch. 335.

I am touching up my *First Book of Jurisprudence* for a third edition: luckily not much to be done for it.

> Yours ever,
> F. POLLOCK

LONDON, May 12, 1911

My dear Holmes:

We have taken passage in the Lusitania for Sept. 9, so we ought to be at New York some time on the 14th–15th and Boston 15th.[1]

The majority of your Court seem to think that a contract between A and Z which on the face of it is not in restraint of trade may be held to be so because B, C, etc. have independently made similar contracts with Z. In other words the construction of A's contract may be affected by the existence of other contracts to which A is not party or privy.

A ma entente ceo est merveillous ley.

> Yours ever,
> F. P.

LONDON, June 21, 1911

My dear Holmes:

Ecce sum e consilio secreto domini regis — whereof I had private notice ten days before — and I have had some score of letters to answer. It is one of the few honours open to a man who has neither official position nor wealth nor political ambitions. Huxley had it, which pleases me all the more. The functions of the Privy Council as a whole are, as you know, long since atrophied. Modern Orders in Council all depend on statutory powers I believe: it is not very likely that I shall ever take part in passing one at a formal meeting.

> Yours ever,
> F. P.

---

[1] Pollock had been invited to deliver the Carpentier Lectures at Columbia University in the fall of 1911.

BEVERLY FARMS, July 6, 1911

Dear Pollock:

Nothing could delight me more than the honor that you
have received. You have deserved it on every ground, character, gifts, achievement, — and it gives me real happiness to
know that you have been appreciated. All the better if it
doesn't call for extra work.

The only event in my quiet life here is that last week I broke
silence for the first time, bar the required Oxford few words,[1]
on the 50th Anniversary of our graduation. Some one always
speaks for the Class and I was asked to do it by the Class officers. I enclose what I said.[2] Apart from that, but far from
strenuously, I try to enlarge and deepen the channels for the
great forces of which I spoke, by reading a *little* philosophy,
science, economics, etc. Bill James's posthumous book[3] did not
impress me much except as literature. I don't know that it
doesn't prove that I fail to appreciate a real difficulty, but his
recurring treatment of Achilles & the tortoise, etc., etc. as real,
serious problems always amazes me. The argument as I understand it is that five minutes is conceptually infinitely divisible,
an infinite series cannot be run out short of eternity, therefore
five minutes equals eternity. That strikes me as bosh. If
infinite divisibility be conceded at all, and I think it well may
be suspected to be an unreal conception, it must be a divisibility
and a series consistent with the postulate, five minutes, and if
you can't state it consistently with that, you can't state it.

A queer thing apropos of my reference to Longfellow.[4] I
had a misgiving that it ought to be *salutant* and asked John
Palfrey to verify for me. He answered that Longfellow's poem
had *salutamus* as I said. I didn't know that Longfellow had
written a poem on it, and on reference found that he had
delivered one at Dartmouth. I certainly never heard him there.
But for many years I have had a visual memory of a man saying

---

[1] See *supra*, p. 155, footnote 1.
[2] See *Speeches*, p. 95.
[3] *Some Problems of Philosophy* (1911).
[4] In his address to the Harvard Class of 1861 Holmes said, "The last time that I
remember witnessing the periodic semi-centennial plunge of a college class was when I
heard Longfellow say 'Morituri salutamus'."

that on Commencement, and for many years I have attached the name Longfellow to the picture in my mind. I can see about where the man stood in the Hall, and I referred to it on the strength of that memory. I wonder what the explanation is — whether it was Longfellow apropos of something else than fifty years out or some other man quoting Longfellow to whom memory had attached his name. I was at a distance and may have been deceived at the time. At all events it is no recent error bespeaking advancing years and failing powers. . . .

Yours ever,
O. W. H.

London, July 19, 1911 [1]

My dear Holmes:

Thanks for your speech, one of your best I think. I know no one else who can strike the right note in few words like that. What you say about making ideals [2] just touches the difference between you and the Pragmatists, who are afraid of making ideals at their own risk and protest loudly that they are making fact: now when the maker of ideals does make facts it is the gift of God, or the Devil, or genius. Muhammad made his ideal a big fact; on the whole, I fear, a bad one. . . .

It is curious about Longfellow and *Morituri te salutamus.* I see no reason why he should not have said it in public twice or oftener: we don't know but that it was a favourite tag with him.

My lectures are getting written in the interestices of other work. I suspect that the nearer I go to professional platitudes the better I shall please my audience.

There is a nest of young pigeons on a windowsill in my chambers in a cupboard full of little used books cut off from the working room. I have verified that your sucking dove is in truth a

[1] A letter from Pollock dated July 19, 1911, is omitted. In it he informed Holmes that Lady Pollock would not accompany him on his trip to the United States, and described briefly the procedure followed at meetings of the Privy Council.

[2] "Man is born a predestined idealist, for he is born to act. To act is to affirm the worth of an end, and to persist in affirming the worth of an end is to make an ideal." *Speeches*, p. 96–97.

fierce and suspicious fowl, being armed with a beak almost as big, for the first fortnight, as the rest of him, which he drives at anything that comes near. The old birds are much tamer.

Yours ever,
F. POLLOCK

I suppose Wm. James's point on Achilles & Tortoise is of this kind. Of course it *is* bosh, but it is very difficult to prove it so in solemn dialectic form. We know it is bosh because it won't fit into the conduct of life, and that is our only real reason. Contrariwise we cheerfully accept paradoxes when we do find them useful. That is all we really know about anything — hence the pragmatic test of truth.

I believe this is a roughly fair statement of his process — not sound in my opinion but easily made plausible. Does the puzzle, or that of summing a series, which is essentially the same, assume infinite divisibility? It is enough if the series (say $1 + \frac{1}{2} + \frac{1}{4} + \ldots \cdot \frac{1}{2^n} + \frac{1}{2^{n+1}} \ldots = 2$) has a number of terms greater than any assignable finite number, which is not the same thing for a mathematician (though I believe the number of terms *is* mathematically infinite). But I doubt if it matters.

BEVERLY FARMS, July 28, 1911

Dear F. P.:

Many thanks for your kind letter, this moment received. I am deeply pleased that you like my speech. I also intended to express a difference from W. J. when I said that we were parts of the whole. I look on man as a cosmic ganglion.

On the Achilles business I still don't see why the supposed logic of the paradox doesn't postulate that an infinite series will take an infinite time to elapse, and so that five minutes supposed to be infinitely divisible equals eternity, whereas the postulate is five minutes, and whatever its divisibility, it has got to be finished in five minutes. Everything else is less certain than that, because it is the postulate on which you work.

I have been reading a recent work on political economy by

my friend Ely of the Wisconsin University [1] which touches on all the burning themes with fairness and moderation. But in all such books I find not much more than the negation of fallacies that I don't believe. I do not get much nourishment except when the writers become sociological (I remember getting much pleasure from Adam Smith) — because there he gives his general views of life. So I have been excusing myself from reading your Marshall [2] of whom I had thought, and instead at this moment am full of Fairfax's Tasso. I did not think it necessary as with Dante to have the Italian alongside as I don't know the language. There is a lot of fine Elizabethan English in Fairfax as I dare say you know. I have noted many quotable lines, and not a few with a poetry of their own: "His face seemed fierce and sweet, wrathful and fair"; "He saw war dim the starlight of his eyes"; "So Latmus shone when Phoebe left the chase, and laid her down by her Endymion's side," etc. Also one or two plays by Brieux and various odds and ends. Flinders Petrie strikes me as an eccentric but a man of ideas. It always is amusing to read suggestive men whom you don't feel bound to believe. I liked his *Janus* though I have forgotten what it said, and now his *Revolutions of Civilization*, with incidental instruction, tickles me with the formula that they culminate first in art, then in riches, then democratize, and then goodnight. When I read old books, I always have a horrid misgiving that I am wasting time, but one of the results of experience is to be able to get more or less of the right pleasure from them. I think the inexperienced generally "dilate with the wrong emotion," like the good ladies who think that they are enjoying Euripides when they take just pleasure in Gilbert Murray's Swinburne & water. I read a while ago the *Oxford Book of French Verse* and renewed my old affirmation that we must correct the judgment of posterity by that of the time. For to posterity it is amazing to see what has hit men where they lived, in the past — bar Villon & Ronsard. Also I refreshed my memory of Flaubert a little. [3] I still don't see why the story of a bourgeois that bored him while he wrote it (see his letters to G.

---

[1] Richard T. Ely, *Outlines of Economics* (2nd ed., 1911).
[2] Alfred Marshall, author of *Principles of Economics* (1890).
[3] From Holmes's Journal it appears that he had recently read *Trois Contes*.

Sand), and bores me when I read it should require long attention although I see in his sentences the result of his writing by
the ear. They would read well aloud — a good test. Love to
all.

Yours ever,

O. W. H.

BELMONT
RYE, SUSSEX
August 11, 1911

My dear Holmes:
What I meant about the Achilles and Tortoise puzzle is
that it does not, on the face of it, involve the mathematical
or metaphysical problems as to the nature of infinity, though
I am not at all sure it does not at bottom. It asserts (and
truly) that, if you insist on counting up the parts of a finite
magnitude in a particular way, you will never have done counting. The practical refutation (of the supposed consequences) is
that if the puzzle is an honest puzzle for a mile it is equally so
for an inch or the $\frac{1}{10^{n+1}}$th part of a millimeter: if it proves anything it proves motion impossible altogether: but motion does
happen (and, as you most truly say, five minutes are done in
five minutes); therefore there is certainly something wrong with
the logic. That, however, may have been precisely the inventor's point — that we have not a satisfying logic for the first
principles of measure and number: which, so far as I make out,
is just what the high mathematicians are now telling us in
formidable books. I don't think they are all agreed that there
is *any* complete logic to be had. B. Russell and Whitehead are
constructing one on a grand scale.[1]
Our Marshall is in fact, if I remember right, a good deal more
sociological than most economists. I read his vol. 1 long ago
when it was new, rather think there has never been a vol. 2.
Some of it is stiffish reading.
With Tasso I have no acquaintance in either original or
translation. I like medieval Italian and can admire good mod-

[1] *Principia Mathematica* (1910).

ern Italian when it is not too full of new words. The 17th century elaboration leaves me pretty cold. I should not wonder if
the Fairfax were quite as good as the Tasso.

Nothing of Flaubert's here: I suppose you refer to *Bouvard
& Pécuchet*: most people do judge it tedious: worth reading
once, all the same. F. always worked with groaning and travail-
ing. I think *L'éducation sentimentale* on the other hand is a
book I mean to read again some day. But don't you think the
Trois Contes a jewel, any way? Loisy,[2] by the way, writes very
well, but he seems to me no more scientific than other people
with the Gospel narrative. They all pick out what suits their
theory and give pretty bad reasons for ignoring the rest. Salomon Reinach agreed with me herein when we met in Paris at
Whitsuntide. . . .

Yours ever,

F. P.

BEVERLY FARMS, August 21, 1911

Dear Pollock:

This in reply to yours. I drop Achilles, even though
tempted to add a word. Have you read Bergson? I did a year
or two ago and lately have reread, this time by accident in a
translation, his *Creative Evolution*. I don't think I spoke of it
when writing to Lady Pollock.[1] If I did, I probably said that
it recalled *Rejected Addresses*: "Thinking is but an idle waste
of thought." I take as little stock in trying to think outside the
intellect as ditto outside time and space. He is suggestive however — among other things, of my old conjectural formula for
the universe as a spontaneity taking an irrational pleasure in a
moment of rational sequence. Also I think his criticism of Greek
philosophy, at the end of the volume, fine. I reread also Tarde's
Psychologie Économique the other day with less delight than I
expected. I think he is a trifle improvisatorial. Now I have
dropped those themes for the moment and have been rereading
the *Purgatorio* in that most convenient little edition published

---

[2] Alfred Loisy (1857–   ); Catholic theologian, excommunicated in 1908 following the publication of his *Évangiles Synoptiques*.

[1] This letter is missing.

by Dent, which I think you mentioned to me, and of which my friend Canon Sheehan of Doneraile [2] sent me his copy, dear man. Less surprise and excitement than the first time of course, but with renewed conviction that D. was the greatest singer ever. But I think one would realize that he was dead if one read only the translation. Do you remember my sending you a memorandum by a certain Franklin Ford [3] (not Lester Ford [4] the sociologist) in which you, like Senator Aldrich and myself, couldn't see much? He sends me newspaper clippings to keep me informed of the movements he is interested in, and the other day a note of some 30 or 40 pages on his views, in which he plainly says, as he has before, that he has done more than Darwin and is a second Copernicus. I believe he has done something and therefore treat him seriously, but I wrote to him that I wished he would tell me what, especially if he has any original transfiguring thought. I have wanted for some years now to find out what it is. He has a burning sense of the greater importance of the organizations not called government, such as the N.Y. clearing house etc. than that of Congress, and his big feeling seems to me to delude him with the idea that he is a great discoverer. I am afraid he is mainly a crank — but cranks sometimes are suggestive. I was much disturbed in mind by your strikes. [5] I know nothing of the particular merits, but it emphasized to my mind that while I believe the economic advantage is on the side of the organization of capital *over* against the organization of labor, labor sees it mainly *against* — and labor has the votes. Hence it is inclined to destroy as an antagonist what is really the most powerful co-operative force. I forget exactly when you sail but I think this will reach you before you do. Love to Lady Pollock and the children. . . .

Yours ever,
O. W. H.

[2] Letters from Canon Sheehan to Holmes and one from Holmes to Canon Sheehan are printed in Herman J. Heuser, *Canon Sheehan of Doneraile* (1917).

[3] See Holmes to Pollock, April 23, 1910.

[4] Probably Paul Leicester Ford (1865–1902); historian and novelist; author of *The Honorable Peter Stirling* (1894).

[5] In June a seamen's strike, joined by dockers and carters, had been called, and on August 17 a national railway strike was called, which, however, was temporarily settled on August 19.

WASHINGTON, December 31, 1911

Dear F. P.:

A happy New Year to you and yours.[1] . . . Your impression as to Ashley on *Contracts* is more favorable than mine. I haven't read it but it seemed to me from casual glances to be a professor's book, without much actuality beyond a certain not very effective sharpness. But I only opened it at random. Just now taking it up to make sure of the name I happened to open on a criticism of a decision of mine that seemed to me not very intelligent — but that had nothing to do with my expression and I stand ready to correct my notions from further knowledge or your more instructed judgment. Harriman in his day struck me as a man of different and very superior timber, and I was confirmed by seeing him last summer. I hope I am not growing dyspeptic in my judgments, but the worthy Bigelow strikes me as appearing in the undisguise of an ass in his later politico-economic lucubrations. It is well enough for Brooks Adams to *pontifier* on matters he doesn't understand, because Brooks after all is an extraordinarily suggestive and interesting man and writer, but he is about the last whose judgment I should follow, and when Bigelow begins to prophesy in his name to my mind he pitiably drools. The two best men that I know of, of the generation or half generation after us, in this country are Wigmore and Roscoe Pound (the latter, I am told, also a distinguished botanist). I was rejoiced that Harvard should have got Pound and wish it had Wigmore as then I should have thought it better equipped than ever. There is a Philadelphian, Bohlen, who is well thought of in Torts. I remember two articles of his — the fact, but not the content, except that he thought he knew more than I did about taking the risk, apropos of a case here, and I thought he didn't.[2] But somehow the Philadelphians while not infrequently having the manners of the great world always have struck me as hopelessly injected with the second rate, when I have seen them in their law, on which they pride themselves — but I would not breathe this aloud.

---

[1] Pollock had visited the United States in the fall of 1911.
[2] Francis H. Bohlen, "Contributory Negligence," 21 *Harv. L. Rev.* 232, 249 (1908), commenting on Holmes's opinion in Schlemmer v. Buffalo, Rochester and Pittsburgh Ry. Co., 205 U. S. 1 (1907).

... I have been working like the devil almost all the time. Now being finished up to Tuesday next I have taken up *Vita Nuova* with Rossetti's translation alongside. Rossetti justifies to my mind my proposition that everything is dead in 25 years. What seemed to that lot (and very likely to all of us, then), exquisite and passionate speech now produces somewhat the effect of the fashions of the same time — self-conscious and faded and more or less bogus. Only the classic simplicity of the *naïf* who know no better and of Mephistopheles who knows enough, last. The rest is like shaking hands with your elbow up to your chin, which tells your neighbor that you are thinking of yourself and not of him — or told, while it was a fashion. As to Dante, as I was saying to someone else, his discourse seems in equal parts from the heart and through the hat. Out of respect for Kohler [3] I have got a new ed. of Hegel's *Philosophy of Law*, and may reread him, though methinks he has not succeeded in convincing me that the King of Prussia was God, in his day.

Do give my love to Lady Pollock and the children and believe me

Ever affly yours
O. W. H.

In my leisure moments in bed or at food I speculate without conclusion whether I had better leave the bench when my ten years are up next year.

London, January 30, 1912

My dear Holmes:

Our Commission on Records is now incubating its first report: [1] the business of the Chairman as I conceive it is to insist on the text being short and readable, to relegate details and authorities to appendices, and if possible to avoid asking for legislation. Incidentally we visit the archives of offices very little known to the public, such as the Ecclesiastical Commis-

---

[3] Joseph Kohler (1849–1919), German jurist.

[1] The First Report of the Royal Commission on Public Records, of which Pollock was chairman, was published in September 1912.

sion and Queen Anne's Bounty: and I plead the work of the Commission to essoin myself from miscellaneous appeals to attend meetings and put the world to rights, and just now Persia in particular. . . .

I have for review in *L. Q. R.* a volume of lectures on reform of procedure by Moorfield Storey:[2] rather pessimist in tone, but it seems to me mostly unanswerable. If I knew of a good young American lawyer who would review it I would gladly turn it over to him. Roscoe Pound in *Amer. Law Rev.* ascribes much of the trouble to the Puritan antinomian or at any rate anti-Common Law spirit, in the main rightly I think.[3] . . .

I have ordered my ascension robe, *viz.* Privy Councillor's uniform — should not grudge the cost if it was ornamental, but it is not — you must have seen it on Bryce once and again. And John Morley, being Lord President, will present me at a levee: which we should scarcely have believed if it had been prophesied to us 40 years ago. Well, if one has not a vocation to go forth and cry in the wilderness — with a big chance of crying the wrong things — one must take the show as it comes!

Yours ever,

F. POLLOCK

Beyond question Ashley is not on the level of Harriman, but he is clever enough to be worth looking at, and knows too much to write mere rubbish, as an English lawyer of the same temper well might. If you see the *L. Q. R.* you will find my review of him there.[4]

WASHINGTON, March 21, 1912

Dear F. P.:

In answer to your, what some people here call, in'-quĭries, I didn't know that Wharton had spawned a book on Contracts.[1] As you intimate, his German reading gave him ideas that hardly became part of his substance and that were too good for

---

[2] *The Reform of Legal Procedure* (1911); noted, 28 *L. Q. Rev.* 225 (1912).
[3] "Puritanism and the Common Law," 45 *Am. L. Rev.* 811 (1911).
[4] 28 *L. Q. Rev.* 100 (1912).

[1] Francis Wharton, *A Commentary on the Law of Contracts* (1882). The letter from Pollock to which Holmes refers is missing.

him, but still there is not infrequently suggestion in his loose fibred books. . . . I am weary with work and some slightly worrying incident of the job, *e.g.* a week ago Monday the C. J. dissented with Hughes & Lamar from a decision by Lurton under the patent law.[2] I didn't care a straw about the case one way or t'other and thought I could have written a better opinion on either side. But the Chief has Irish blood — he is naturally a politician and a speaker — and much as he abhorred the outbreak of Harlan in the Oil and Tobacco cases,[3] I thought he made a stump speech that was no better and that had more tendency to hurt the Court. The result was that while the point decided had been accepted as law in the Circuits for ten years, the newspapers have been flaming and it has been suggested that if the recall were in operation the majority might get the benefit of it. I am too near the time when I can hop off, if I want to, to care personally, but I regretted the performance very much, especially as I thought it not only bad in tone but very thin and beside the point in the reasoning. The printed dissent is more moderate and gives no idea of his oral discourse, though I think it very poor work. All this of course just between ourselves. Some other things have annoyed me. On the other hand, in an opinion a month or two back, I got a chance to pay a compliment to Girard (*Droit Romain*) and sent the opinion to him without more.[4] He sends back his last edition and a charming letter — the last received this morning — after I had written to him, as *non obstant* your advice I didn't venture to, when I read his book some years back. As to strikes present or impending,[5] inasmuch as capital only means society buying,

---

[2] Henry v. A. B. Dick Co., 224 U. S. 1 (decided, March 11, 1912). The complainant in this case, owning the patent on a certain machine, attached to the machine a notice that it could only be used in connection with certain unpatented materials which he manufactured. The defendant, knowing of this restriction, sold to a purchaser of the patented machine unpatented materials of the class described in the license restriction, expecting them to be used in connection with the patented machine. A majority of the Supreme Court, with Holmes concurring, held that the defendant was guilty of contributory infringement of the complainant's patent.

[3] Mr. Justice Harlan wrote dissenting opinions in Standard Oil Co. v. United States, 221 U. S. 1, 82 (1911), and in United States v. American Tobacco Co., *id.*, 106, 189 (1911).

[4] Ker v. Couden, 223 U. S. 268, 276 (1912).

[5] From January through March, 1912, the textile workers in Lawrence, Massachusetts, had been on strike, and throughout the same period there was considerable likelihood of a strike being called by employees of the United States Steel Corporation.

and as I devoutly believe that all such wars are really contests between the different bodies of producers, unfortunately without their realizing it, I possess my soul in patience and expect the limit to what possibly can be done. I must go to work on a mining case,[6] as already I have delayed too long in your agreeable company. My love to Lady Pollock.

Yours ever,
O. W. HOLMES

April 26, 1912

My dear Pollock:

... I received your book[1] and thanked the Columbia people from whom it purported to come. I should have thanked you before this, but you knew my opinion and the press of work made me forget to write. I have had no chance to reread it, though I must confess to having read one book in the interstices of a balled up time — *Present Philosophical Tendencies* — by a young man Perry[2] — very good though I don't agree with all his conclusions. He is a disciple of Bill James and has an appendix on his philosophy which to my mind pretty nearly reduces it to platitudes by freeing it from the ambiguities of the original discourse. It may be that W. J. made a valuable contribution in pointing out that ideas were not necessarily faint pictures of original experience, but on the Will to Believe he seems to come to this, that the body of compulsory truth is admitted, subject to the profound remark that we test it by experience, and that the will comes in in those cases where the result depends on our effort, in which cases our belief may help to bring about the result, *and* that we are warranted in choosing what seems to us the most effective and helpful view in cases where we have no proof either way. The first half of which hardly startles and the last is fishy. The alliance of philosophy with religion and the dogmatic foothold that it gets from a morality from which to bully *nous autres* seems to me to weaken

---

[6] Probably Swanson v. Sears, 224 U. S. 180 (argued, March 15; decided, April 1, 1912).

[1] *The Genius of the Common Law* (1912).
[2] Ralph Barton Perry.

its significance for us hard-headed ones. But just as preachers like Robertson and half way lots like M. Arnold and Clough filled a want half a generation ago, W. J.'s softness to spiritualism and other isms fills one for many now. He was a human being and a temperament and so he charmed the world — with his Irish blood he really contributed to psychology — but I don't think he was strong in logic or in that kind of abstract thinking that needs it. His father before him was bothered with the thought that there were such things as science and rational sequence, and being altogether a man of dramatic *aperçus* wasted pages in trying to be what he wasn't made for. I speak from impressions of many years ago.

Naturally we all have been thinking about the Titanic on which were lost men like Millet the painter, war correspondent, etc. and Archie Butt who were known and loved here. I am afraid the Senator in charge of the investigation [3] has shown a want of good taste and has opened himself to some ridicule. I know him but slightly, but have a kindly feeling toward him. I haven't read the proceedings. Bryce seemed a little stirred up before he left.[4] Perhaps there was a touch of international pride involved, that I didn't think of when we were talking. I am afraid we shall have some pretty hard work and perhaps differences on important matters before we finish but I don't know. I am interrupted by an opinion from Hughes that I must read at once. Poor man — he was kept at work all summer on a post office investigation that the President asked him to go into and he has had no rest since last year.[5] I notice that he says he won't be a candidate unless the President asks him to be — or something like that. *Entre nous* I have noticed a certain reserve in his speech that seems to leave possibilities open. I think a judge should extinguish such thoughts when he goes on the Bench. Love to Lady Pollock.

Ever yours,

O. W. H.

---

[3] William Alden Smith, United States Senator from Michigan.

[4] On a trip to Australia.

[5] By a joint resolution of the Senate and House the President had in 1911 been authorized to appoint a Commission of three persons, one of whom was to be a Justice of the Supreme Court, to investigate the cost of transportation and handling of second class mail. President Taft had appointed Mr. Justice Hughes to the Commission.

LONDON, June 12, 1912

My dear Holmes:

I wish I had known your formula about the action for deceit earlier,[1] though I believe it is better than our ancestors deserve: on the whole I have a poor opinion of their pleading logic. I suspect they shied for a long time at suing in assumpsit on a warranty because they could not believe that a single consideration could support more than one promise, nor yet evade this imaginary difficulty by supposing the consideration for the warranty to be not the contents of the principal contract, but the act of entering into it (a needless fetch, perhaps not wholly sound, but much less sound fictions have passed muster). . . .

Yours ever,

F. P.

BEVERLY FARMS, July 9, 1912

Dear Pollock:

This is begun under the imminent shadow of having my portrait painted for the Mass. Bar [1] but at least it is begun. I sent to you this A.M. opinions and dissents in two conspiracy cases which interested me.[2] The Chief asked me to see if we couldn't

---

[1] In the ninth edition of his *Law of Torts* (1912), Pollock, at page 298, said: "No one now regards an express warranty on a sale otherwise than as a matter of contract; yet until the latter part of the eighteenth century the common practice was to declare on such warranties in tort." In the tenth edition (1916), at page 303, Pollock added to footnote M the following comment on this sentence: "The explanation is concisely given in a judgment of the Supreme Court of the U. S. by Holmes, J., *F. L. Grant Shoe Co. v. Laird*, (1909), 212 U. S. 445, 449: 'No doubt at common law a false statement as to present facts gave rise to an action of tort, if the statement was made at the risk of the speaker, and led to harm. But ordinarily the risk was not taken by the speaker unless the statement was fraudulent, and it was precisely because it was a warranty, that is, an absolute undertaking by contract that a fact was true, that if a warranty was alleged it was not necessary to lay the *scienter*': *cp.* the same learned judge's remarks as a member of the Supreme Court of Massachusetts, *Nash* v. *Minnesota Title Insurance and Trust Co.* (1895) 163 Mass. 574, 587." It would seem likely that Holmes in a letter which is now missing had brought these cases to Pollock's attention.

---

[1] This portrait by Robert Wilton Lockwood, 1861–1914, is now in the custody of the Supreme Judicial Court of Massachusetts.

[2] Hyde v. United States, 225 U. S. 347 (1912); Brown v. Elliott, *id.* p. 392 (1912). In each case Holmes wrote a dissenting opinion in which Lurton, Hughes, and Lamar,

stop the hardship and injustice of snaking men across the Continent for trial as you will see was done and as has been done, and then he wobbled to and fro and lit on the other side—I suspect on his usual ground of the consequences, — that many convictions would be shown to have been without jurisdiction. For thirty years it has been regarded as established doctrine that under the Statute,[3] as at common law, the overt act has no part of the crime. I was able to fire off one or two words and phrases that tickled me a bit. Also, a week or so ago, I went to Williams College to take a degree (beautiful place) and took occasion to let out some of my economic beliefs, which I was glad to do, with Roosevelt talking about the Trusts and the crowd believing what I think fool things.[4] I told them that most people reason dramatically not quantitatively and never ask how much is withdrawn from the total by the palaces and dinners at Sherry's. I am told that 85 per cent of the annual product here and in England is consumed by people with not over 1,000 dollars a year, and whether the figure is right or not I believe that the crowd has substantially all there is. The portrait man has come and gone and begins to paint in the barn across the way at 10 tomorrow — a severe tax on the bowels to be ready at that hour. You remember the New York man Franklin Ford, some exposition of whose I sent to you and you despised? He sent me a long statement of his views that leaves me in doubt whether he is a crank or a genius — with the benefit of the doubt — *quoad* answering etc. He also sent me a German book on Proudhon [5] that I find interesting. . . . Also to finish my affairs I have lately received a German translation of my

---

JJ., concurred. The majority opinion in each case was written by McKenna, J. In the Hyde case the majority held that the defendants who had conspired in California to do illegal acts there, but who had caused the performance of overt acts in the District of Columbia, could be tried for conspiracy in the District of Columbia. Brown v. Elliott presented substantially similar issues.

[3] Rev. Stat., Sec. 5440: "If two or more persons conspire either to commit any offense against the United States, or to defraud the United States in any manner or for any purpose, and one or more of such parties do any act to effect the object of the conspiracy, all the parties to such conspiracy shall be liable to a penalty of not more than ten thousand dollars, or to imprisonment for not more than two years, or to both fine and imprisonment in the discretion of the court."

[4] This speech, it is believed, has not been published.

[5] Arthur Mülberger, *P. J. Proudhon, Leben und Werke* (1899).

book [6] — a very respectable looking volume that I never shall read. All books are dead in 25 years, but luckily the public does not always find it out. . . .

Yours,

O. W. HOLMES

LONDON, July 20, 1912

My dear Holmes:

Thanks for your opinions which I may have a little more time to consider than I should have had a few weeks ago, the First Report of our Commission on Public Records being now signed. The rather intricate etiquette of presenting the report to the King and laying it before Parliament will be satisfied just in time before this session ends, and will constructively cover a lot of appendix stuff still in the printers' hands: then, when Parliament meets in October, the whole thing will be distributed among the estates of the realm, of whom the great majority will never read a word of it, after which it can be published. How every M. P. got the perquisites of having a free copy of the report and proceedings of every Royal Commission I don't know, but in substance it must be that such is the condition express or implied on which the House of Commons makes good the expense.

In octavis S. Petri ad Vincula — vel post gulas Augusti — Anglice, on or about Aug. 7 — we purpose to take our car abroad for the first time and see the castles of Touraine, and then go south to the Tarn country, perhaps running out as far as Toulouse.

Per Roosevelt on a visit to Harvard — authentically related to Jack: It is a privilege to live in a simple community like Arkansas, where you can plug a man in the stomach. He had been infuriated by boys trying to snap-shot him. . . .

I have been reading Wm James's *Essays in Radical Empiricism,* much more fruitful to my mind than the Pragmatism business. . . .

[6] *Das Gemeine Recht Englands und Nordamerikas* (1912), translated by Rudolf Leonhard.

We are perhaps going to have a fight with a Scotch pirate about copyright in the *Law Reports*. It seems to me off hand that the reporter has a good copyright in his report of an *unwritten* judgment (*Walter* v. *Lane*)[1] even if written judgments once handed down are *publici iuris*. But *de his alias*.

Yours ever,
F. P.

LONDON, July 22–23, 1912

My dear Holmes:

I have taken your opinions in *Brown* v. *U. S.* and *Hyde* v. *U. S.*[1] into the country, Rye to wit. . . . For once I am disposed to agree with the majority of the Court: though I am not familiar with the authorities on criminal conspiracy, and the only one I can add is a legendary headnote said to have been made by Sir Gregory Lewin in his *Crown Cases*: Hayricks may be burnt in any county.

On principle it seems to me that conspiracy must be a continuing offence, like trespass, and continues as long as the common unlawful design is in being and capable of execution. Otherwise the offence would be complete and closed at the moment of the first agreement, and nothing happening afterwards would be more than evidence of that specific agreement: and every renewal of the agreement with any addition or variation would be a new offence, creating a theoretic possibility of multiplied and vexatious prosecutions. If it is a continuing offence then every act done in pursuance of the unlawful common purpose is the act of all the conspirators, and (as proof of a continuing agreement then & there) makes a good venue at the place where it is done. This view may be supported by the analogy of the doctrine of continuing trespass in the law of larceny.

The objection that this involves a fiction of constructive presence does not seem to me well founded. Surely there is no

[1] [1900] A. C. 539.

[1] See *supra*, pp. 193–94.

doubt that if I stand in D. C. and throw things at a man in Virginia, or shoot across the Potomac at him, that is an assault in Virginia: and I suppose the offence of demanding money by threats is committed both where the blackmailing letter is written and where it is delivered.

This is in substance identical with the opinion of Marcy, J. of New York,[2] as cited p. 12 of the majority opinion in *Hyde's case*,[3] and consistent with the English authorities referred to on the same page, assuming them to be correctly stated.

So far as to the common law doctrine, which, however, was not directly before you, the indictments being statutory, as I suppose all indictments in Federal jurisdictions are in fact (whether necessarily, I am not competent to say, though I should rather think so if the Constitution itself is counted as a statute).

Nunc ad literam, as medieval commentators say. The text of Section 5440[4] might be literally read as creating two distinct factors of the offence — conspiracy and act — which must concur to found the jurisdiction: and it might further be argued that the act is not merely the completion of the offence, but an independent necessary element, so that Section 731[5] does not apply. The result would be that both the conspiracy and the act must be within the same district. But this would practically reduce the statute to impotence, and so inconvenient a construction must be avoided by any reasonable means. Anyhow no one seems to have maintained it.

If the conspiracy and the act are so connected, according to the plain understanding of a reasonable reader, that the act is the completion of the offence, then Section 731 applies and there is a choice of venue. On the whole this appears to me the common-sense reading.

If the conspiracy is the whole offence, and the act only statutory evidence (a needlessly artificial view to my thinking), then,

---

[2] In People v. Mather, 4 Wend. 229, 261 (1830).

[3] 225 U. S. at p. 365.

[4] See *supra*, p. 194, footnote 3.

[5] "When any offense against the United States is begun in one judicial district and completed in another it shall be deemed to have been committed in either, and may be dealt with, inquired of, tried, determined and punished in either district, in the same manner as if it had been actually and wholly committed therein."

according to the view of the Common Law which I take, the act is still part of the conspiracy and the conspiracy is well laid at either place.

I do not understand the supposed Common Law rule or presumption that a man cannot act at a place where he is not. As a presumption of fact it is contrary to common experience, even before there were mails and telegraph. As a proposition of law it is unworkable without a lot of artificial definition.

It is not for me to form an opinion — even if I had time to make the attempt — whether the weight of modern American decisions and learned opinion is with the majority or the minority.

As for the danger of practical oppression, surely the procedure of Federal courts has some provision for change of venue on cause shown? Anyhow it was about as long a journey from York to Exeter in Blackstone's time as from Portland, Maine to Portland, Oregon at this day: so the Common Law and the U. S. statutes may be tarred with the same brush if they are tarred at all.

I say nothing of the questions which might arise, at Common Law or under the statute, if it were found as a fact that a particular act done by one or more of a number of conspirators in intended furtherance of the common purpose was done without the authority and against the manifest will of others.

Tu. 23 — Coming back to Lincoln's Inn, I do not find that further recourse to the books would enable me to add anything without a more extensive search than I have time for. . . .

Yours ever,
F. P.

BEVERLY FARMS, August 2, 1912

Dear Pollock:

Just time for a line. Of course conspiracy is a continuing offence. I wrote a decision to that effect that I think was not the worst I ever wrote [1] — and I start with that assumption. The whole question turns on the overt act being part of the

---

[1] Probably United States v. Kissel, 218 U. S. 601 (1910).

offence, which it was not at common law *non obstant* doubts &
the custom of laying one in the indictment. For many years it
had been held not to be by our court under the statute. As my
dissent was originally an opinion I did not rub in the decisions
as much as I should have done. On the point of constructive
presence I can't better what I said as I remember it. I think
you pass from presence *secundum quid* to presence *simpliciter*.

I have spent a fortnight in standing for a portrait for the Bar
Association — great success — then this last week in lum-
bago — better now & so haven't read much, a German book &
also Ste. Beuve on Proudhon, a man of insights, who ends by
boring you as all men with isms and panaceas in their head do,
especially if you think you know the answer.

I liked to have him walk into Karl Marx as a plagiarist and
a humbug, after K. M.'s bullying everybody else as a bourgeois
intelligence.

Do you know J. H. Fabre, *Souvenirs Entomologiques*, 10 vols.?
I have them & have read a very little with the impression that
they are truly golden books. V. Hugo called him the Homer of
the insect world I believe. Since my wife got the books there
has been a letter in the papers from the Mirieu [*sic*] poet [2] (I
can't think of his name in a hurry) saying that he was dying of
starvation (which he promptly denied). I believe he is about 90.
Love to all.

Yours,
O. W. H.

VALENCE, le 4 sept. 1912 [1]

My dear Holmes:

We have now turned north from Avignon. You may read
of the Popes' palace in divers authors: we found it being actively restored — not in a bad sense — much fresco has been
rescued from the whitewash of the dark ages (17th–19th centuries to wit), especially a whole room decorated with pleasant

---

[2] Frédéric Mistral (1830–1914); author of *Mirèio*.

[1] A postal card from Pollock dated Poitiers, August 26, 1912, is omitted.

medieval hunting scenes. The Musée Calvet is above the average of provincial collections. . . .

This Valence is a cheerful spacious town finely situated on the Rhône, much open space and a park sloping down to the quay, looks by its extent as if it might have 50,000 inhabitants, in fact about half that number; the only bad thing I have seen in it is a monument to Émile Augier, writer of plays very fashionable under late second Empire and early third Republic, which we could not have made much worse in England. We came here under a brilliant sky with a tearing northerly wind (mistral type) which made driving the car like keeping a ship's head up in a stiff breeze and covered everything with fine limestone dust. *Similiter* on excursion to Nîmes yesterday. The Augustan Temple there is good, but the Pont du Gard, which we took by a very slight deviation on the way back, is better: a magnificent fragment. In the Cévennes we saw a modern French railway viaduct which posterity may perhaps admire as much, and I am sure the Roman engineer of the Nîmes water supply would appreciate if he could have steel construction explained to him. We find Fabre very much in honour here, and have bought a volume or two of him among us. He is alive, about 90 years old, not starving though poor. I am told he has a small pension.

This Panama canal controversy is queer.[2] The best argument I can think of for Taft's contention is that if the dues on American coastwise navigation were actually collected nobody could prevent Congress from returning them, and remitting them beforehand is only doing the same thing *brevi manu*. To which other people may answer that if American shipping is to be subsidized the Government of the U.S. must find a way of doing it which does not conflict with treaties, and if they can get the same result circuitously without breaking treaties that is no reason for setting the bad example of treaty-breaking or

---

[2] In the Hay-Pauncefote Treaty of 1902 between Great Britain and the United States it was provided that the Canal, when completed, "shall be free and open to the vessels . . . of all nations . . . on terms of entire equality so that there will be no discrimination against any such nation . . . in respect of the conditions or charges of traffic or otherwise." The Canal Bill of 1912, signed by President Taft on August 24, provided that American vessels, engaged in coastwise trade, might use the Canal free of tolls.

sharp practice, but rather the contrary. I dislike the whole tone of the discussion, so far as I gather it from scrappy notices available in such papers as we see, and fear it tends to play into the hands of the militarists and despisers of good faith among nations.

We have had one disappointment: the spring of Vaucluse, Petrarch's favourite spot, is as cockneyfied as Hampstead heath, and vulgarity in this romantic South is if anything more vulgar than in the north. Still the site cannot be quite spoilt.

Yours ever,

F. P.

BEVERLY FARMS, September 15, 1912

Dear F. P.:

This is the time of your getting home, by your card, and it should be in London to greet you. I envy you the trip. Lately I have been filling my leisure hours with little volumes of the Home University Library which give one more or less the *dernier cri* on various themes from the History of England (250 pages!), or Industrial Evolution — to Architecture, Anthropology, Psychology, or Psychical Research. They generally give one a fillip or a fact. The book on architecture I thought extremely good [1] — and what lots of words I didn't know the meaning of. Bertrand Russell's *Problems of Philosophy* I thought poor. I never read anything of his before, but it seemed to me that I could have added a more fundamental page. I should gather that the series is conducted by gents who believe in the upward and onward rather more than I do. My *pièce de resistance* is Fabre's *Souvenirs Entomologiques*, with which we wind up our evenings. I believe I have said before to you or Lady Pollock — to whom my love — that Fabre seems to me the source of the echo from behind phenomena that for a moment one thinks one hears in Maeterlinck's *Bees*, as well as some features in Bergson's philosophy. I like a book that adds to the known features of the unknown, as this seems to show it, prophecying the future and implanting the prophecy in a worm. You people

W. R. Lethaby, *Architecture* (1912).

have a great advantage in being able to pick up so much history and aesthetics simply by living in your *milieu*, not to speak of the greater number of people of education and insight with whom you talk. By way of exception I dine out tomorrow to meet the President, and a little after you receive this go to a college club that gives me a dinner. I have not been to a meeting of it since I was in college! They once asked me for an inscription for a tablet in the Club, for those who were killed or perished from disease in the wars of Secession and with Spain. I don't think I ever mentioned it. I thought I got out of it rather well. . . . The name of the Club was Α. Δ. Φ. (I don't know what the letters stand for, & now it is called the A. D.):

> "Α Δ Φ
> In this bronze are cast the names of the
> Men of the Club who died in war for their faith.
> 1861–1892 (if the last date is right)
> Lest we forget."

(& then the list of names underneath). I made it years ago before the quotation from Kipling had become so hackneyed. Soon now, that is early in October, I return to Washington but feeling so free in the thought that by December I can leave whenever I want to. . . .

Yours ever,
O. W. H.

Sussex ss., September 24, 1912

My dear Holmes:

We got a volume of selections from Fabre (I think I told you) and very good stuff it is, with a little touch of unfamiliar constructions as if he would rather have written in Provençal: which I am emboldened to think because a learned friend of Toulouse and a good writer on French legal history, Brissaud, told me when we met in Paris in 1900 that he did not regard French as his real mother tongue. Compared to Fabre's insects of sorts Maeterlinck's bees are thin artificial creatures, posing for irrelevant biped moralizing. I don't find that Fabre has much to say about the fantastic prodigality of devices in the insect world, which to me is even more striking than the ingenuity. But as to the wastefulness of nature Berkeley said long ago (in effect, much more elegantly of course): "Why should the Creator economize unlimited resources?"

As to Bertrand Russell's little book I do not agree, not meaning thereby that I do agree with all his opinions, but that his business was to explain to an assumed intelligent reader, knowing little or nothing of philosophy, what philosophy is about, what the main questions are, and why you are driven to them in one shape or other when you try to get behind rule of thumb in anything whatever. Speaking from recollection, for I read the book before the vacation and have left it in London, I think he has done that very well: perhaps there is a want of artistic uniformity in the extent to which he discloses his own preferences at different points, but I don't believe any man could help it. I am free to confess however that Whitehead's *Introduction to Mathematics* in the same series is even more interesting to me (he is another youngish and very able Cambridge mathematician, and jointly with B. Russell has produced a work which only about a dozen men are competent to judge, if so many).[1] One learns from him that even in the exact sciences correct results have been arrived at by processes which were inadequate or indeed wrong, so that some of our leading cases are no worse than Taylor's theorem (we fudged even the binomial theorem in our youth, so Russell once told me), and yet the outsider's criticism is generally not only wrong but on wrong lines. In that volume, again, Whitehead does not profess to teach mathematics, but to show what its methods are and to put the fundamental ideas on a sound footing.

That is a good inscription, but I would not answer for every man who went into the war of 1898 at any rate having done it as an act of faith. It is still the human nature of a good many men to like adventures, and fighting not less than other kinds, international peace societies notwithstanding. Just now the Ulster Orangemen offer a complex bit of psychology:[2] how

---

[1] *Principia Mathematica* (1910).
[2] On September 6 an open-air meeting, presided over by Sir Edward Carson, was held in Enniskillen to protest against the Home Rule Bill. In a riot at Belfast on September 15 one hundred persons, more or less, were injured.

much of their talk is genuine fanaticism, how much Irish devilry, how much calculated bluff to impose on the peace-loving Englishman? Someone has been reminding them that in fact the Pope wholly disapproved James II's conduct and went as near blessing William III as he could with a heretic. Your true blue Protestant is incapable of seeing nice distinctions between different sorts of Papishes.

Yours ever,
F. P.

I wonder if the expansion of Α Δ Φ is as bad Greek as that of Φ Δ Φ (the specific secret of which is safe enough with me, for I have forgot the words but I know they are ungrammatical).

Where did I write from last, Tours or Avignon? anyhow before we were at Fontainebleau and saw the rooms Napoleon occupied as First Consul, left — or perhaps a little restored — exactly as he used them: one has to make interest with the custodian to discover that they exist — to me much more interesting than the rather overblown Francis I decorations freshened up by Louis Philippe. . . .

WASHINGTON, December 15, 1912

Dear F. P.:
Your letter and documents received yesterday.[1] As to the difference between civil and criminal contempt [2] there is a discussion by Lamar in *Gompers* v. *Buck Stove and Range Co.*, 221 U.S. 418. Early in my judicial experience I wrote a decision on the extent of the privilege in publishing legal proceedings, *Cowley* v. *Pulsifer*, 137 Mass. 392 (in 1884). I remember that *The Nation* pitched into it and don't remember much else.[3] In a divorce case once I remember saying that if reporters saw fit to withdraw out of hearing I thought it would be a very proper and considerate thing, and I let the woman testify in a very low voice. I think some of my predecessors had heard cases *in camera* but I don't think I ever did.

[1] The letter and papers referred to are missing.
[2] 29 *L. Q. Rev.* 8 (1913), discussing Scott v. Scott, [1912] P. 241.
[3] See 39 *Nation* 7 (July 3, 1884).

I have been pretty busy and still am. This last week besides sitting in Court I wrote two decisions to be fired off tomorrow,[4] and had to be ready on about fifty cases (including those argued) for Saturday's conference. We dined out nearly every night, but I don't work at night.

Last Sunday, December 8, was just ten years, according to the Reports, from the day I took my seat. So now I am entitled to retire, and while I don't I am working for nothing, so to speak, as my pension would equal my salary. I don't intend to hop off while I feel all right and believe that I am as good as ever. When a man has made one outlet his only channel of experience for so many years, and when it is too late to expect to master a new subject and to produce results from it, it seems wise until one is ready for idleness to try to do as much as one can in one's chosen way. I am pretty sure they all want me to stay on.

As to your kitten we had the noblest cat in the world, and it was chloroformed last summer because a horse doctor said some fool thing about what was the matter with him, that all too late we disbelieved. Have you seen Wigmore's Continental Legal History series? I know, yes, for are not you to introduce a volume as I did, one?[5] The translation of Brissaud[6] has a lot of frightful blunders of detail, but the book itself strikes me as making one feel and realize the evolution of law and correspondence of change to change of circumstances more than any history I ever read. I observed with pleasure that he constantly cites Pollock and Maitland. . . .

I must shut up & go to work.

My love to Lady Pollock & the children.

Yours ever,
O. W. HOLMES

A Merry Christmas to you all.

---

[4] Robertson v. Gordon, 226 U. S. 311; Murray v. Pocatello, *id.*, 318 (1912).

[5] Holmes wrote an introduction to the first volume of the series, *A General Survey of Continental Legal History* (1912), reprinted *C. L. P.*, p. 298; Pollock wrote an introduction to the eleventh volume, *The Progress of Continental Law in the Nineteenth Century* (1918).

[6] Jean Brissaud, *A History of French Private Law* (1912), vol. 3 in The Continental Legal History Series.

LONDON, March 1, 1913

My dear Holmes:

Thanks for the New York Speech.[1] I am very glad you have put your ideas of the real economic facts into print. I only hope they will get adequate hearing.

The further practical question is: If the State undertook the irrigation of society with the stream of products, the State would have to be paid for it, and would the work on the whole be done better or cheaper or even more justly than by the selfish (but unconsciously automatic) distribution of the capitalist? To which I see no universal answer: it varies with the nature of the goods to be distributed and other conditions. Evidently you can't turn competing capitalists loose on the water supply of a city. So far I go with the Socialists as to think it a pretty general rule that, where monopoly is necessary, it is better in public hands. (And so, I think, is the spirit of the Common Law.) You regard the visible luxuries of the rich as mere brilliant shavings from a great machine tool, quite rightly I think. But the world has to learn that the actual pleasure derived from such things is of rather low quality on the whole, and less even in quantity than it looks to those who have not tried it. This is what the East can teach us, and is beginning to teach us though not always in the wisest way. I should like to meet an American Baháist—there are said to be many. We have had Abdu'l Bahá (the successor of the Báb) here twice. I did not see him: he seems to be like all official prophets. The keys to that very curious movement are in Gobineau's *Religion et philosophie dans l'Asie centrale* and E. G. Browne's *A Year among the Persians* — both fascinating books. Get hold of one or both if you don't know them.

We have lost Macnaghten, and Parker[2] takes his place, leaping over the Court of Appeal. I have seldom known an appointment so universally expected and accepted as being the obviously right one. Parker's opinions in the House of Lords will be more

[1] "Law and the Court," speech delivered at a dinner of the Harvard Law School Association of New York on February 15, 1913; *Speeches*, p. 98; *C. L. P.*, p. 291. If Holmes wrote to Pollock when sending him his speech, the letter is missing.

[2] Sir Edward Macnaghten, Baron Macnaghten, died February 17, 1913, and Robert John Parker, Baron Parker, was appointed Lord of Appeal in Ordinary, March 4, 1913.

visibly learned than Macnaghten's, not quite so human I should think.

I am full of Public Records for a goodish while yet to come, and the Historical Congress is impending in London a month hence. Gierke and his wife are coming to stay with us. I wonder how much English they can speak; at Berlin we spoke German all the time.

You might be a little interested by my account of our divorce controversies in the January number of the *L.Q.R.*[3] Many of the reformers, unluckily, give themselves away by lack of scholarship.

Yours ever,
F. POLLOCK

BURTON HALL, LINCOLN,[1]
August 13, 1913

Dear F. P.:

... I have been here [2] since Saturday inclusive, and return to Morley's Hotel tomorrow, expecting unless countermanded to pass Sunday with Leslie Scott (the last Sunday on this side). The French trip fell through because he was directed to rest, but it is just as well for I have been having a most delightful time here, with a simple joy in life that heretofore has been strange to me, as I have been a helpless spectator of misery after misery. You know what I refer to in London, and at Doneraile, beside the fact that Castletown has not yet fully recovered from his nervous collapse and sees things with a downward inflection, if I may mix metaphors, the Canon [3] considered himself a dying man and though we had a cheerful daily talk, *that* was in the background. Before I left he asked me to choose a book from his library, with the result that I sent a folio

---

[3] 29 *L. Q. Rev.* 85; reprinted *sub nom.*, "Reformation and Modern Doctrine of Divorce," *Essays in the Law* (1922), p. 279.

[1] Holmes was in Ireland and England in the summer of 1913. A letter dated April 20, 1913, in which he discussed the possibility of making a trip to England in the summer is omitted, as is another from Pollock, dated August 9, 1913.

[2] Burton Hall is the family seat of Baron Monson.

[3] Canon Sheehan.

Suarez *De Legibus* home by parcel post. He thought that Suarez was the *ne plus ultra* of original philosophy, as to which I naturally remain a sceptic till converted. Well, *mon vieux*, I expect to sail on the 23rd and probably this is my last from England. I tried to tell Lady Pollock how much I thank her and you, and I trust you will take that for granted without my attempting to say more. Do give my love to her. This is an ideal spot with family portraits where they belong and reaching a good way back, old books (lots of incunabula), and a host and hostess who are most considerate without your feeling it a burden, also two very nice gairls on the hair trigger to ideas in the way that young women sometimes seem to be here. Goodbye dear old friend. Don't forget the venerable jurist.

Yours ever,
O. W. H.

August 15, 1913

Postal Card, Pollock to Holmes

I never heard before of so much being claimed for Suarez, though he was no doubt the last, or almost, of the eminent scholastic moralists. All I know of him at first hand is the passage supposed to show prophetic insight about the nature and importance of international law — which in my opinion it does not: he thought the duties of princes & rulers to each other a matter of simple deduction from settled ethical principles, and (*semble*) almost too easy to be worth systematic pursuit. But what think you of this for an original law tract? "A false & feign'd Fee Simple truly determin'd, and the estate of paternal authority claim'd by Adults qualified by its proper conditions and demonstrated to be meerly precarious and grounded in wrongful Intrusion. By B. W., spinster, and to be sold at the sign of the Distaff in St. Powles Churchyard." I am sure my granddaughter [1] is meditating this, if I rightly construe her utterances.

F. P.

[1] Elizabeth Mary Williams, born 1913, daughter of Alice Pollock Williams.

CHERRY ORCHARD
FOREST ROW, SUSSEX
August 18, 1913

My dear Holmes:

... My granddaughter is certainly meditating her tract against the usurped estate of adults, the Naughtinesse of Long-Cloaths, the Iniquitie of Needles & Pins, and the damnable Superfluitie of Ribands.

That is only part of the title. It will begin:

"The Disseised Infants Assize — wherein the false and fayn'd Fee Simple of Parental Authority is truly determin'd, qualify'd by its proper Conditions, and shown by plain and perspicuous Reasons to be meerly Precarious and commenced in wrongful Intrusion. . . . And the Cause carry'd by way of just & necessary Appeal to the High Court of Natures Originall Lawes. Together with the Restoration of Wisdom despis'd in the Mouth of Bottle-Sucklings. By B. W., Spinster, to be sold by Mrs. Freeborn at the sign of the Distaff in Powles Churchyard."

By way of something to bite on, I have here Sir W. Jones's *Essay on Asiatic Poetry* — a wonderful performance for a young man — written in good Latin and giving extracts in Arabic, Persian, Turkish and Hebrew: and this when Oriental texts, at any rate secular literature, had to be read in ms. and the apparatus of lexicons, etc. (far from perfect yet) was extremely defective and cumbrous. The mistakes in transcription and printing are enough in the Persian (probably also in the other tongues of which I know nothing) to give one a fair amount of critical exercise. Jones worked largely with copies made by himself, at Oxford I think, which he was unable to collate with the originals afterwards. (Many years later he tackled Sanskrit at Calcutta, and was the first Englishman who really knew much of it.)

You are like to have a fair wind for your voyage, which nowadays makes little difference to the ship, but counts for something in the amenity of the promenade decks. By the time you are home we shall be touring in Wessex.

Yours ever,

F. P.

LONDON, October 17, 1913

My dear Holmes:

Thanks for the photograph of your picture. We think it makes you look too ancient and solemn, as if dissenting, and exercised in your conscience about it. Now your dissenting judgments are to me joys forever. And (if the photograph is not unjust) your painter has left out the joy. . . .

We have Indian summer here after rain and chill at Madrid: but the climate of that capital is nearly as bad by the act of God as its roadways are by the act or rather default of man (much worse than New York).

No more this mail.

Yours ever,
F. P.

LONDON, January 9, 1914

My dear Holmes:

Santayana's last volume[1] is quite brilliant — we read it some months ago. I quite agree with you that he scores neatly off the Pragmatists and also Bergson.

Just now we have been reading C. Eliot Norton's letters. I am glad I knew the man, for the letters do leave a certain taste of flatness (in the sense that *Superficies* or Flat = *longuenso* × platitude) which was not in his converse. But anyhow I should think well of him for two things: that he was a friend of Leslie Stephen's and that he mistrusted Froude at sight. And one feels a rather special respect for a man who, not being of the robust mood to which it is all in the day's fun, is not afraid of sticking to an unpopular opinion. Then his scholarly faculty was re- markably sound: though I don't know that he would have admired the Middle Ages so much if his medieval studies had extended to judicial records.

Your ambassador[2] and his wife were at lunch with us to- day — excellent company both — to meet the Grand Duke

[1] *Winds of Doctrine* (1913).
[2] Walter Hines Page.

Michael of Russia and his morganatic wife who can only be called Mme. de Brassova, for marrying whom he is at present in disgrace at his very inferior brother's court. . . .

Yours ever,
F. P.

P.S. I see a story about your Chief retiring and Taft succeeding him. But why should White want to go? And how about the cost of reconstructing your bench?

WASHINGTON, January 28, 1914

Dear Pollock:

Until the next adjournment I am no good for a correspondent. This last week, while sitting, I wrote three decisions (not that I wrote while arguments were going on), and right along I have been at it about as hard as I can be. The average interest beyond the general one of untying knots has not been high. That depends on what we have and the Chief Justice, but still I have had amusement and plenty of occupation. I am glad that we agree as to Santayana. . . . C. Eliot Norton *was* a flat, a very cultivated one, one having some good as well as some bad qualities, and representing or retaining a Boston tradition that made him speak in public like a gentleman — but still a flat. Bill James used to say that in one hundred years he would be the dark planet believed to be greater than all the shining ones, because of the many correspondences with the illustrious, all treating him with deference, and of his having had the wit to suppress his answers. Now I suppose they are out. I will speak of him no more, except to note that no doubt many or some were indebted to him for kindness, and for a contact with cultivation otherwise inaccessible to them. But Oh Lor — Did you ever hear of his beginning a lecture to one of his classes: "Probably none of you ever has seen a gentleman"?

I am glad you like Page & wife. They both impressed me very favorably. I don't believe he walks softly before (a) Lord, and she seemed to me simple, self-possessed, not pretending to be other than she is, and knowing her own mind. If I think of it tomorrow I will try to get copies of one or two of my late cases that may interest you a little; one showing the hair trigger working of business in N. Y.,[1] the other having a slight touch of long abandoned antiquarian conjecture in the interest of a principle.[2]

At present I read nothing. Fanny has read to me some letters of Mme Calderon de — — in Everyman's Library,[3] astonishingly vivid yet the better part of a century old. Also a notice of an American poet, Holmes, who with the vendor of pies, of that name, in Washington, has done something to make the name worthy of remembrance. No relation of mine, so far as I know, dead, but in his life time playing weird and tragic variations on Mother Goose, which from the extracts I much desire to see.[4] I have not yet got the book. I must shut up. Love to Lady Pollock.

Yours ever,
O. W. H.

LONDON, March 18, 1914[1]

My dear Holmes:
Those cases of your are both interesting. In *LeRoy Fibre Co.* v. *Chicago M. & St. P. R. Co.*[2] I think you and the Chief Justice are right. But I find it hard to understand how nine men can ever agree in judgments depending on the precise effect of saying Yes or No to clumsy and involved questions.

---

[1] Perhaps National City Bank v. Hotchkiss, 231 U. S. 50 (decided Nov. 3, 1913).
[2] Probably Trimble v. Seattle, 231 U. S. 683 (decided Jan. 5, 1914).
[3] Madame Calderon de la Barca, *Life in Mexico* (undated).
[4] Daniel Henry Holmes (1851–1908), author of *Under a Fool's Cap* (1884).

---

[1] This letter appears to be responsive to one from Holmes which is missing.
[2] 232 U. S. 340 (decided February 24, 1914). The plaintiff in this case sued for the destruction of straw by a fire negligently set by one of the defendant's engines. The majority of the Court, in an opinion by McKenna, J., held that the plaintiff's act of storing inflammable straw on its own premises near an operating line of the defendant's railroad was not evidence of negligence on the plaintiff's part which should go to the jury. Holmes, partially concurring, said that the question could not be answered in such categorical terms as those used by the majority, and that if the plaintiff's straw was stored unreasonably near the defendant's tracks then plaintiff's negligence might bar it from relief. White, C. J., concurred in Holmes's opinion.

Fire carried in locomotives has apparently long ceased, on your side, to be treated as an "extra-hazardous" risk — whether by statutes, charters of railroad corporations, or otherwise.

In the Seattle case [3] I should have thought it arguable that the State, as a matter of public law, cannot deprive itself of the right to tax, but that the State, as a landholder, is under the rules of private law and can covenant by express words to indemnify a lessee against future taxes imposed by its own public legislation, and if by express words why not by necessary or usual implication? Assuming good faith of course: an unjust steward might conceivably play tricks on an intolerable scale. Contrariwise I suppose Henry George's school think it would be all right for the State to make leases and then tax the lessee out of them (though, on the economic rules accepted by that school, the total amount the State could get anyhow in rent plus tax would have a constant maximum).

. . . Vinogradoff has brought out an interesting Shillings worth of *Common Sense in Law*: & Baldwin of Vassar a learned study of the King's Council [4] — almost too many trees to make a wood, perhaps.

Our Commission on Public Records is in travail of a Second Report dealing with the archives of Government Departments. It will give the fullest list of departmental offices & sub-offices — including some obscure judicial survivals — known to have been yet published. . . .

Yours ever,

F. P.

[3] Trimble v. Seattle, 231 U. S. 683 (1914). In this case land had been leased by the plaintiff from the State of Washington. Such a lease ordinarily contained an implied covenant that the lessor would pay all taxes and assessments levied on the property. Subsequently, acting under newly adopted statutes, the defendant city assessed the plaintiff for certain local improvements. The Supreme Court of the United States, in an opinion by Holmes, affirmed the decision of the state court that the assessment was valid and did not unconstitutionally deprive the plaintiff of contract or property rights.

[4] James Fosdick Baldwin, *King's Council in England during the Middle Ages* (1913).

London, May 20, 1914

My dear Holmes:

Behold I too am a judge — of a sort: A. Cohen's [1] successor in the venerable office of Admiralty judge of the Cinque Ports: and a fellow came yesterday to photograph me for the press, but I prefer my own sketch in the Cubist manner as enclosed. The work apparently consists of about one case in four years,

, The Lord Warden's Official

and the ceremonies of installing the Lord Warden when there is a new one, which now there is, and I shall have to do it in July. I feel that there ought to be silver oars and three-cornered hats but am waiting for information. The books say the Court is older than the Lord High Admiral's, and I look forward to amusing times of grubbing in the records, which I have already seen in a superficial way on behalf of the Commission on Public Records. Cohen resigned, being very old and hardly fit to go through a ceremony. The fees are like nominal damages, too small to count in the category of assignable quantity. When you are here next I shall try to drag you to Dover.

[1] Arthur Cohen (1830–1914). Pollock wrote an obituary notice of Cohen in 113 *Spectator* 669 (Nov. 14, 1914).

Haldane [2] asked me last week to a tobacco talk of *Derry* v. *Peek* [3] and the possibility of minimizing its consequences. The Lords are going to hold that it does not apply to the situation created by a positive fiduciary duty such as a solicitor's,[4] in other words, go as near as they dare to saying it was wrong, as all Lincoln's Inn thought at the time.

Also there has been a great exposition of money had and received and following assets, in the final appeal on the Birkberk bank smash. This should be published in July.[5] *Dominus Cancellarius* says to me privily that counsel nowadays don't know their authorities properly: I wonder how you find it at Washington.

A volume of Rudolf Eucken (in a seemingly competent translation) has come from the circulating library. I have never read anything of his but have a suspicion of *squish.*

Yours ever,
F. POLLOCK

WASHINGTON, May 28, 1914

Dear F. P.:

I salute my brother Judge! I always rejoice at every honor or pleasure that comes to you, of course, and I do doubly as this brought out your gifts as an artist. I am delighted at the cubist portrait and, but that it might make a wrong impression on the vulgar — I cannot confine the entrance to my library to the elect — I think I should frame it with the letter on the reverse. . . . As to your silver oars, after my late brother Brown persuaded us that the admiralty jurisdiction extended to the Erie Canal [1] I suggested that a donkey, or at [least] mule shoes, would be more appropriate, but it hasn't been acted on. As to *Derry* v. *Peek* my memory is not fresh enough for me to

---

[2] Richard Burdon Haldane, Viscount Haldane, Lord Chancellor, 1912–15.

[3] 14 App. Cas. 337 (1889).

[4] Nocton v. Ashburton, [1914] A. C. 932.

[5] Sinclair v. Brougham, [1914] A. C. 398.

[1] The Robert W. Parsons, 191 U. S. 17 (1903); Brewer, J., Fuller, C. J., Peckham, J., and Harlan, J., dissenting.

recite. My impression is that it illustrated what I like to show everywhere in the law that every distinction is a matter of degree and that controversies are apt to be fierce in proportion to the nicety of the question. The average lawyer wants the absolute, and I have shoved my notion upon my brethren here as formerly in Mass. *ad nauseam.* This morning I shall circulate an opinion on that theme which in its original form was received with silent loathing and which as rewritten I doubt if the boys will like much better.² Otherwise I am in good shape; everything written and delivered, except one little case just given in, which I think will go through without much objection, though I have put in a phrase or two that I have some hope may give pain.³ On Monday I fired off a decision that the owner of the *Teutonic* [*sic*] was entitled to the benefit of the American limitation of liability as to suits brought here.⁴ Our first impression was otherwise or doubtful, but when I got pen in hand I thought there was no doubt, and all but McKenna came in, Lamar absent making peace with Mexico,⁵ and Lurton not taking part. It is very hot here but the papers say hotter at other places on the Atlantic Coast, with snow west of the Mississippi, so I am glad my work is done. I find myself thinking of the quiet field in the rear of your house and the little children playing there. I do not omit the inhabitants of the house at such moments. I have not yet had time to read much. Livingston, *The Greek Genius & its Meaning to Us,*⁶ I think charming. It puts more forcibly and strikingly what one knew in a general way, and

---

² Perhaps International Harvester Co. v. Kentucky, 234 U. S. 216, (decided June 8, 1914), McKenna and Pitney, JJ. dissenting.

³ Probably Keokee Coke Co. v. Taylor, 234 U. S. 224 (decided June 8, 1914). The court in this case sustained the constitutionality of a Virginia statute which forbade miners and manufactures to issue orders for their face value in lawful money of the United States. In disposing of the contention that the statute unconstitutionally discriminated against certain classes of employers, Holmes said: ". . . . while there are differences of opinion as to the degree and kind of discrimination permitted by the Fourteenth Amendment, it is established by repeated decisions that a statute aimed at what is deemed an evil, and hitting it presumably where experience shows it to be most felt, is not to be upset by thinking up and enumerating other instances to which it might have been applied equally well, so far as the court can see." *Id.*, at p. 227.

⁴ The Titanic, 233 U. S. 718 (1914).

⁵ Justice Lamar in May had been sent by President Wilson to Niagara Falls, Canada, as a commissioner to the mediation conference to adjust the differences between the United States and Mexico which grew out of Wilson's refusal to recognize Victoriano Huerta as President of Mexico.

⁶ By Richard Winn Livingstone. The first edition of the book was published in 1912.

in stating what we should have to give up if we had their direct-
ness he hardly recognizes the distinctively modern and that
our losses would not only be bogus Latin pastorals, — *Idylls of
the King*, etc. — but *Hamlet, Tristram Shandy, Faust* & *Mona
Lisa*. But the book is delightful. I would rather read it than
Plato, but I frankly prefer the modern straight through. As to
Eucken, I remember seeing somewhere that the three leaders
of European thought were Bergson, Eucken & another that I
forget. That led me to look at a book of Eucken's when I saw
it, but I surmised that it was not for me. Bergson I think in
the main a humbug agreeably pinned to paper by Santayana.
Give my love to the kindest of hostesses and the beloved
friend of

Yours ever,
O. W. H.

V

1914-1918

My dear Holmes:

Here we are in a general European war. The cables will anticipate anything I could say about its present state. I will only observe that the discipline of the press has been fine. Everybody was talking in private about the departure of our expeditionary army, and not a word of it in print till yesterday morning when it was announced that it was actually in France and on its way to the front, guarded by the silent pressure of our sea power — about which we hope for a profitable commentary from Mahan in due season. At present we know of just six shots fired by our fleet, all effective; they sunk a mine layer and a submarine, exactly where is not disclosed. Guesses at the length of the war vary from six months to three years. Paper currency of £1 notes and postal orders (become legal tender) are all the signs of war in this rustic inland region, which is off the military routes. Trade is much less disturbed than was expected. I am wondering whether I may have to exercise the prize jurisdiction of the Cinque Ports Admiralty Court. William of Berlin is like to make a united Ireland whatever else he makes or destroys. Well, if it had to be I am content that it comes while I am alive and have my wits still about me. Official German mendacity seems to be making wonderful flights, of which you probably see more than we do. Our French friends on the contrary are keeping their heads admirably.

Yours ever,
F. POLLOCK

BEVERLY FARMS, *August 30, 1914*

Dear Pollock:

A line from you this morning. I wrote a few days ago to Lady Pollock telling how I, like the rest of us, prayed for your success against this march of Tamerlane. I suppose that every week's delay is to your good as enabling Russia to bring her pressure to bear. There is no use in talking about it, but my heart aches with you all.

Have you taken to reading prize cases? Sprague's decisions had much repute in that direction. He was a Mass. U. S. District Judge, who could read nothing, having to keep his eyes screened, but had so trained his memory that I believe he never made a mistake about the testimony & facts of a case.

I have been reading philosophy and economics and Everymans Library. Much of August was taken up with the *Nicomachean Ethics*, Descartes, Berkeley, Ricardo and Malthus. Think of my never having read the *Nic. Ethics* before. I was amazed to see how much later thinking and even English law had been affected by him — or rather had found their seed in him. Even John Adams in the Mass. Constitution "that this may be a government of laws and not of men" — though he may have got it indirectly through the French, as I have seen Quesnay quoted for the same thought.

Malthus pleased me immensely — and left me sad. A hundred years ago he busted fallacies that politicians and labor leaders still live on. One thinks that an error exposed is dead, but exposure amounts to nothing when people want to believe.

I could talk for an hour, but I am ashamed to speak of anything else while your struggle is on, and as to that can utter little more than an ejaculation. If I had the religious gifts of the German Emperor I should give up books for my knees and pray all the time between meals. I certainly should not be afraid of the form, God defend the right.

Yours ever,
O. W. H.

My most affectionate remembrances to Lady Pollock.

LONDON, September 15, 1914

My dear Holmes:

Thanks for your letter. At its date the German advance
to the west had about reached its farthest point; now we feel
easy about the immediate future. It is premature to talk of
marching into Berlin: the Germans are not so broken but that
they can make a decent stand on the Rhine. On the other hand
the unexpected collapse of the Austrian armies in the east has
made their work much harder. The practical blockade of the
German fleet continues, and nobody (outside the Admiralty)
knows whether the Germans think the odds of a general action
too much against them to be risked, or have had to divert a
considerable proportion of their strength to the Baltic to observe the Russian fleet there and prevent any landing of troops.
Our expeditionary army has done its work, of a highly trying
kind for many days, thoroughly well: some units suffered losses
which would have reduced any but highly trained soldiers to
insignificance (on which the Germans apparently counted).
Americans could have done the same, and possibly Japanese.
The German mechanical method of attacking with huge masses
to overwhelm the defence at all costs has clearly failed. So
many reports say the Germans have all the individuality drilled
out of them and won't face the bayonet that I think it must be
true.

The conduct of their troops in Belgium — *and by order* — was
clearly abominable. In France one has heard of nothing so
bad. Their official counter-charges appear to be pure invention.
The systematic lying of even high official persons goes beyond
everything one thought possible. As to expanding bullets I
know we have none and doubt whether the Germans have any.
I suppose some officers *might* by mistake have bought revolver
ammunition of private manufacture open to objection, but I
doubt that too.

Where are Sprague's prize cases reported? I shall get none
in my Cinque Ports court: there were none in the Napoleonic
war.

Aristotle's *Ethics* have been the foundation of many things,
and a good one too. So far as I know there is no really satis-

factory edition for general use: Grant's is old-fashioned and meagre. I have never read Malthus.

Yours ever,
F. P.

The story of a body of Russian troops (250,000!) having come through Scotland & England from Archangel is one of the strangest legends in modern history. It is now formally denied.

BEVERLY FARMS, September 24, 1914

Dear F. P.:

A note from you this morning adds to the pleasure of the day — one of my last here. . . . I find it hard to believe in atrocities having been authorized but one can't but hold the side answerable from which they come. Louvain and Rheims present in a less debatable form the question suggested by P. Loti's *La Mort de Philae*. What amount of material gain warrants the destruction of one of the world's unique spiritual treasures? So far as my choice goes I would rather see a million fellahs go hungry, or (apart from my sympathies with you) a German army corps wiped out, than lose what we more or less have lost. . . .

As to dum-dum bullets, whatever may or may not be the objections to them, I didn't believe the story. The Southerners at the beginning of our war in like manner howled about our using explosive bullets — which of course was pure humbug. I apply more or less to your side also the rule not to believe enemies' accounts of enemies' outrages, but I have heard so many stories of hands cut off that, though I thought them absurd at first, I am shaken. It seems incredible.

Flinders Petrie's (as it seemed to me rather feebly supported) notion of 1000 year cycles of civilization, generally ended by an incursion from the north, comes up to one's mind, since the Germans have brought us all back to the rudimentary animal qualities.

Since my little cycle from Aristotle to Malthus via Descartes, Berkeley, etc. I have been rather light in my demands on my intellect, but have got amusement or stimulus here and there rather by chance. I went off my beat to read the life of Sir A. Lyall [1] all because Fanny Morse sent it to me and because by your kindness I met him *chez vous*. I value everything that shows the quiet unmelodramatic power to stand and take it in your people. I have quoted once or twice Lord Salisbury's immortal, "We shall muddle through it somehow," in the Boer War, for the same thing. All the great efforts of life are prose while they are on. When they are over we can let the ivy of romantic feeling grow upon the ruins, but it takes a deeper thing to carry them through, as I believe you will.

Please give my love to Lady Pollock.

Yours ever,

O. W. H.

LONDON, Oct. 24, 1914

My dear Holmes:

It is curious to see in the press that you have received a long letter from the learned Gierke,[1] composed it seems mostly of the official piffle about German culture. I can't believe he wrote it all out of his own head, and suspect that the substance if not the language was dictated by higher authority.

Certainly Germany is under the great Illusion of our age. Do you know George Meredith's *Shagpat*? If not, you must. Shibli Bagarag the predestined Barber is not one but many. Still the prophecy is good in the main, and we look with growing confidence to the day that shall dawn on the baldness of Shagpat.

This war is full of surprises for the military student: a war of entrenchment and siegecraft, artillery fire preponderant, fixed forts condemned: but sea power has come out all right and Mahan is more than justified. We never expected to get a working command of the sea so promptly.

---

[1] Sir Henry Mortimer Durand, *Life of the Right Hon. Sir Alfred Lyall* (1913).

[1] In the London *Times* of October 23, 1914, at p. 6, there was included in a story concerning German propaganda an excerpt from a long letter of von Gierke to Holmes, dated September 26, 1914. It was stated that an English lady had received a copy of the letter from an acquaintance in Berlin.

The Germans are using old single-loading rifle ammunition: this is not gossip: General Neville Lyttelton (my old tutor's pupil with me at Eton) told me he had seen one of the cartridges taken in action and knew the pattern. . . .

A certain Judge of our High Court lives in such a state of war panic that the leaders of his Court have given him a plain piece of their minds. If a German air raider were to blow up our Law Courts and not touch St. Mary-le-Strand or St. Clement Danes the profession (if not in the building at the time) would be rather grateful than otherwise.

Yours ever.
F. P.

WASHINGTON, November 7, 1914

Dear F. P.:

What an extraordinary thing that you should see that Gierke had written to me. I received the letter only within a week and beyond letting two or three of my brethren read it have made it public in no way. Indeed your letter was written more than a week before I had received the other. Do you mean that Gierke published the fact? Surely he can't have published the *letter* which had a personal side. It is quite true that a part of it had the inspired official sound, but other parts had the personal note of one old soldier talking to another and the passion of a man wholly believing in and devoted to his side. It was difficult to answer for I love the old boy in all that I have seen of him, and sympathize with him very much, though I have to wish that his country may be beaten. I told no lies, and in truth I should grieve only less to have German than to have English civilization broken up or hampered, which does not mean, of course, that I waver or slacken in my paramount wish that England may not lose her place. But your knowing that Gierke had written shows what I knew must be true, that along with whatever friendly feelings may have led him, there was an official impulse. I believe the Smithsonian men have received letters from any German professors they happen to know. The Germans certainly seem to me an object lesson of a race fit for domination. They have a single ideal. They are trained to fight and ready to die for it. How they pull every string. I get scared about your navy once in a while but on the whole am feeling encouraged at this writing.

I am working as hard as ever now that Court sits once more. I fire off two cases next Thursday [1] as I did two last Monday [2] — which means dyspepsia at night if I don't look out. Of course I read nothing to speak of here, but one of the young men I delight in has just sent me *Drift & Mastery*,[3] "an attempt to diagnose the current unrest," that I think devilish well written, full of articulation of the impalpable and unutterable, discussing labor with insight, touching the absurd Sherman Act with Ithuriel's spear — not without the superstitions of a young come-outer as to capital, and quoting foolish things about the Courts — altogether a delightful fresh piece of writing and thinking. He and Croly,[4] one of the strongest of the young men, also author of a remarkable book, and some others, are going to start a weekly, *The New Republic*, to which I have subscribed with hope.

My love to Lady Pollock and the children. I heard that you had done generous things to refugees and your government, which did not surprise me.

Yours ever,
O. W. H.

LONDON, February 10, 1915

My dear Holmes:
Without doubt you are right in lamenting the captivity of the real Germany we knew [1] — and shall hardly live to know again — as the greatest spiritual tragedy of this war. I have

[1] DeJonge v. Breuker, 235 U. S. 33; Missouri, Kansas and Texas Ry. Co. v. United States, *id.*, p. 37 (both decided Nov. 9, 1914).
[2] Pullman Co. v. Knott, 235 U. S. 23; United States v. Portale, *id.*, p. 27 (both decided Nov. 2, 1914).
[3] By Walter Lippmann (1914).
[4] Herbert Croly, author of *The Promise of American Life* (1909) and *Progressive Democracy* (1914).

[1] The letter referred to is missing.

given just a hint of it in my pamphlet.[2] The worst of it is that apparently the German people as a whole were not unwilling to be deceived. The enormity of the deception and of its consequences would make me believe in an active devil if anything could. I suppose sailors of other nations must be almost as much shocked to see the German fleet ordered to commit piracy. There is some reason to fear that one merchantman has already been torpedoed and sent to the bottom without warning.

It seems to me the German Admiralty is doing its best to run its head against a coalition of neutral states which might be formidable even if confined to European Powers of the second rank. One of the curious political incidents is the open way in which the intervention of Rumania is talked of — chiefly by Rumanian ex-Ministers & the like — as merely a question of time, without any remonstrance or inquiry from Germany or Austria that we hear of. Estimates of the possible length of the war are still speculative and variable. There is nothing to show that the German public does not still expect, at worst, to retain Belgium or a good piece of it.

Two learned Finns — Prof. Reuter of Helsingfors (Sanskrit) and Mr. Kihlman, ex-Procurator General, are sailing for New York next week. I have given the lawyer an introduction to you. They are going to study public libraries, *ac etiam* to sound American opinion, very discreetly, as to the prospects of Finland getting some good out of the post-bellum settlement, as I hope she may. Not a word of this purpose, of course, to anyone capable of making mischief with it. Our liberal Russian friends would no doubt sympathize but not feel free to say much openly just yet. They all seem to believe in a real awakening of Russia — which is grand if it comes off. But even so there is danger of Finland being not exactly oppressed, but forgotten.

Yours ever,

F. POLLOCK

---

[2] Presumably his *German 'Truth' and European Facts about the War* (undated) published by the Central Committee for National Patriotic Organizations.

LONDON, May 19, 1915 [1]

My dear Holmes:

Your *habeas corpus* from Georgia [2] is one of the things that bewilder the insular legal mind. I could not see it in any proper atmosphere: for one little point, I never heard of polling a jury and don't know whether it is archaism or innovation. On principle I should suppose a man who goes for a Federal *habeas corpus* should first exhaust the justice of his State courts, which the applicant had seemingly done in this case. Then I should expect you to hold the final judgment in the State court conclusive as to all matters of form and local procedure, but not as to extraneous matters going to the jurisdiction or to the fundamental conditions of justice: and I should conceive, if that distinction is sound, that a question whether the jury was in fact intimidated was extraneous to the record and not concluded by the production of a record regular on the face of it: therefore not to be disposed of on any formal grounds. But I feel myself on strange ground and dare not have any confident opinion.

I have just done revising a new edition of *Torts*. The only very interesting new case is *Hurst* v. *Picture Palaces* [3] where the rule in *Wood* v. *Leadbitter* [4] was eviscerated by the modern predominance of equity. This is ingeniously discussed in the *Law Quarterly* by Miles of Oxford,[5] a good young or youngish teacher of law. Yesterday cometh from Woodbine of Yale a sumptuous first volume of his restored *Bracton*, elaborate critical prolegomena with graphic devices to expound the families of the forty odd mss. Perhaps Woodbine knows by this time how the

[1] A brief letter from Pollock, dated March 6, 1915, is omitted.

[2] Frank v. Mangum, 237 U. S. 309 (1915). The petitioner in this case, having been convicted of murder in the courts of Georgia, brought *habeas corpus* proceedings in the Federal Court, upon the ground that the trial, dominated by mob violence, did not constitute due process of law. The majority of the Supreme Court, in an opinion by Pitney, J., held that the District Court had properly dismissed the petition, saying that because the Supreme Court of Georgia on writ of error had determined that the trial was not dominated by violence, the Federal Court could not review that question, and that the conviction did not deprive the petitioner of any rights secured to him by the Fourteenth Amendment. Holmes wrote a dissenting opinion in which Hughes, J., concurred. *Id.* at p. 345.

[3] Hurst v. Picture Theatres, Ltd., [1915] 1 K. B. 1.

[4] 13 M. & W. 838 (1845).

[5] 31 *L. Q. Rev.* 217 (1915).

printers of 1569 lighted on any ms. bad enough to produce the
text they gave us, but so far I can't see that he tells. As I have
written to him, Bracton is now taken in charge by a *gens
robusta et longinqua* but happily not *cuius linguam ignorabunt*.
After the war I doubt not that Woodbine will furnish
many German doctoral theses with the crumbs from his
table.

The report of Bryce's Committee on German outrages was
published last week.[6] I directed a copy to be sent you: not
the appendix because (1) it is too disgusting for anyone to read
except in the strict course of duty: (2) you would not have
time anyhow: (3) if you do want to verify the damning facsim-
iles of German diaries, it will be accessible enough in Washington. The committee was too large in my opinion: five men
would have done it better than seven, but in the main it is
thought to be well done.

The New York *World* (I think it was) asked me for a short
appreciation of the President's Note to Germany,[7] which I
gave.[8] Moses was very meek until he smote the Egyptian, as
I wrote about a week earlier to an impatient friend in your
State. According to rumour by way of Holland, the Lord is
hardening the Egyptian's heart. It would be bad for us to lose
your good offices in Germany and Austria as powerful neutrals,
but good to have some of your modern battleships helping the
Queen Elizabeth, from which good ship my son-in-law,[9] now
with the H. Q. staff doing cipher work, saw the landing of our
troops,[10] his cap blowing off at every shot of the 15-in. guns. A
wonderful change from being a clerk in the House of Commons.

[6] See *Report of the Committee on Alleged German Outrages* (1915). Other members of
the Committee, which had been appointed in 1914, in addition to James Bryce, the
Chairman, and Pollock, were Sir Edward Clarke, Sir Alfred Hopkinson, Mr. H. A. L.
Fisher, Mr. Harold Cox, and Sir Kenelm E. Digby.

[7] On May 13 President Wilson demanded that the German government disavow the
sinking of the Lusitania and, so far as possible, make reparation.

[8] "The Right Hon. Sir Frederick Pollock, another member of the Commission on
Belgian Atrocities, one of Britain's highest authorities on international law, and author
of numerous legal textbooks, said: 'President Wilson's note is excellent in both matter
and form. Less would not have befitted the dignity of the United States or been adequate to the wrong inflicted on its citizens. More would have exceeded the bounds of
sincere desire to preserve friendly relations on terms consistent with honor and justice.'" New York *World*, Sunday, May 16, 1915, p. 2.

[9] Orlando Cyprian Williams.

[10] In the Dardanelles Campaign, February–May 1915.

Jack is dispensing relief to distressful Poles in Galicia [11] —
last heard of by telegraph from Peremysl, the more pronounce-
able Russian variant of Przemysl, which is a sneeze and a swal-
low, and he has twice been motored out for a visit to the Russian
front from Warsaw or thereabouts. I seriously think I must try
to learn Russian and make a start in the summer vacation.

Next week the Commission on Public Records will profit by
the short Whitsuntide holiday for a circuit in the Severn country
and the marches of Wales. We are a frugal Commission and the
Treasury does not threaten to cut us down in war time.

Yours ever,

F. Pollock

London, December 9, 1915 [1]

My dear Holmes:

 . . . *Definitions.* The said Roscoe [2] is monstrous learned,
but I am not sure that he perceives what definers constantly
overlook, the existence of two quite distinct problems.

You may want to analyze the past and present uses of a term
(let x = Right, or Possession, or anything) to find out what
idea, if any, is really common to all the significations, and
whether you can make a pedigree of them — this is what, I
think, French philologists call *sémantique* as distinct from the
natural history of sound and inflexion.

Or you may want to decide whether any and what conventional limitation of the term will be useful for the particular
job you are upon: to which your *semantic* results will no doubt
have much to say, but the object is quite different. Plain
enough, but many writers muddle it.

Dentists. I have found them fairly human and been thankful
for good American ones as far away as Rome and Bombay.
Have you only of late become familiar with the species? I have

---

[11] John Pollock, from 1915 to 1919, was in Poland and Russia as Chief Commissioner
of the Great Britain to Galicia Fund under the Russian Red Cross.

---

[1] A short letter from Pollock, dated November 25, 1915, is omitted.

[2] Undoubtedly Roscoe Pound. The letter to which this one of Pollock's is apparently responsive is missing.

been more or less in bondage to them this quarter of a century
tho' I shall be only 70 tomorrow. . . .

Henry James has had a stroke, not quite so bad as was feared
at first. Mrs. Bill James,[3] who by the way is adorable, is coming over to look after him. But I guess you will know more in
a week's time, one way or other, than I do now. . . .

Yours ever,

F. P.

WASHINGTON, December 29, 1915

Dear F. P.:

. . . We are getting through the two weeks Xmas adjournment. The time has been so broken up that I have little to
show for them. I read a little book, *The Freudian Wish*, by
Holt, Harvard College, who seems to think that psychology is
reborn between Freud and him but from whose work I derived
less nourishment than Walter Lippmann who sent it to me
seemed to have done. Monstrous clever lad, W. L., and only
26 and he has done much. But these young men are so damned
solemn that I have been philosophising anew on emotional
weather and its independence of what might be expected to be
the causes, *e.g.*, workingmen oppressed before the French Revolution, yet seemingly gay (Restif de la Bretonne), workingmen
now in the saddle, yet groaning and grunting and seeming to
be having a worse time than ever.

The first half of the 19th Century was unhygienic but jovial.

We now have improved hygiene and all manner of intelligent
isms but don't seem to get a good time out of it.

At times I think the men in the trenches are the gayest
people left. Possibly gaiety is the miasmic mist of misery. I
was rather gay in the army when certainly I was unhappy
enough. *Que sçay je?*

Apropos of Pound perhaps I said before that I keep all his
essays. I have one volume bound and the stuff for another. I
admire his learning and his command of it, but as yet have not

---

[3] Alice Runnells James, daughter-in-law of William James.

perceived a very strong personal reaction upon his knowledge — as one does in Wigmore — whom I hope to see here on January 1. . . .

Yours ever,
O. W. HOLMES

I didn't remember what a lambkin you were — only just 70! Welcome to the higher story and may you live on it many years. I shall be *75* March 8.

LONDON, January 30, 1916

My dear Holmes:

It is a very true "observe" that people cry aloud not when they are worst off but when a beginning of better things has given them a little spare strength to cry with. I seem to remember that Maine pointed this out somewhere in the case of the French peasants before the revolution, but I can't lay my hand on the place. Similarly the demand for reform in England after the Napoleonic war did not become intense till 1825–1830.

Have you seen Taft's scheme for establishing a real international jurisdiction?[1] I think very well of it and hope to say so in print before long.[2] The Assistant Editor of the *Law Reports*, who was there because he had been independent editor of the Common Law (King's Bench and Probate and House of Lords) sections, and was a kind of fifth wheel in the coach, retires at the end of this month and his place is not filled, so I shall get the whole thing more under my direct control and I think a nominal increase of work will on the whole be more than made up for by abolishing friction and circuity. Also our ancient Admiralty reporter is in *misericordia*, having taken on himself to suppress a number of prize cases without consulting me, or any one, because (*sicut dicit*) he feared they might offend neutrals. A queer example of misplaced diplomatic astuteness if the excuse was genuine. Jack is still hard at work

---

[1] The American League to Enforce Peace was inaugurated on June 17, 1915, with William Howard Taft as its president.

[2] Probably "The American Plan for Enforcing Peace," 119 *Atlantic Monthly* 650 (May, 1917).

with his refugees in Petrograd and I suppose learning Russian faster than I can here even with a good teacher. It is a fascinating language, but one ought to have several months with little else to attend to, which of course I cannot have.

Another professional item: I have written a short introduction to a new edition of Wheaton's *International Law* which should be out very soon.[3] I wish you and I could have our fingers in the new pie that will have to be baked after the war. It will be a great pie and need a slow oven — say about five years' baking: may we live to see it.

Today I have been with Haldane who told me the whole story of his visit to Berlin early in 1912 and showed me the Foreign Office print recording his conversations there.[4] Sooner or later it will be published, and then it will be seen that he told some very plain truths, and the German military party, when they forced on war, did so in the face of most explicit warning that they could not count on our neutrality. The inference I had already drawn from public materials that the said party got the upper hand over the German Chancellor[5] and Foreign Office only in 1913 was right. Till then the chances of peace were quite promising. Short of publication, there is no need to regard the main facts as secret. . . .

Yours ever,
F. P.

Dear Pollock:

A welcome line from you comes this morning. I have not seen Taft's scheme for international jurisdiction. I am glad if he has said anything worth saying when so many drool. Also I am glad at what you tell me about Haldane whom I have liked for many years.

As for myself there is little to tell. I am having a breathing

---

[3] Henry Wheaton, *Elements of International Law* (5th ed., 1916).
[4] See 6 *British Documents on the Origins of the War* (1930), p. 676 *et seq.*
[5] Theobald von Bethmann-Hollweg (1856–1921), German Chancellor, 1909–17.

space — adjourned till next Monday and my work done. I have taken the moment to read a little Fichte [1] and Aristotle [2] and Remy de Gourmont's *Le Latin Mystique*. I can't believe that R. de G. was a great poet in spite of Amy Lowell's account of him in her *Six French Poets*. I am confident from my own reading that he is superficial as a philosopher, but as a dilettante and scholar with horizons and scepticisms he has much to give pleasure, and in this book he is at home. I was pleased to learn that the *Dies Irae* was the final incarnation of motifs previously existing, as when I was young it pleased me to notice the same as to the *Dance of Death* and some of the great religious pictures, and then remembering *Faust* to suggest that the Supreme was likely to be some final expression of popular legend. Doesn't it happen to you sometimes to realize a poetic phrase that but for some accident you might have passed unnoticed? Somehow I was transfixed by "*Ave Stella Maris.*" *In primis* how came the image? I bet through the suggestion of Maria — but anyhow the picture brings tears to my eyes. The one great star in the sky and the expanse of the ocean beneath, vivified by the reflection of the gleam. Similarly I have been rearrested by two lines of a Southern poet recalling the war:

> "And only in our dreams the guns
> peal, and the flag is seen."

You hear the cannon in the word guns, and how ghostly the flutter of the lost flag. Well, I must go and attend to business. I think much of you in these days.

Give my love to your wife.

When you receive this I shall be near to turning the corner of my third quarter century.

Yours ever,
O. W. HOLMES

[1] *The Vocation of Man* (Journal).
[2] *Metaphysics*, Book I (Journal).

LONDON, March 1916

My dear Holmes:

Remy de Gourmont was a mere name to me. I don't think he counts very high now: the present champion of that sort of spiritual reaction is Paul Claudel, and I think you would find him more profitable. However, I have got *Le latin mystique* from the London Library. As a historical anthology of devotional Latin verse down to *saec.* XIII it is well enough, but the scholarship is hardly up to the mark. There are lots of misprints and some blunders. On p. 161 the common adjective *crebra* appears in the teeth of both sense and metre as *cerebra* and is translated *cérébrale*. Even if R. de G. found *cerebra* in the text, the correction should have been obvious. But the main fault is that he never brings out the essential facts of the conflict between decadent, would-be classical, and rising popular Latin, and the resulting compromise, and all but ignores the influence of the Vulgate. He actually quotes examples — after official medieval Latin had taken form — of the same man writing something as near classical style as he could make it, or frankly popular canticles, with quite deliberate choice, and has nothing to say about it. That is not much better than the frame of mind of 18th century antiquaries to whom all medieval writings were just "monkish" in the lump. Apparently the gulf between Prudentius and the *Dies Irae* seemed irrelevant to R. de G.: from a merely devotional point of view that may be so, but if so his title is misleading. It ought to mean a study of the language of specially mystical writers in Latin: such writers had a specialized vocabulary in all languages where such literature is found. But the book is certainly not that, and I doubt whether R. de G. realized the difference between mystics and ordinary ministers to edification. By the way, it is a pity Wm. James did not know more of the Middle Ages when he wrote on varieties of religious experience. Huysman's preface belongs to an offensive kind of affectation which already stinketh. Would the war have made a man of that creature?

The learned Baty has published a clever paradoxical book on *Vicarious Liability* (my own term invented thirty odd years ago), denouncing employer's liability *in tort* as all wrong. I am dealing with it politely but faithfully for the April number of the *L. Q. R.* However, it is good for current doctrine to be vigorously winnowed now and again. B. is of the school who think you can reduce law to rigorous chess problems: so he never reflects that the most certain result of the law being as he would like would be a huge expansion of implied, *i.e.* fictitious contracts, to no great advantage of either law or conscience.

Talking of anthologies you should see Bridges' (now Poet Laureate) *The Spirit of Man*, marked with the character of a real poet and scholar, and mixing new with old matter very prettily. A learned Persian of Oxford [1] has helped him to some fine pieces of Jalālu ddīn Rūmī and of the Indian Kabír, lately Englished by Rabindranath Tagore and my friend Mrs. Stuart Moore.[2] This anthology is published by Longmans, who have a house in New York.

I am getting to read Tolstoy's infantile moral tales — as straightforward and idiomatic as Grimm — in an excellent edition with scholarly notes and vocabulary. I had to wait for it to come from Chicago.

Yours ever,
F. Pollock

Is there anywhere, outside big books on the Constitution, a compendious account of the manner in which Abraham Lincoln understood and exercised his executive war power? Some folks here need to learn it.

Washington, March 24, 1916

Dear F. P.:

A hurried line to catch the mail. You abase and amaze me by your ever present and available learning. I had noticed some things in Remy de Gourmont that made me say he must have had an ignorant clerk or a scissors man to help him, but I could not have delivered your admirable discourse.

I am just reaching a moment when I hope to read a little for a few days of adjournment; first, *Twentieth Century Social-*

---

[1] Hasan Shahid Suhrawardy.
[2] Evelyn Underhill, 1875– .

ism, Edmond Kelly — deceased. From time to time I read things of that sort as I read a good deal of philosophy I don't believe, to get all sides, and perchance damn intellectual titillation. It seems on the opening pages to be cocksure — and the introducers [1] also are cocksure — a frame of mind that makes me puke, and I probably shall think his fallacies not less obvious than those of Karl Marx. Did you know that Proudhon, who was a man of ideas, though I don't believe most of them, pitched into Marx as a humbug and a charlatan?

My wife is reading aloud to me a clever novel *The Real Adventure* by Henry Kitchell Webster, which hasn't yet flatted as most novels do when half way through. It is the first I have read for some time. I was amused, and thought my wife was chaffing till I looked at the book, to hear her read of the hero telling of his discovery "of a real legal problem, a problem that for its nice intricacies and intellectual suggestiveness, would have brought an appreciative gleam to the eye of Mr. Justice Holmes, or Lord Mansfield, or the great Coke himself." Is it not fame for a judge to be referred to by the lay gents in that way?

I can't answer you — or rather I can't tell you any such book on the war powers of the President as you ask for, though there was a book on that subject that I believe went through many editions, but that I never looked into, by Whiting I think, written early in the war.[2]

I read last night a notice of Charles Francis Adams's (the younger) *Autobiography* just published. Those brothers, especially Charles and Henry, with great talents have a gift of turning all life to ashes, that does not do justice to their own good points.

I have made a note of your Bridges anthology to get at once. My love to Lady Pollock and the children.

Yours ever,
O. W. HOLMES

I passed 75 on the 8th.

---

[1] Franklin H. Giddings and Rufus W. Weeks.
[2] William Whiting, *War Powers of the President* (1st ed., 1862).

April 7, 1916

Dear F. P.:

Many thanks for your 10th edition [1] and still more for the touching and unexpected honor of your suggestive article in the numbers of the *Harv. Law Rev.* dedicated to me.[2] I have been much moved by this kindness, as well as surprised. My love to Lady Pollock and to you.

Yours ever,

O. W. H.

I reopen this, dear Pollock, the few words I have written are so inadequate. You have been one of the great encouragements of my life. I am sure I need not write many words to tell you of my ever living gratitude.

O. W. H.

LONDON, June 29, 1916

My dear Holmes:

These few lines are not exactly to condole with you on the loss of a colleague,[1] since it may turn out to be for the good of the commonwealth — thereafter as may be. It seems to me a strange taste that leads a man to leave your Bench and plunge into political conflict.

As Editor of the *Law Reports* I lament that paper and printing have gone up and litigation has not gone down in proportion. The cases of prize now being reported are interesting.

Yesterday a point of law was raised on the Statute of Treasons on Roger Casement's trial,[2] but so far as I collect from the newspaper reports there was very little in it.

I found a nice story of a bear for my granddaughter in my

---

[1] Of his *Law of Torts*, recently published.
[2] To the April 1916 issue of the *Harvard Law Review*, dedicated to Holmes, Pollock contributed an article, "Cosmopolitan Custom and International Law," 29 *Harv. L. Rev.* 565.

---

[1] On June 10 Charles Evans Hughes accepted the Republican nomination for the Presidency and, on the same day, resigned from the Supreme Court of the United States.
[2] See Rex v. Casement, [1917] 1 K. B. 98; noted by Pollock in 33 *L. Q. Rev.* 109 (April 1917).

Russian reading book (being a collection of Tolstoi's short stories & apologues)—though I can hardly say it was worth while to learn the language for that purpose alone.

Yours ever,
F. P.

BEVERLY FARMS, July 12, 1916

Dear Pollock:

It was not preference but simply and solely, as I believe, a sense of duty that led Hughes to accept the nomination. I shall miss him consumedly, for he is not only a good fellow, experienced and wise, but funny, and with doubts that open vistas through the wall of a non-conformist conscience.

I have not yet quite unhooked from the law, for after reading a volume of cases on constitutional law [1] — Lord, Lord, how long-winded even though the editor cut out a good deal — I have taken up *An Economic Interpretation of the Constitution of the U. S.* [2] S. Patten set an example years ago in seeking the origins of new philosophies in economic changes and to that end studied the biographies from Hobbes to Darwin to find the original *aperçu* that started them, by which they broke in, subsequent system-making being immaterial. This cove in like manner studies the accounts of the members of the Const. Convention. To find out what? He mentions the amount of U. S. or state scrip held by them. Why? It doesn't need evidence that the men who drew the Constitution belonged to the well-to-do classes and had the views of their class. The writer disclaims the imputation of self seeking-motives yet deems it important to constate all the facts. Except for a covert sneer I can't see anything in it so far. I am a little worried about the submarine that has got here, [3] but your affairs are looking so promising now that it takes less hold on me.

[1] L. B. Evans, *Leading Cases on American Constitutional Law* (1916).
[2] By Charles A. Beard (1913).
[3] On July 9, 1916, the submarine merchantman *Deutschland* arrived in Baltimore. Great Britain and France, although the vessel was unarmed, protested against her presence in an American harbor, asserting that she was potentially a warship.

Did you know Harold Laski, an astonishing young Jew, whom Frankfurter brought over here the other day?

My love to Lady Pollock and the children. I wrote to her a while ago to make sure she understood that if ever I talked in a detached tone it was only that such is my nater from time to time, not that I don't long heart and soul for your success.

Yours ever,

O. W. H.

WASHINGTON, October 16, 1916

Dear F.:

Many thanks for the pleasant essay on Shakespeare.[1] It furnished me an agreeable distraction for a short time from the rush in which I now am, and the 100th occasion to wonder helplessly at your collateral knowledge. The summer ended with no epoch-making reading — such as Malthus was a year or two ago — but with a tolerable number of odds and ends. I reread, for the first time with real and amazed appreciation the *Oedipus Tyrannus* with Sir G. Young and a dictionary by my side, and got a lot of pleasure out of Hazlitt whom heretofore I had supposed to be one of the reputations made for domestic consumption but not for foreign export.

I did a certain number of legal and economical books without great profit and with some *ennui*. Did you ever read Abel Hermant's *Famille Valardier*? I think it the best thing I have read apropos of the war, with a tenderness and kindly humor that I think it took the war to bring out in one whom I had regarded as a *boulevardier*.

We have a lot of assigned cases on, under the Sherman Act, rate cases, etc.; things I loathe and to listen to which I now must depart. Give my dear love to Lady Pollock and tell her not to forget me even in the present, I am glad to believe hopeful circumstances. To you my lifelong affection.

Yours ever,

O. W. HOLMES

[1] Presumably, Pollock's "War and Diplomacy in Shakespeare," 114 (41 N. S.) *Cornhill Magazine* 400 (October 1916).

LONDON, November 23, 1916

My dear Holmes:

Nothing particular happens here except tightening of postal and other regulations — quite right no doubt, but now we can't send a scrap of print to your side without special leave. We now have (this morning) authentic photographs of the "tanks," and I wonder whether those published elsewhere were so far from the real thing as an official answer declared. The striking feature is that the caterpillar business runs all round the frame, so that the body, so to speak, is all chassis.

Concerning the presidential election, being a lawyer and not a schoolmaster, I feel rather like Sir Perceval when in his dream he saw a lion and a serpent fighting and decided to help the lion as being "the more natural beast of the two." Apparently the majority find the serpent more profitable. We shall see.

The House of Lords is going to affirm that "the death of a human being cannot be complained of as an injury," thinking the rule inveterate.[1] Damned bad law in my opinion, whatever kind of historical pedigree may be made for it. Strange that a proved series of blunders should be more sacred than one. . . .

Yours ever,
F. POLLOCK

WASHINGTON, December 5, 1916

Dear Pollock:

I would that you wrote πολλάκις, (do you get it?), as it always is such a pleasure to hear from you, and I always am wanting to know how things are going with you. . . . I believe the tanks barring the coat of mail are an American invention. As to the House of Lords decision, the heralds used to say, I believe, that old disgrace is better than new honor.

I am working along as usual. On Monday I fired off a decision that an acquittal of a man on the ground of the statute

[1] See Admiralty Commissioners v. S. S. Amerika, [1917] A. C. 38.

of limitations (a decision subsequently held wrong in another case) was a bar to another indictment.[1] It seemed to me sufficiently obvious, but the habit of expressing the criminal immunity in the terms of the Constitution (that a man must not be brought twice into jeopardy) has led to the notion that unless there was jeopardy there was no bar, and by our decisions there is no jeopardy till a jury is empanelled. As one Judge couldn't sit the Court was evenly divided at first (between ourselves) but I ultimately persuaded all but one and he was silent. There has been a fair number of hard nuts to crack and several remain uncracked still. They keep me very busy so that I have no chance to do more for the moment than send a bulletin. Do give my love to Lady Pollock. My feelings go up and down as things seem to be going well or ill with you — but the Lord knows I am anxious enough about my own country.

Yours ever,
O. W. H.

I just hear of Asquith's resignation[2] but don't know what it means. I also hear that the Roumanian troubles have followed on their refusal to coöperate with the general staff of the Allies, but am quite unable to estimate the importance of the German success against them. But the day begins with sadness.

London, January 25, 1917

My dear Holmes:
    The decision of the House of Lords in the *Amerika case*,[1] affirming the doctrine that in a civil court the death of a human being cannot be complained of as an injury, is passed for press for the February number of the *Law Reports*. . . . Parker and Sumner (formerly Hamilton L. J.)[2] delivered elaborate opinions — the sum of them being

---

[1] United States v. Oppenheimer, 242 U. S. 85 (1916).
[2] On December 5, 1916, Herbert Henry Asquith, First Earl of Oxford and Asquith (1852–1928), resigned as Prime Minister.

---

[1] Admiralty Commissioners v. S. S. Amerika, [1917] A. C. 38.
[2] Sir John Andrew Hamilton, Lord Justice of Appeal, had been appointed a Lord of Appeal in Ordinary by title of Baron Sumner of Ibstone in October 1913.

A. (1) Trespass would not lie at common law for an act which was on the face of it felonious (appeal being the proper remedy in such case).

(2) But all homicide, not being clearly justified like execution of legal sentence etc., was felonious

(3) Therefore homicide, wilful or not, could not be a cause of action in trespass

(4) nor could an action on the case be allowed to give a more extended remedy for the same kind of injuries

(5) nothing has happened to alter the rule.

B. If this rule is anomalous the action for trespass *per quod servitium amisit* is more so and ought not to be encouraged.

The Lords disclaim reliance either on the maxim *"actio personalis"* etc. or any rule of public policy.

Our learned friend Holdsworth of Oxford came to a different conclusion on substantially the same materials, *L. Q. R.* xxxii. 431 (last October number). His argument is not so well constructed as Parker's, but I am not sure that it is not really the sounder. If you have time to look at the report — which you probably won't — I should like to know how it impresses you.

A curious book by Prof. Husband of Dartmouth College — a classicist — has been sent me for review:[3] *The Prosecution of Jesus: its date history and legality.* His points are that (1) the received date of the Crucifixion is three years too early, (2) there was no trial or sentence under Jewish law, but the Sanhedrin acted as prosecutor on a charge of treason under Roman Law (in effect, the story is correct in Luke but not in Mark or Matthew, though the author does not say so quite plainly), (3) the proceeding before Pilate was regular according to Roman provincial practice and the sentence legal if unjust. (H. does not seem to know that the competence of Pilate's jurisdiction and the formal legality of the sentence are essential in scholastic theodicy, *sicut per Dantem De Monarchia.*)

Qu. whether it was worth a whole book to make those points, but it is not a large book and he writes like a scholar. He takes no notice of the radical sceptics who treat all the details as unhistorical or even doubt, like Salomon Reinach, whether there

---

[3] See 33 *L. Q. Rev.* 199 (1917).

was any Crucifixion at all. The question of date does not interest me.

Once on a time a Leopard and an Ethiopian were fighting on the sea-shore, and a learned Fish put his head up from the sea and spoke to the other fishes, but so that the Leopard and the Ethiopian could hear him: "My friends, the fighting of these creatures is unseemly, and their noise disturbs us even in the sea. If only the Ethiopian will change his skin and be a white man, and the Leopard will change his spots and be a tame cat, we can help them to make an excellent peace and be friends again." The Leopard said softly: "I thought this was my fight," and crouched for another spring. The Ethiopian grinned for a moment, thinking the Leopard, who was already giving him all he could do with, would be put off; but when he saw it was not so, he cursed and swore by Mumbo Jumbo. But the learned Fish, when he saw that, went down into the water and began to compose another discourse.

Does the history of the late unlamented Rasputin interest you? Perhaps your press gives it more freely than ours. I have from Russia some unprinted matter which goes pretty far. I should think Old Testament false prophets and medieval pretenders to crowns, when they were not mere puppets in stronger men's hands, were made of the same kind of stuff. And so is, on a humbler scale, the common Indian Fagír, to be distinguished from the real, learned, holy man who is moral and clean. Russians like Indians condone every kind of vice and excess — especially sexual, as to which there are many tales of R. aforesaid — in any one who has once acquired a reputation for sanctity. It is also rather like incidents in the Book of Judges.

I am looking with curiosity for the developments of our new constitutional practice. Jumping from a cabinet of twenty-three to a cabinet of five with never a Secretary of State in it is a feat calling for some agility.[4] Now I should have said the number of your Honourable Court was about right for a supreme executive body as well as for a supreme judicature.

Yours ever,
F. Pollock

---

[4] In December 1916 the Prime Minister, Mr. Lloyd George, superseded the ordinary Cabinet by a War Cabinet of five members.

WASHINGTON, February 18, 1917

Dear F. P.:

It is good to see your fist and I am interested by what you tell about the action for causing death. I will try to take a look at the case, but being now in recess with my work done I find my time so occupied minute by minute that I won't promise. We have had all manner of interesting and important cases — the two are not the same — but nothing very special has fallen to my pen. One case, important but hardly interesting, which I have disposed of in a comparatively few sentences, I don't get back from my brethren, which leads me to wonder whether I have failed to satisfy them.[1] It occurred to me that some would think that it was not pompous and longwinded enough for the matter involved. But Lord, when all you really have to say can be told in two pages and your argument is A. B. C. why dilate?

You hammer, as you so often have, on the essentiality of Pilate's competence and the legality of the sentence in, *e.g.* the *De Monarchia*. But I am so much nearer to Salomon Reinach than to the gent from Dartmouth College that his discussion would only amuse me like a game of tit tat too. If you don't believe the miracles and think it obvious that speech of diverse origin is put into Christ's mouth, as all the indecent stories used to be attributed to Lincoln, I don't see how one can discuss even the character or life with profit. And as to the death, if it happened, as told in the best of ancient tragic pages, I suppose A. France's short tale of the talk with Pilate probably is true to the atmosphere of the time. We had here over Sunday a youth whom I wonder if you remember: Harold Laski, an unbelieving Jew with a *specialité* for church history. He was distinguished at Oxford I believe, then lectured at Magill and now does at Harvard. Beat the American champion at tennis, is one of the very most learned men I ever saw of any age, is in his 20's and an extraordinarily agreeable chap. He goes with some of the younger men like Frankfurter and the *New Re-*

---

[1] When the Court sat on March 6, 1917, Holmes delivered three brief opinions: McDonald v. Mabee, 243 U. S. 90; Pennsylvania Fire Insurance Co. v. Gold Issue Mining and Milling Co., *id*. 93; and The Five Per Cent. Discount Cases, *id*. 97.

public lot, who make much of your venerable uncle and not only so, but by bringing an atmosphere of intellectual freedom in which one can breathe, make life to him a good deal more pleasant. Your remarks touching the learned fish please me, and although just now the voice seems to have another tone I don't feel sure of anything till it happens. Personally I distrust fish talk, even inspired. As to your Rooshan, again I can't recite. But I have reached the time when I am content to be frankly ignorant on most themes. I may succeed in sucking up a bit of culture in the next few weeks, in which case I may be articulate for a page. My love to Lady Pollock.

Yours ever,
O. W. HOLMES

Western Union Cablegram

April 7, 1917

JUSTICE HOLMES
    SUPREME COURT WASHINGTON
GREETINGS OLD FRIEND AND ALLY

POLLOCK

LONDON, May 14, 1917

My dear Holmes:

We are awaiting your impressions of the Allies' mission.[1] I suppose you knew Balfour at any rate already. The one doubtful spot in the general outlook is Russia, but Vinogradoff is hopeful and I have great confidence in his judgment.

While as editor of the *Law Reports* I am trying to keep down the bulk — subscriptions falling off in wartime and cost of production mounting — Lord Shaw must needs deliver a portentous opinion about the liberty of the subject in the House of

[1] In the middle of April the French and British Commissions arrived in the United States. The British mission was headed by the Foreign Secretary, Arthur James Balfour.

Lords.[2] My private opinion is that there is no liberty of the subject in time of war within the realm.

Yours ever,

F. P.

I am in office in the Royal Colonial Institute Lodge and on the way to the chair thereof next year: a pretty tough task for a septuagenarian memory, for some of the forms are longish.

WASHINGTON, June 1, 1917

Dear Pollock:

The Allies' mission I should suppose was a marked success but you will have heard more authentic accounts before this answer to your line can reach you. I had a few words with Balfour but nothing much, supposing the kindest thing I could do was to let him alone. I did offer to take him to the Great Falls of the Potomac, a real sight within relatively short motor distance, but he was afraid to make an engagement. I met the Mussoos also at dinner, tried a few feeble words on Viviani as to French legal literature but gathered that his interests were elsewhere, and I believe amused Joffre by telling him that the C. J. & I had been enemies.[1] But I speak not the French and the rest was silence. I am pretty well through my work — altogether, except what may be handed to me at the last minute — and one page dissents from opinions of from twenty-one to twenty-four pages. Long wind hasn't given out on this side any more than on yours, nor so much, though the tendency is towards shorter opinions. I abhor, loathe and despise these long discourses, and agree with Carducci the Italian poet who died some years ago that a man who takes half a page to say what can be said in a sentence will be damned.

I have discovered the pleasure of soft shirts and collars during the undress season, and they have removed one misery from life. By the by I wonder if your people would agree with a de-

---

[2] Rex v. Halliday, [1917] A. C. 260. The opinion of Lord Shaw of Dunfermline was a dissent. See, *id*. p. 276–305. The case was noted, presumably by Pollock, in 33 *L. Q. Rev.* 205 (1917).

[1] Chief Justice White had fought in the Confederate Army in the Civil War.

cision I rendered not without dissent letting off the *Kronprinzessin Cecilie* from liability for turning back at 11 P.M. Greenwich time July 31 from a voyage to Plymouth & Cherbourg.[2] I haven't yet seen the House of Lords decision on *Mitsui & Co.* v. *Watts, Watts & Co.*[3] (They seem to get the reports much later here than they do at Cambridge.) I should be hard to convince of a different conclusion whatever the intimations of the House of Lords might be. I have been interested in some other questions of rather more local character, such as the power of the states to impose liability for death by accident two feet from a wharf on a gang plank over the water and so within the admiralty jurisdiction.[4] Four of us dissented in favor of the state's power,[5] and I can't understand the decision, *et superest ager.* I must off with my wife to lunch, as our servants have gone and we have renewed our annual reliance upon the venal ravens. Love to all.

Yours ever,
O. W. HOLMES

LONDON, July 2, 1917

My dear Holmes:

Just a line to say I have not seen any proper report of your Court's decision concerning the *Kronprinzessin Cäcilie*, but from such account of the facts as I have seen it looks like a case rather on the line, in which differing opinions might be expected. I don't understand our Courts either to have laid down that no apprehension or restraint will equal actual restraint of princes or to have defined how much apprehension will do. One suggested test is whether the adventure is still insurable, but it is only one. The subject however is not very much in my line.

Amen to your damnation (and Carducci's, tho' I can't fix the passage for you) of prolixity. Likewise of starch.

Yours ever,
F. P.

---

[2] The Kronprinzessin Cecilie, 244 U. S. 12 (1917). Pitney and Clarke, JJ., dissented.
[3] [1917] A. C. 227. The issues were somewhat similar to those in The Kronprinzessin Cecilie. [4] Southern Pacific Company v. Jensen, 244 U. S. 205, 218 (1917).
[5] Justice Pitney, concurring substantially with Holmes's dissent, wrote a separate dissenting opinion. Brandeis and Clarke, JJ., concurred in both dissenting opinions.

WASHINGTON, October 12, 1917

My dear Pollock:

It is ever a joy to see your fist in a letter.

Yours of the 20th found me here a day or two ago,[1] just gathering breath from the most crowded beginning of a term that I have seen. Not matters incident to war, but in consequence, partly, of a part of our jurisdiction having latterly been made dependent on our discretion, some 60 or 70 applications for *certiorari*, in each of which we had to familiarize ourselves with the case so far as to decide whether it was a proper one to come up, a question that I, at least, generally answer with very little regard to whether the case seems to me to have been decided rightly or not. But counsel who don't know the ropes generally argue the merits at length in their briefs, and that common American long-windedness presents us with volumes like the Bible. I don't read more than is necessary, but on top of the work in Court it is a job. Also I have written my first decision for the term, to be delivered tomorrow.[2]

Did I tell you that in the vacation I recurred *inter alia* to Virgil? I read all there was in the Loeb edition which unfortunately stops with the 6th book of the *Aeneid*, and thought a good deal more of the old man when I finished than the recollections of boyhood led me to expect. There are some awfully fine lines, fit precursors of Dante, in the descent of Orpheus, 4th Georgic, and of Aeneas. I was struck incidentally with the seeming sincerity of Virgil's worship of the national gods, and with the reflection that very likely it never occurs to him to question them, and then that the same is true of the run of men today *non obstant* modern scepticism in many matters. "I always have heard so" is a sufficient reason for their belief.

I also reread the first part of *Faust* with difficulty — greater than I have with law German — and with notice of what seemed to me incoherence in the scheme as to Mephistopheles and Faust, etc., but with the feeling that Margaret is the most touching figure I know in fiction. Is H. James's unfinished

---

[1] The letter referred to is missing.
[2] United States v. Leary, 245 U. S. 1 (decided Oct. 15, 1917).

novel published, I wonder.[3] Some one told me yesterday that
my uncle John Holmes's letters to J. R. Lowell had been.[4] I
must get them. I hope they do him justice for he had a very
charming inconsequent humor of his own. I simply allow myself time to come to the surface and blow (like a whale) and as
soon as I have lunched shall plunge below into the law again.
Please give my love to Lady Pollock. You speak of Gerard's
revelations.[5] More published here by the State Department as
to Bernstorff's underground doings while we were supposed to
be friends [6] make one chuckle from the point of view of our
people knowing and keeping a quiet face till they were ready
to tell.

Yours ever,
O. W. H.

London, October 15, 1917

My dear Holmes:
   The time has come for me to think of the contribution I
have promised to a festival number of the *Illinois Law Review*
to be dedicated to Wigmore next year. Not being able to settle
down to a serious theme in war time, I must try to dress up
some kickshaw as prettily as I can. My title at present is
"Lay Fallacies in the Law," [1] and incidentally I see my way to
vindicate Cicero and Horace from current and exceedingly
stupid perversions of their meaning by people who would not
attend to the context of their tags.

---

   [3] Henry James had died on February 28, 1916. His uncompleted novels, *The Ivory
Tower* and *The Sense of the Past*, were posthumously published in October 1917.
   [4] *Letters of John Holmes to James Russell Lowell and Others* (William Roscoe Thayer,
ed., 1917).
   [5] Ambassador James Watson Gerard had recently published *My Four Years in
Germany* (1917).
   [6] On September 21 Secretary of State Lansing made public a message from Count
Bernstorff to the German Foreign Office, dated January 22, 1917, in which he had
sought authority to spend $50,000 "to influence Congress" for the prevention of war.
On September 22 Lansing supplemented that publication with the assertion that the
Department of State possessed conclusive evidence that when Bernstorff requested the
authority to spend $50,000, he knew of his Government's intention to begin unrestricted
submarine warfare on February 1, 1917.

---

   [1] The article, under that name, appeared in 13 *Illinois L. Rev.* 147 (1918). It is
reprinted in *Essays in the Law* (1922), p. 258.

Air raids have driven my daughter and granddaughter to winter in the country: not that Alice fears our own shrapnel fragments, against which a good roof over one's head is enough, or the enemy's bombs, from which the chance of injury to any one under cover or even not under cover at any given spot is extremely small, but because it is not good for small children to be hauled out of bed in their first sleep. The last time the guns were pretty loud for about two hours and a half, and we were glad Betty was not in the house. As for us old folks we are pretty callous.

I hear that sundry of your less discreet men in France are swaggering in their talk about coming in to finish the war, and thereby offend ours and will offend the French too if they have not done so already. There have been one or two ugly little rows, it is said, but I will not repeat details for which I cannot vouch. Only I am sure it is not merely gossip, and this kind of boasting is obviously not wise before the thing has come off, and to the face of the men who have borne all the rough work these three years.

The woman novelist May Sinclair (much read on your side, I believe) has broken out into a book on philosophy which looks rather brilliant.[2] I have only glanced at it but mean to read it.

Jack's volume of collected papers on War and Revolution in Russia[3] is well advanced in the press, and should be ready for publication some time before Christmas if paper does not give out and there is not a strike of printers or binders.

Yours ever,
F. POLLOCK

Your State Department is doing admirable work in exposing the methods of Boche intrigue not only during but before the war.

[2] *In Defence of Idealism* (1917).
[3] The book was published under that title in 1918.

WASHINGTON, November 3, 1917

Dear Pollock:

Your letter adds to the sadness I was feeling about my countrymen, for I agree with Roosevelt for once that we had better keep our mouths shut until we have done a damned deal more than we have yet, and you aggravate my fears that we have done some odious blowing. Also I hear that our manners in the tropical countries to the south have been such as to make us hated while the Germans have been knowing enough to conform to local ways, etc.. That even the Germans should teach us manners is hard.

I am just finishing *Le Feu* (Barbusse), very real and striking. The notion of a lot of chaps who never have smelt powder swaggering to such as Barbusse portrays, makes me puke — while I recognize that probably it does not mean anywhere near as much as it does harm, mainly, probably, inexperience and want of manners. I am assured that his material is good. Well, I hope we shall be able to count in other ways as well as by forking out cash, and I believe the administration means to do its best. But I wish a different man had been elected when Wilson first came in. It seems as if the fight was with you and France and us after this, but perhaps it will turn out not so bad as it seems in Italy. Even my detachment and would-be impartiality are shaken somewhat and whatever I may think privately I would do what I could to cherish in my countrymen an unphilosophic hatred of Germany and German ways.

What you say about Wigmore pricks me. I ought to write something and I don't see how I can. I am very busy when not taking needed rest and haven't anything in particular to say. I repeated what you say to my wife and she said that our men were not solely to blame, that they repeated what had been said in our newspapers (which I don't read) and also, which I should think not unlikely, that they got side from the English — in which case it was right to pay it back — so I will suspend judgment and hope that we may learn discretion. I imagine from some things I have heard that there is not absolute smoothness between the French and you.

I am much interested to hear that Jack has a volume to come

out, and also am curious about May Sinclair, philosophess, though I never heard of her that I remember, in any capacity. I indulged myself this week by buying one of Nanteuil's engraved portraits — he was the king of the business. In former days I used to long for an example but never expected to have one. I may say similar things of two etchings by Van Dyck that I got in the spring. Strange that a very satisfactory impression of a Van Dyck should cost less than the average, I think I may say of the run of etchings by living men of any standing, though only fit to black his boots. You will not blame me, I am sure, for being able even now to take pleasure in a print. Love to my Lady.

Yours ever,
O. W. HOLMES

LONDON, November 1, 1917

My dear Holmes:

That yarn about Cecil Rhodes's will exceeds even the usual stupidity of German inventions. Possibly German agents have suggested that the Rhodes scholarships were intended to work British propaganda in the U. S., and this, by a process of "Russian scandal" through a series of ignorant people, may have grown into the wild fiction you report.[1]

This morning the Boches gave us a post-midnight instead of an evening alarum, the change of hour presumably due to later moonrise. Our guns were lively for about an hour beginning a little before 1 A.M. So a good many people had what Mr. Hicks[2] of Bodmin's friend called "a indifferent zort o' night." Nothing published about it yet. . . .

---

[1] The letter from Holmes which Pollock mentions is missing. Possibly it had referred to the publicity given, during the war, to the provision in a tentative draft of the will of Cecil Rhodes, dated September 19, 1877, by which he proposed to leave a fund "to and for the establishment, promotion and development of a Secret Society, the true aim and object whereof shall be the extension of British rule throughout the world . . . and especially . . . the ultimate recovery of the United States of America as an integral part of the British Empire. . . ." See Sir Lewis Michell, *Life of the Right Hon. Cecil Rhodes* (2 vols., 1910), I, 72–73.

[2] William Robert Hicks (1808–1868); humorist and story teller, superintendent of Bodmin Asylum.

My *First Book of Jurisprudence* is going into a fourth edition. The life of an edition has been almost exactly seven years since it was first published (1896) — not so bad for a book which does not cater for the examination appetite or pretend to make hard things easy.

Yours ever,
F. POLLOCK

P.S. One enemy machine was brought down at Folkestone and one at Roxford (Kent). Total number out probably not large. Our 2-gun battery in the park fired, as I am credibly informed, 350 rounds, so we had a good noise (and I hope some of the execution) for our money.

WASHINGTON, November 19, 1917

Dear Pollock:

It always delights me to get a letter from you, especially does it at this moment when I had heard a rumor that you were ill. I felicitate you on the deserved success of your *First Book of Jurisprudence*. At this time the very few moments I have for reading are given to, *horresco referens*, a *German* abridgement of Marsilius of Padua's *Defensor Pacis*,[1] which Laski (formerly of Oxford — do you know him — diabolically clever and omniscient), mentioned to me. It is wonderful to see a chap about 1320 arguing with something of the form and detachment of mathematics that the law-making power is the body of the community or the major part of it, that sovereigns should be elected, *non obstant* the objection that they will have the arrogance of the *nouveaux riches — nouveaux riches* in 1320!—, that no ecclesiastic should have temporal power, and that they may marry — citing 1 Epistle to Timothy 3, 2, & *Sextus* 3, 2, for the last. He seems to expect persecution. I also have just received the life of my friend Canon Sheehan of Doneraile, (Longmans),[2] which to me at least is moving and charming. I read the proofs some time ago. . . . But in the main of course my job takes all my time. . . .

[1] Edited by R. Scholz.
[2] Herman Joseph Heuser, *Canon Sheehan of Doneraile* (1917).

Letters from your side don't tell any particulars as to the damage done by air raids. I rather have the impression that they cost the Germans as much as they come to.

I believe that we are building airplanes as fast as we can. I suppose it would be a great gain if we could get in enough to wipe the Germans out of the air and I should think it might be hoped for after a time. Hitherto I have not supposed that one need feel anxious about friends in London. I take it that the damage is infinitesimal. I thought the Cecil Rhodes yarn incredible, and wish I could remember who told it to me as an undoubted fact. Well, dear boy, the clock admonishes me to go to work so I must shut up. Please give my love to Lady Pollock.

Yours ever,
O. W. HOLMES

LONDON, December 6, 1917

My dear Holmes:

Concerning air raids, we had one this morning about 5 A.M. — lively in London for only half an hour or so. This completes the round of night hours or nearly so. I hear two of the enemy were brought down; as usual the material damage is much less than might have been expected considering the number of bombs dropped, and where. The Germans who escaped other damage must have had a mortal cold time getting home. It came on to freeze hard about 6 A.M. having been comparatively mild with southerly wind before. If you lump in the Zeppelin account with the rest I am sure the balance would be rather heavy against the Germans. Taking airplanes alone I don't know: it depends on the unknown and speculative value to them of keeping a certain number of aircraft, guns, & munitions here ready to deal with raids when they come. The direct damage they have done is practically of no military importance. There have been appreciable military casualties only twice, once in naval barracks and once in a camp.

My son's advices from Petrograd come down to the middle of November. Things were pretty confused then and the citizens (encouraged thereto by a proclamation of the town council,

which the so-called government of Lenin & Co. has since purported to dissolve) taking measures to guard their houses
against possible marauders. In the house where Jack lodged
they were taking the watch in turns and had 25–30 armed men.
Vinogradoff, having concluded that there is no law for a lawful
man to abide in Russia, is applying for naturalization here and
I made a declaration in support of his memorial yesterday. At
present everything seems uncertain there. A curious question
arises in Finland. Did the Finnish Diet mean to include a Russian republic among the successors of Alexander I. to whom
Finland by the Diet commended itself, and in any case is there
now a Russian government in being, of any form, capable of
discharging the duties undertaken by Alexander I. as Grand
Duke? *De facto*, the Finns must in common prudence look out
for themselves.[1]

John Morley's *Recollections* have some admirable passages,
specially about G. Meredith. The bulk is, I should think, too
much entangled with our domestic politics to interest you.

Of Canon Sheehan I seem to know nothing: I must find out
about him.

Yours ever,
F. Pollock

P.S. Wilson's message to Congress is quite first-rate and covers
every point both good and bad of Landsdowne's rather enig-
matic epistle.[2] It was very bad form of the *Times* not to print
L's letter all the same. It had merit, like the curate's egg, in
parts.

---

[1] On November 15, 1917, after the October Revolution in Russia, the Finnish Diet declared that it possessed supreme power in Finland. On December 6 the Diet formally declared Finland to be a sovereign, independent state.

[2] In his message read before Congress on December 4, 1917, President Wilson de- fined the purposes for which the United States was fighting. Lord Lansdowne, in a letter submitted on November 27 to Mr. Geoffrey Dawson, editor of the London *Times*, had restated what he conceived to be the purposes of the Allies, and had denied the existence of a desire to annihilate Germany as a great power. Mr. Dawson questioned the propriety of publishing the letter at that time, and Lord Lansdowne, consequently, sent it to the *Daily Telegraph*, in which it appeared on November 29. See Lord Newton, *Lord Lansdowne, A Biography* (1929), pp. 465–467.

WASHINGTON, December 27, 1917

Dear F. P.:

Your letter brings warmth on a cheerless day when coal is scarce. I am glad to hear that Wilson's message was good. I have some fundamental personal doubts, while I don't doubt that now we are in he is doing his best. I grieve and sweat to think of all the time we have let go by and fear disappointments still, but some things are in good shape and I am hopeful. I met one of our ablest old admirals yesterday who thought that the German nation was pretty well worn out. So may it be. I sent you some letters of my Uncle John Holmes the other day thinking that you knew enough of the atmosphere to get some pleasure from them, though my impression was that the attempt to portray him and his talk was flat. I have only glanced at it as I am busy all the time. I seem to be getting a certain fame among the Catholics from the evidences of my friendship with Canon Sheehan in his life. If you ever are curious about him I thought *Under the Cedars and the Stars* a beautiful rhapsody on the seasons as he sees them in his garden. I never read *My New Curate* which was translated into various languages I believe. His novels, while having certain merits and recommended by the Church I was told, are meant for somewhat less complex tastes than ours.

Since the last word I have gone to a funeral (of a Senator)[1] in the country and have returned too frozen to have ideas.

The other day I bought Rembrandt's etching of Janus Lutma, and by a queer coincidence in looking over my engravings found one by Janus Lutma of Vondel which my father bought because of the suggestion of Wendell. The Wendells came from Holland, and Vondel, the portrait assures us, was *Olor Batavus*. I am having a mild revival of my love of prints as a boy now in my old age — or rather of my attention to them. I always have loved them.

I must shut up. Love to Lady Pollock and the children.

Yours ever,
O. W. HOLMES

[1] Francis Griffith Newlands, United States Senator from Nevada, died December 24, 1917.

LONDON, January 2, 1918

My dear Holmes:

With our best New Year's wishes, and a better prospect in my opinion than things look like on the surface. Thanks in advance for the book of your Uncle's letters. You must have had a very early copy of Canon Sheehan or a special American edition: the book is only now announced here.

We are back from a very pleasant ten days' holiday in a bungalow near Sandhurst that my daughter has taken for the winter, and the most complete holiday I have had for a long time. I read there the life of Stopford Brooke,[1] a genial eloquent (but not sentimental) Irishman with a true vocation for art and criticism — whereby he produced much good and some very good work — and a false one for theology, as he discovered late in life, but seemingly his biographer has not. Also I found among the lessor's books, mostly rubbish, Macaulay's *History*, and read again after many years the story of the Revolution of 1688. M. was supreme as a narrator whatever else he was and was not. To Penn he was of course unfair, not seeing how little cause a Quaker of that time had to respect any established tradition good or bad.

I have been almost under fire in the basement of Lincoln's Inn. The last air raid, December 18, surprised the Benchers just sitting down to dinner. A high explosive bomb fell in Stone Buildings, fortunately in the open, and did little damage beyond smashing glass. Ultimately we drank the King's health after the "All clear" sounded, and so departed with content. It was a unique farewell for the outgoing Treasurer of the year, Muir Mackenzie. I don't know whether you have met him.

I sent you the Jane Austen centenary booklet as a New Year's card, in the hope that you are good Austensians.

My new hobby is masonic history — a curious tangled skein. Next week I am to be installed as Deputy Master of the Royal Colonial Institute Lodge, which has become a great centre for overseas soldiers, so I feel bound to know something of our origins.

Yours ever,
F. POLLOCK

[1] By L. P. Jacks; published in 1917.

The Paris *L'Illustration* — the best illustrated journal in the world, I believe, has lately paid a well deserved tribute to American public spirit in the matter of rationing on honour.

No intelligence from my son for some time — he is still at Petrograd and his good work seemingly not impeded beyond the general hindrances to travelling and communications. We are having our share of winter — I write on my knee over a rather weak gas fire. . . .

WASHINGTON, January 24, 1918

Dear F. P.:

Many thanks for the Austen pamphlet, which has our full sympathy. We have done our part in reading the lady, though I must admit that my last experience was when I was playing solitaire which is unfavorable to listening acutely. Stopford Brooke I remember seeing and liking. I think Bryce took me to his house — and have a vague recollection that he had one or more etchings hanging there that excited my interest. *Liber studiorum*? Also I read with pleasure many years ago a book of his. Of course Macaulay was a big fellow, bigger in my humble opinion than Arnold who pitched into him. A man who could write his history and essays, the verses of the Old Cavalier, the Benthamite notes to the Indian penal code and all the rest, of course was big, even if not quite very great. I am moved by your air raid experience as putting it with others I infer that they have dropped shells all over the place and I can't help fearing that more damage has been done than is told. I do not suppose the personal danger is enough to worry over. Your Masonic hobby makes me smile. I had supposed that Masonry in these parts prevailed with people who liked to be called Worshipful or Knight and wear aprons in processions, and with lawyers who hoped to get an advantage from it with juries. But I know that it is taken more or less seriously in England, and no doubt by many here. . . . I am pleased to see that you share the trouble we have had in keeping warm. There is a great shortage of coal and an unusually severe winter. The poor have suffered and the well-to-do have been uncomfortable.

Luckily we have an economical cook and the supply laid in last spring is not yet exhausted. We use gas heaters when the pipes are not frozen, as they have been twice, and electric contrivances, and have had little ground to complain, as compared with most.

Did I tell you of allowing myself a little extravagance in buying Rembrandt's Jan Lutma, 3d state, not quite so good I fear, as the second, but I think better than the first of which only four examples are known, sold, two of them for $5,000 & $10,000! The third state is not very expensive. I have little time for such things but it is good not to forget art in these days, and last night I received a copy of the volume on the *Great Painter Etchers from Rembrandt to Whistler* with admirable reproductions. It renews my youth. My last purchases before some Van Dycks last spring were made during our war when I was in with Theis,[1] who made a great collection for one of the Grays.[2] He let me have some ripping A. Dürer woodcuts and his St. Jerome in a room and other things. When I came back wounded and went to Cambridge he opened his arms and embraced and kissed me and produced a bottle of wine and cigars. I had good times with him and with a queer old collector at the South End of Boston with whom I used to sit up till all hours. Both shades long ago. Do you lament your failure to ask questions of the old when you were young? I do from time to time now. But as usual I am absorbed in decisions. The boys generally cut one of the genitals out of mine, in the form of some expression that they think too free. They have badly cut down this week's.[3] And now comes in the income tax return. Truly I am not idle — but my secretary has got to do that last.

My love to Lady Pollock.

Yours ever,

O. W. H.

[1] Louis Theis; curator of the Gray Collection of Engravings, Harvard University, 1862–70.

[2] Francis Calley Gray, 1790–1856.

[3] Perhaps Greer v. United States, 245 U. S. 559 (decided Jan. 28, 1918).

LONDON, February 3, 1918

My dear Holmes:

Last Wednesday I made acquaintance with Santayana at a lecture he gave to the British Academy on the state of philosophy in America. He was in England at the beginning of the war and has been living at Oxford ever since: whence I infer that he has few or no domestic ties. His discourse was brilliant and in parts amusing — of course one could not appreciate it properly off hand but we shall have it in print.[1] This put me on reading the first of his four volumes on the *Life of Reason* which you gave me a dozen years ago. I doubt whether I examined that one at the time, anyhow it seems new to me now. There is a curious contrast between the complex style, which I do not find easy, and the core of hard Latin demand for definiteness in his way of thinking, and also a certain Latin dogmatism which tries to explain systems in terms of absolute value with little regard to their surroundings. This makes him unjust to all the 18th century philosophers and grossly unfair to Berkeley, for whom he seems to have a special aversion. He quite forgets that if B. was superficial on some vital points the people he was controverting were much more so. The same is true of Butler (of the Analogy) whom I think S. does not touch at all. However, a man either has a historical mind or he has not.

All I can say about Father Heuser's biography of Canon Sheehan is that he has contrived to make it, for any one not already acquainted with Sheehan's person or works, a pretty dull book. One has glimpses of an interesting figure through a sort of ground mist. Which are Sheehan's best books to give one a notion of him? but perhaps you were content with knowing the man. I would rather not dip at a venture among a dozen unknown volumes.

We have recent telegrams from Jack showing that he is holding on to his relief work in spite of all difficulties, and communication between Petrograd and Moscow is not suspended though liable to uncertain delays — but no letters for two months. Probably several mails are held up somewhere. The Foreign Office continues to take charge of ours, but we don't know how

---

[1] See *Proceedings of the British Academy*, 1917–1918, p. 299.

long it takes for the Embassy bag to get through. Some telegrams have certainly gone missing, but on the whole it is possible to cable and receive answers. The whole situation there is
still extremely obscure. Jack's book was passed for press before Xmas but printers' and binders' delays are still unknown
quantity.

Do journalists really not understand that the ablest man at
the head of an army or anything else has to work through more
or less stupid underlings and can't make them different, or do
they ignore it on purpose because it would spoil their copy if
they did not? Unluckily a lot of the stupidity seems to have
percolated into the War Office censorship from the first. The
supposed mystery about Cambrai [2] is, I hear, simply that our
men — the same who had taken the position — were dead tired
and lost their heads. I presume the German counter-attacking
troops were fresh. Such things have happened in all wars.

Signs of a break-up from within are increasing in the Austro-
Hungarian empire and beginning in Germany: and experts
say the financial crash can't be kept off much longer. *Fiat.*

Yours ever,
F. P.

WASHINGTON, March 1, 1918

Dear Pollock:

Yours of February 3 comes this morning. I am much interested in the impression Santayana made on you. He has
seemed to me to hit, more subtly than other philosophers,
points as to which I was disposed to agree with him. His *Winds
of Doctrine* has a delightful criticism of Bergson. There seems
to me something repellant as well as something attractive in
him personally. His style which you don't like has pleased me,
although after a time you seem to see the trick of it. . . . As
for me I have had a week of freedom and have read vols. 3 &
4 of Merz's *History of Thought in the Nineteenth Century*, with

---

[2] In the battle of Cambrai (Nov. 20–30, 1917) the initial successes of the British
troops were effectively wiped out by a strong counter attack of the Germans.

the profit that comes from a general view of the different streams of thought. It makes one realize that *aperçus*, one's own or of others, that seemed to indicate a new point of view were but particles in a current. Among other things the notion of the discontinuity of the universe which had struck me first in Newman and later in W. James and which I had accounted for by their desire for the interstitial miracle, Catholic or spiritualistic, by their wish for a chasm from which might appear a phenomenon without phenomenal antecedents, I was interested to see went back to Du Bois-Reymond. Or again, I have often thought of the superfluity of energy that makes it necessary for man to act, as it makes a kitten play with its tail, as carrying with it a destiny to idealize, *i.e.*, to persist in affirming the worth of ends — since every act has an end. I learn that Schiller laid hold of play and its implications to found his theory of aesthetics, etc., etc.. I am more than ever impressed by the thoroughness of the Germans in systematizing, while I believe that the real contribution of the system-makers was one that was shared in by outsiders — *viz.*, a certain number of *aperçus* or insights. The systems disappear, the insights remain; but probably the great body of insights that we have, touching life and the world, comes in large part from an unknown multitude, not mentioned in the histories of philosophy. In which connection I am rereading Patten's *Development of English Thought*, a work of *esprit* with generalizations that a lifetime could neither prove nor disprove, but interesting as making specific suggestions as to previous economic changes that he thought led to Hobbes, Locke and the rest down to Darwin and Spencer. I remember that years ago it amused me hugely and I think it still will. On Monday we come in again for six weeks of argument after a recess in which I had only one case [1] and one dissent [2] to write, and I am not quite sure of the case going through. The recess gave me the chance to read a little. I wish I had more. I hope you received the letters of my Uncle John Holmes that I ordered sent to you. I don't remem-

---

[1] Gulf, Colorado and Santa Fe Ry. Co. v. Texas, 246 U. S. 58. (Chief Justice White and Justices McKenna and McReynolds dissented.)

[2] Denver v. Denver Union Water Co., 246 U. S. 178, 195. Justices Brandeis and Clarke concurred in the dissent.

ber your mentioning it. There is a little streak of amusement
in spite of rather flat editing. My love to Lady Pollock.

Yours ever,
O. W. HOLMES

WASHINGTON, March 22, 1918

Dear Pollock:

Your last letter has disappeared in some mysterious way
from my table, whether burned by mistake or hidden undis-
coverably I know not.[1] Jack was at Moscow I think, which I
understood to be good; I am wobbly as you see about the place,
being very shaky in my geographical notions — which I would
fain hide from you if I could. The news this morning, *ex rel.*
my secretary, sounds encouraging, but I am anxious as to a
general German attack. I have heard very good accounts of
the present morale of the French army about which I was more
apprehensive than that of yours. I think our men will do as
well as can be expected of beginners, but we shall know more
before this reaches you.

I am kept as busy as possible with my work and that keeps
me from dwelling on the war with futile fidgets. The particular
cases have been nothing tremendous — this week rather an
interesting little point (*entre nous* as the case is not decided), of
allowing a charterer to recover full damages from the owner
for loss of cargo belonging to third persons, on the warranty of
seaworthiness,[2] although there was not a demise of the ship, so
that the owners seemed to be the technical bailees, the ground
being that the cargo owners looked to the charterers who controlled the whole business and that the time-honored ground of
the right of bailees to recover full damages in tort (established
here), whatever may be said of it as history or theory, is applicable to an express contract which reasonably may be said to
have contemplated what happened. I only distributed the
opinion yesterday, but I rather think it will be agreed to as I

---

[1] The letter referred to is missing.
[2] Pendleton v. Benner Line, 246 U. S. 353 (argued, March 11, 12; decided March 25, 1918).

probably am rather more conscious of the difficulties than anyone else. I struck out from my proof a reference to Pollock's
Torts 10th ed 536 as I thought that fairly taken it didn't quite
come to my point.

I have no time to read any of a lot of books on my table.
Julien Benda, *Les Sentiments de Critias*, I began in recess and
sympathized with its intellectual detachment (or effort after
it) and its prejudice against Bergson. . . . Please give my love
to Lady Pollock and tell her that I am such a law machine at
this writing as to be unfit for human intercourse.

The good time will come I hope.

I must off to the dentist who pulled out a tooth last night —
eheu fugaces — and who wished to inspect. I think of you
much.

Yours ever,
O. W. Holmes

London, April 18, 1918

My dear Holmes:

Certainly I wrote to you about the John Holmes book,[1]
agreeing exactly with your judgment of it, I think. But nowadays, as one never knows when mails are to be dispatched (only
the heads of the Central Post Office here know it, and carefully
do not tell the postmasters of subordinate offices), so one cannot be sure that they will arrive. I hear a consignment of the
Law Reports went to the bottom some months ago, which is a
nuisance with the present shortage of paper. (The other priva-
tion I feel most is not being able to get a taxi save by luck on
a very wet day or when one is in a hurry. Complaints of war
diet leave me very cold — though of course high prices are
an evil.) . . .

For unprofessional reading I have completed a course of
Miss Austen with *Sense and Sensibility*, which has marks of
immaturity especially in the first of the three original volumes
but also has great merit, and am now re-reading *Tom Jones*,
for a contrast, after an interval of about forty years. Certainly

---

[1] The letter referred to is missing.

Fielding was a big and spacious man though his scene, as his last editor, the learned Saintsbury, observes, is almost wholly in London and on the western road. I see no reason to doubt that Somersetshire squires really talked the local dialect in the third quarter of the 18th century and even later: seemingly it has not changed much. . . .

Some days ago I had a beautiful letter from Paul Sabatier which I have made bold to send to the *Times Literary Supplement*, published today. See it if you can.

By the time you get this I hope both military and political tension may be relieved. The British Government that does not make a mess of Ireland has yet, I fear, to be born, — not much distinction of parties to my mind.[2]

Yours ever,
F. POLLOCK

WASHINGTON, May 16, 1918

Dear Pollock:

. . . The only book I have read at all lately is *The High Court of Parliament and its Supremacy*, by Charles Howard Mc-Ilwain, a professor at Bowdoin College, published by the Yale University Press. . . . You are far more competent to criticise it than I am, but it seemed to me in every way admirable. . . . You tempt me to recur to Miss Austen when I get a chance — not to Fielding. When I was hit in the foot I thought I was going to do a lot of reading and took *Tom Jones* and the *Novum Organum*, but they both had to wait for better days. Later I read the former through aloud with my wife and thought F. a great man. But my life is too short now for such voluminous leisurely work. And in the main I hover round books more or less related to my job, including philosophy on occasion. I envy you your letter from Sabatier but I have not seen it yet. I have to go too far afield for the *Times*. My time has been

---

[2] During the month of April there had been much debate in Parliament on the proposed extension of the conscription laws to Ireland. On April 16 the Commons passed a bill with such an extension included and on the 18th the Bill became law. During the debate on the bill the government promised shortly to carry through a Home Rule Bill for Ireland.

filled with my work. I have just circulated an opinion that has interested me more than most this year and hope that I may fire it off next Monday,[1] if some Judge doesn't ask time to write a dissent. . . . I wish I could tell you of the spring and one or two little *Vicar of Wakefield* incidents here, but I have to cut this rather short. Before long, *i.e.*, in a little over a month, I hope to be in Beverly Farms and at leisure. Meantime please give my love to Lady Pollock. The old friends grow fewer all the time now, but I remain in good shape so far as I can see. Mind that you do.

Yours ever,
O. W. HOLMES

LONDON, May 30, 1918

My dear Holmes:

The *Law Reports* account shows loss, tho' not so much as last year — price of paper and printer's charges having risen hugely, as you know — but publication has been punctual within a day or two. Is it not curious that I have more matter in hand for the *L. Q. R.* than I ever had in time of peace? and by no means all of it arising out of the war. . . .

I am reading *Gil Blas* for the first time, a little 18th century edition, 6 vols. in 3, given me when I was at Eton. A rather dim memory seems to tell me I tried it then, in the early 1860's, and could not get on with it. Partly, maybe, because I could not read French as easily as I can now, but that style of desultory novel of adventures rather loosely strung together, with interpolations of casual stories related by this or that person and having nothing to do with the main narrative, is, it seems to me, naturally not attractive to young readers who have not yet acquired any critical or historical sense of literature. That way of intercalating wholly irrelevant sub-adventures as it were in *oratio obliqua* is I suppose of Asiatic origin (the object, presumably, being to keep up a continuous flow of some kind of story for as long as the occasion may require). It left

---

[1] On May 20, 1918, Holmes delivered the Court's opinions in Carney v. Chapman, 247 U. S. 102, and Western Union Telegraph Co. v. Foster, *id.*, p. 105.

its mark on *Tom Jones* and is traceable as late as *Pickwick* —
I don't know of any later case. By the way, when one considers
the halting steps of narrative fiction, in point of structure,
down to Fielding's time, and the prevalent formlessness of
serious historians down to the Renaissance (even in the classical epochs Thucydides, Livy, Tacitus are rather brilliant exceptions than normal), does not the *Odyssey* seem a marvel of
pure story-telling art?

Also I am reading Santayana's volume on Religion.[1] I like
his detached humanism and absence of any desire to grind any
axe in particular. Yet somehow there is something elusive
about him. His analysis of Augustine's view of the world is a
singular, fine piece of historical-philosophical criticism.

Yours ever,
F. POLLOCK

This is the last time I can write to you for a penny. Of the war
nothing to say but that those confounded Bolsheviks have for
the time being let us down rather badly.[2] The French grit,
however, is admirable.

WASHINGTON, June 14, 1918

Dear Pollock:

Your letter of the 30th of May finds us on the eve of departure, next Sunday, for N. Y. and a day or two later for Boston and at the end of the week for Beverly Farms. I feel a
little of the sense of hurry, although it is only Friday, incident
to my being a bad case of train fever. The conveniences of
travel are curtailed and as I write my wife comes in to say that
I am to give my tickets to the messenger today and that our
trunks will go tomorrow. Such things make one twitter — no,
not *one* but *me*. Apropos of *Gil Blas* and his interjected story,
I wonder whether Washington Irving was not one of the latest

---

[1] *The Life of Reason* (1905), vol. III: "Reason in Religion."

[2] On March 3, 1918, the Treaty of Brest-Litovsk was signed. Thereafter it was
understood by the Allies that the Czecho-Slovak troops in Russia would be allowed to
leave the country to join the allied forces on the Western front. On May 26, however,
the Russians at Irkutsk attempted to halt the transportation of these troops out of
Russia.

to practise it. Do you ever read those in *Pickwick*? I haven't for many a long year.

My last two cases in Court were marked by two dissents that I imagine the majority thought ill timed and regrettable as I thought the decisions.[1]

The decision in the first case held an act of Congress void that provided that products of mills employing child labor in disapproved ways should not be carried in interstate commerce. I said that as the law unquestionably regulated interstate commerce it was within the power of Congress no matter what its indirect effect on matters within the regulation of the states, or how obviously that effect was intended. I flatter myself that I showed a lot of precedent and also the grounds in reason. The second case was when a Judge, after the event, punished a newspaper and its editor by a summary proceeding that he ordered instituted and tried himself without a jury, for contempt — such summary proceedings being limited by Statute to misconduct in the presence of the Court or so near thereto as to obstruct the administration of justice. I thought the performance wholly unwarranted and the last thing that could maintain respect for the Courts.

We stood 4 to 5 on the first — and 2 to 5 on the last — two Judges[2] preferring not to sit because of their relations with the Judge etc. One of them at least agreed with me, as Brandeis did openly.

The term has not been a specially interesting one, though after we had decided the *Draft Cases*[3] Hannis Taylor made a pompous row in the effort to show that drafted men could not be sent abroad.[4] I was told when I last was at Oxford that he was trying to get a D. C. L.! I think they understood him however. The interruptions multiply and I must go in person to the Express Office to get some whiskey that I am allowed to order from Baltimore (we being dry in the District), upon my affidavit before a Notary Public etc. etc. As John Ropes once remarked, "The Notary Public like the domestic dog is found

[1] Hammer v. Dagenhart, 247 U. S. 251, 277 (1918); Toledo Newspaper Co. v. United States, *id.* 402, 422 (1918).
[2] Day and Clarke, JJ.
[3] Selective Draft Law Cases, 245 U. S. 366 (1918).
[4] See Cox v. Wood, 247 U. S. 3 (1918).

everywhere." So I must cut this short with my love to you both.

Yours ever,
O. W. H.

LONDON, July 18, 1918

My dear Holmes:

. . . I should like to see your judgment in the interstate commerce case you mention. It looks a pretty question. By the way, one Fletcher Dobyns gives so to speak the toast of the Fourteenth Amendment coupled with your name in the *Illinois Law Review* for June:[1] it seems there are conflicting schools: naturally I bet yours is right. . . .

Now I am in the middle of *Jonathan Wild* — a grim and terrible rogue, very different from *Gil Blas*, but a masterpiece. These oddments I read for half or three quarters of an hour before I get up, which gives quite a fair lot of reading from year's end to year's end.

That blessed Indian Specific Relief Act is still with me[2] — not quite so bad as the corresponding sections of the New York Civil Code, on which it was partly modelled. It is strange how little harm bad codes do. I have not heard that even the New York abortion has done very much in the States where it has been enacted. *Quaere* however what would happen if it were turned loose on a virgin jurisdiction where there were no professional traditions.

My son was last heard of by cable from Moscow a little over a month ago. Last week I had advices in writing (a diplomatic bag having found an opportunity of dispatch — there has been no regular letter post for months) down to May 15. He has the very worst opinion of the Bolsheviks and not much better of Kerensky. See, if it comes in your way, his article in the July *Nineteenth Century*.[3] . . .

Yours ever,
F. POLLOCK

---

[1] "Justice Holmes and the Fourteenth Amendment," 13 *Illinois L. Rev.* 71 (1918).
[2] Probably in preparation for the 4th edition of his and Mulla's volume on the Indian Contract and Specific Relief Acts.
[3] "Under the Bolsheviki," 84 *Nineteenth Century* 114 (July 1918).

LONDON, October 14, 1918

My dear Holmes:

We are wondering at the completeness, to all appearance, of the Germans' climb down,[1] and whether there may not be some crooked trick behind it — hope that Great Britain, France, & U.S. may differ, or that somehow valuable time and freedom to use it may be gained for the battered German armies. Foch and the allied staffs may be trusted to look after the latter risk, but there will be more certainty before you get this.

We are very sorry to see the report that Page is ill, but pleased to hear from Lucy Clifford that you give a good account of his successor.[2]

I have just finished for the editor of *La revue politique internationale* of Lausanne a short paper on Spinoza's supposed Machiavellism [3] — not a subject I should have chosen myself. B. d. S's genius was not for political science. His political ideas are archaic as compared not only with Locke's but with William Penn's: he seems, *e.g.*, unaware that there is such a thing as representative government (but his *Treatise of Politics* is unfinished).

The cumbrousness of life under war conditions has been increasing. I now have to keep an eye on the readings of the gas meter, an instrument I had never looked at in my life. The cook was told off to read it, but it soon appeared that neither her rudimentary arithmetic nor her sight could be trusted. Three times I tried in vain to explain to her that if she reported a less figure for today than yesterday's there must be something wrong in her reading — consumption of a negative quantity of gas being impossible. Now it is turned over to the parlour maid but I see her return every morning. The real trouble however is locomotion. In this part of London one can't get a taxi, and

---

[1] Following the resignation of the German Chancellor, von Hertling, and of Foreign Secretary von Hintze on September 30, 1918, and the appointment in their stead of Prince Max of Baden and of Dr. W. S. Solf, the German Government by a series of pronouncements indicated a new willingness to negotiate for peace.

[2] John W. Davis had recently been appointed Ambassador to Great Britain to succeed Walter Hines Page, who had resigned in August 1918.

[3] "Spinoza et le Machiavelisme," 11 *Revue politique internationale* 3 (January-February, 1919).

when something on wheels is indispensable the only way is to hire regardless of war prices — the result being generally one-horse in every sense. Also jam and the like are now rationed. . . .

Yours ever,

F. P.

WASHINGTON, October 31, 1918

Dear F. P.:

What a centre of energy you are! Just as I was lamenting a sort of flabbiness in my soul and wishing for some pungent spur you write verses as spirited as if you were a young man.[1] Well, I suppose you are a young man compared with me. At all events since I have been here I have got nothing out of such leisure as my duties left me except to finish up a few odd jobs and tuck in some loose ends. We have been adjourned on account of the epidemic as it was not thought right to require lawyers to come, often across the continent, to a crowded and infected spot. . . .

The Congressional Library, even, has been shut. I profited by my position I suppose, in getting them to let me in to go to the print rooms and wallow in potentialities. I could have a very good looking young lady (I believe a grand-daughter or niece of General Meade) produce any portfolio I called for and bear me company in turning over the contents. She told me that they had a Goya of her great (?) grandfather supposed to have been painted over some other painting of value to get it out of the country, but the family naturally was contented with grandpa and Goya.

I hope in a few days to reciprocate for your verses by sending you a few remarks suggested by reading volume two of Gény, on something or other I forget what, that leads him to give an account of the views of a lot of modern jurists on Natural Law, etc. in which Gény believes. I don't and have taken the oc-

---

[1] With his letter of October 14, Pollock had enclosed a copy of his poem "The Victory of Samothrace," which was published in 45 *Cornhill Magazine* (New 3rd Series) 586 (December 1918).

casion to state a part of my creed. I wrote them as [*sic*] some years ago a little piece for the *Illinois Law Review* & Wigmore, *currente calamo*, in a kind of rage of writing one day, and Laski when I showed them to him impounded them for the *Harv. Law Rev.*,[2] which I had not intended. After I sent back the proofs the other day I was depressed to think that one little phrase "for the joy of it"[3] was an echo of Ruskin. I hate to drop into something ready made that is not the immediate expression of one's thought, organizing every word; but as I wrote to Laski, not having the proof before me I would let it stand, feeling as our officers did who had gone through a number of battles unwounded. They expected to be killed outright. So I hoped this small note of infamy might save me from greater ruin. I have read half of Lord Charnwood's *Life of Lincoln* under the compulsion of its being sent to me by a cousin. It seems to me artistically done but I hate to read of those times. This morning brings me *The Development of the United States* by Max Farrand, which I want to read, as the author, my secretary tells me, is a very competent man. Whether I shall have time now, I know not. Give my love to Lady Pollock. I think much of you both in these days.

Yours ever,

O. W. HOLMES

LONDON, November 4, 1918

My dear Holmes:

You should get hold of Alfred Loisy's *La Religion* (Paris, Emile Nourry, 1917, 3.50 f.). Enclosed is the first paragraph of the introduction whereby you may see how far an excommunicated Catholic Modernist has removed from orthodoxy. I have done it out of pure malice into the English of the kind of 17th century learned persons who would have been horrified to think a learned clerk should ever write so. That bit might

---

[2] Holmes, "Natural Law," 32 *Harv. L. Rev.* 40 (1918); reprinted, *C.L.P.*, p. 310.

[3] "We shall still fight — all of us because we want to live, some, at least, because we want to realize our spontaneity and prove our powers, for the joy of it, and we may leave to the unknown the supposed final valuation of that which in any event has value to us." 32 *Harv. L. Rev.* at p. 43; *C.L.P.* at p. 316.

almost be Anatole France — but Loisy's general attitude is not merely negative. He harbours — like every one who has been through the Roman mill — some regret for the comfort of a dogmatic atmosphere (whereas our great Anglican moralist Butler frankly recognized your favourite principle that life in this world is a choice of risks). The traces of this in Renan are familiar. In the history of ethics he is rather out of his depth, lumping all the Greek moralists as individualist: which is true only of the post-Aristotelian schools. He must have forgotten or never known Plato's *Republic*, which starts from the necessity of defining social justice first, and Aristotle's *Politics*, where the family not the individual is taken as the primary unit. Still he is an interesting phenomenon; it is a common view, certainly, that Modernism in the church is a backwater, but I think it exceedingly rash.

Now that Austria is out of the war I don't see how the Germans can either fight or bluff:[1] . . .

Yours ever,

F. POLLOCK

Enclosure in Letter of November 4, 1918

"Lorsque Noé fut sorti de l'arche avec sa famille et tous les animaux qu'il avait sauvés de la deluge, il érigea sur la montagne un autel où de toutes les sortes de quadrupédes et d'oiseaux purs il offrit a Jahvé un grand holocauste. Et Jahvé, dit la Genèse, flaira l'odeur agréable du sacrifice, et Jahvé pensa en lui-meme: 'Je ne maudirai plus la terre à cause de l'homme; car la penseé de l'homme est mauvaise dès sa jeunesse.' Ainsi le vieux dieu, s'avouant que la leçon du châtiment ne servirait jamais à rien, laissait dorénavant aux humains le soin de s'exterminer eux-mêmes: ce à quoi ils n'ont pas manqué."

"*Noah,* having come forth from the Ark with his household and every creature he had saved from the Flood, set up an altar on the hill, where of all manner of clean beasts and fowls he offered unto *Jahveh* a great burnt-offering. And *Jahveh,* as the book of *Genesis* saith, smelled the pleasant smell of that sacrifice, and thought within himself: *I will not again curse the ground any more for man's sake; for the imagination of man's heart is evil from his youth.* So that ancient god, now discerning that the discipline of punishment should never serve the purpose, left unto mankind for time to come the concern of extirpating one another: wherein they failed not."

---

[1] The armistice with Austria was signed on November 3, 1918.

WASHINGTON, November 24, 1918

Dear Pollock:

Many thanks — how many times in my life I have had to thank you for greater things — for the extract from Loisy, which with your recommendation makes me want to read him. I can't just now, for I have my hands full of Court work. I well know the Catholic desire of which you speak for a support *ab extra*. . . .

Let me put to you a pretty point in Sovereignty upon which at the moment I stand alone. The U.S. conveys some [of] its land in Kansas to a private person, who thereafter holds the land as any other holds any other land. Subsequently it is seized on execution for his debt as any other land might have been and as this land might have been for any debt incurred after the execution of the patent to him. But an act of Congress provided that no lands acquired as that was should "in any event become liable to the satisfaction of any debt contracted prior to the issuing of the patent therefor." Assuming that the statute is construed to cover this case I ask myself on what theory it can be given effect — on what theory past legislation can operate where present legislation would be powerless. There is no retention of any interest, no condition such as the U. S. could have attached as owner — it is purely a legislative fiat as to the disposition of the land in what *pro hac vice* is a different sovereignty. I suppose it to be manifest destiny that the law will be held effective if construed as I have assumed. The State Courts have said so, I believe, many times. But I am hanged if I see any satisfactory reasoning for the result. I could frame a form of words, I suppose, to cover it, but as yet I see no ground that I really believe to be adequate.[1]

Nov. 25. I go to Court this morning for a two weeks adjournment which will give me time to write a long case under the Sherman Act.[2] It will be preceded and followed by a conference which I expect will give me some other things to write but nothing so bothery. Think of a case that took five months steady

---

[1] See Ruddy v. Rossi, 248 U. S. 104, 107 (decided Dec. 9, 1918). Holmes wrote a concurring opinion sustaining the validity of the statute but emphasizing the difficulties here suggested.

[2] Buckeye Powder Co. v. DuPont Powder Co., 248 U. S. 55 (decided Dec. 9, 1918).

work to try. I have read nothing to speak of, though in a few spare moments I got through some chapters of a little book on Mysticism in English Literature.[3] The theme interests me. I am a mystic in the sense of believing myself to be an intelligible moment of the unintelligible, but not at all in that of supposing that by purging myself of all activities that the Cosmos has implanted I can get nearer to the central power and have a private conversation with God. I don't believe that Wordsworth thought that he lapsed into sin or into a lower state when he wrote a poem in place of a pure emotional receptivity. But I always remember that one of the first adult books that gave me pleasure as a boy was *Hours with the Mystics*. Alas, I must turn from you and get ready to depart. I hate early conferences and in general anything that disturbs my quiet before eleven — at which time I should like to lie down to recover from the fatigue of getting up — but then I am ready for the world.

Give my best love to Lady Pollock.

Yours ever,
O. W. HOLMES.

LONDON, December 20, 1918

My dear Holmes:

The *Harvard Law Review* is to hand with your remarks on Natural Law as set forth by Gény. Not knowing what he says I cannot fully appreciate your criticism, but if you mean to imply that no one can accept natural law (= natural justice = reason as understood in the Common Law) without maintaining it as a body of rules known to be absolutely true, I do not agree.

See my studies in *Journal of Comparative Legislation* 1900, 1901, of which I think I sent you separate prints at the time.[1]

The Roman lawyers made no such assertions about *ius gentium*, which was simply general custom and for most purposes equivalent to *ius naturale*. As to the exceptional divergences, see opening of the *Institutes*.

---

[3] Caroline Frances Eleanor Spurgeon, published in 1913.

---

[1] See 2 *Journ. Comp. Leg.* (n. s.) 418 (1900); 3 *id.* 204 (1901); reprinted, *Essays in the Law* (1922), p. 31, *sub nom.* "The History of the Law of Nature."

In the Middle Ages natural law was regarded as the senior branch of divine law and therefore had to be treated as infallible (but there was no infallible way of knowing what it was).

If you deny that any principles of conduct at all are common to and admitted by all men who try to behave reasonably — well, I don't see how you can have any ethics or any ethical background for law.

Apparently the ex-German Emperor will have to be tried by a wholly new jurisdiction, if at all, and by some standard which all medieval and not a few modern doctors would refer to natural law. A committee of which I am a member is now hard at work trying to inform the conscience of the Attorney General at the request of the War Cabinet on this group of problems (there are problems with regard to lesser folk also).[2]

Yours ever,

F. P.

[2] Sir Frederick Edwin Smith (1872–1929), later Lord Birkenhead, as Attorney General, had sought the advice of various lawyers, including Pollock, as to the possible methods by which William II of Germany might be tried by the Allies. See Birkenhead, *Frederick Edwin, Earl of Birkenhead* (1935), II, 106.

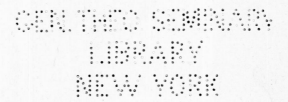